NORTH
ZAMBEZI

A modern missionary
memoir

Fergus Macpherson

THE HANDSEL PRESS

Edinburgh

British Library Cataloguing in Publication Data
A catalogue record for this publication is available from the British Library

ISBN 1 871828 44 9

Typeset in 11 pt. Garamond
at The Stables, Carberry

Printed by BPC-AUP Aberdeen Ltd

Cover design and frontispiece by John McWilliam

Chapter illustrations © Richard Baxter

Published with the aid of a grant from
The Drummond Trust, 3 Pitt Terrace, Stirling

CONTENTS

Dedicated to Myra
in celebration of fifty years together,
and to our six children
and eighteen grandchildren

Chapter 1
'COME WITH HAPPY'

Ngwele and I cycled in September 1952 to a lonely village school in a thinly populated tract of woodland between Zambia's 'great north road' and the River Luangwa to the east of it. We had left the mission vehicle at a roadside shop and spent our first two days at a little village called Mulilabantu ('Where the people weep'). They had probably once known a cruel famine and buried many children in that area.

To shorten our journey we worked by day and travelled by night. There were about 45 miles between Mulilabantu and Chishala. The moon was full and the night air was very sweet. But we had to turn back after about an hour when the hairspring in the crank of my bike suddenly collapsed. The headmaster at Mulilabantu fixed up an ingenious repair by the flickering light of a storm-lantern made in Hong Kong. Two hours later we set off again, not long before the moon slipped from sight beyond the haze of the horizon.

We must have gone about 25 miles by starlight when we saw two glowing eyes ahead of us. It could not be a little animal from the nearby river, we realised at once. The river was dry and the eyes were too far apart. It must be a big cat. We stopped and peered into the deep blue-black darkness that now wrapped around us. The eyes seemed to be moving. I lit a match that shed a bright glow. The creature stood still. As the match died, it started inching towards us again.

Perhaps we could frighten it off by noise, so we shouted and bumped our bicycles up and down. Again the glow of a match stopped it. And again, heedless of our din, it began to advance steadily as the match light died.

"Let's go back to Mulilabantu", said my companion, John Ngwele. But with about 20 miles to go and 25 behind us, there was no point in running away. With eyes as far apart as that, the creature would certainly outrun us.

I had taken my shirt off in the balmy warmth of the night. Before starting to move, I put it on. Why, I'm not quite sure! Perhaps it would not have been consonant with 'the romance of missionary heroism' to die without one's shirt! Then, using our bicycles as shields and singing a lusty song, we went to meet the foe.

As we drew close to it, it stopped; and as we reached it, it did not move an inch. Its stillness halted us and we peered at the unblinking red eyes. "It's the last embers of a grass fire", said Ngwele, and so it was. In the shock of our relief, we roared with laughter, slapped each other's shoulders and shouted for joy.

The hair-spring and the red-eyed beast had delayed us badly. It was in the hour before dawn that we reached Chishala. We were very tired now and glad to rest by a fire in Lex Ngulube's kitchen. His house was full of sleeping children.

Ngulube, the headmaster, and his assistant Harrison Mwamba did not believe me when I said that we had come alone. "He must have carriers", was the thought of their hearts that their faces could not hide. 'Basungu' (as white people were called) always moved on their journeys in 'the bush' with a team of carriers. With tents, tables, chairs and cooking utensils, the team could quickly erect a temporary village for the bwana. Hygiene and differences in eating habits had been the reason given for that mode of travel. Yet the camp outwith the village or the school was a symbol of aloofness, a form of apartheid. And if the missionary Manager of Schools had to rebuke some fault in the teachers' work, his separated encampment would underline the cold formality of his visit. It would then linger as an unhappy memory.

When Ngulube and Mwamba were at last convinced that John Ngwele was my only companion, they were obviously troubled. "Where would you like to sleep?" they asked. "We are your visitors", I replied. "It is for the host and not for the guest to choose the sleeping place". But there was really no space anywhere. The teachers each had big families of young children in their tiny houses. I was, however, squeezed into the Ngulube home, which meant that a bunch of little people would sleep in the kitchen behind the house. The Mwambas made a similar adjustment in order to welcome John Ngwele. You could blame us, I know, for upsetting our kind hosts. But there was no other way through the apartheid, no other means I could find for starting the demolition of what

Paul the Apostle had called "the middle wall of partition between us". (Ephesians 2.14)

"When you are coming again", said Ngulube as we stood, with our packs strapped on our bicycles, ready to say goodbye, "would you please send us word in advance?" "If you like", I replied, "but personally I prefer to find teachers and pupils in their day-to-day situation. Then I can see their problems. And I don't want special preparations made for my visit". I agreed, however, to send word ahead of my next visit if possible - there were no regular postal services in the region at that time - and off we went.

Three months later, with a different companion, I was again on my way to Chishala. As we emerged from thick trees along the stream, some children saw us and raced off to tell their teachers.

It was Harrison Mwamba who heard the news first, and came bounding down to greet us. Taking my fingers in his, he led me up the slope towards the school village and into the area of the teachers' houses and the pupils' tiny dormitories. At once my eyes spotted the back wall of a small building, pink-washed with some tinted river clay and roofed with new thatching grass. "This is for you", said Mwamba as he led me and my companion round to the front of the little house. It had been constructed with neither tee-square nor plumbline. It was to prove an inch too short inside for a light folding camp bed. But it was the inscription on it that I could never forget, written free hand in big bold chocolate-brown letters thus: COME WITH HAPPY.

The Big Pendulum Swings

Only a few decades ago, young people in Britain were inspired by books that told of the romance of lands far away and by vivid tales of heroes whose fearless adventures across the face of the earth had brought glory to their motherland in the high noon of European imperialism.

Among those thrilling chronicles was one that specially kindled the imagination of young folk of Christian background. I can see in my mind's eye the book's broad spine in deep blue, lettered in gold and red, with its bold, alluring title: *The Romance of Missionary Heroism*. Every page of it and every picture brought thrill upon thrill as it told of unarmed men and women who carried the torch of Jesus into heathen lands.

Today there are many who would reject the underlying assumption of that romantic story; the notion of the superiority of what we now call 'the western world', the conviction that men dared not demur at 'the call of God' to a great civilising mission to 'the heathen', the unclouded confidence that European commerce and 'the British way of life' would work hand in hand to bestow on 'the natives' of dark and distant lands the riches of Christendom.

> Can we whose souls are lighted
> With wisdom from on high,
> Can we, to men benighted
> The lamp of life deny?

So they sang with fervour and sincerity.

Then came the Deluge. Two waves of holocaust swept out in our century within 'the western world' to carry desolation far and wide across the earth. What we call for convenience the First and Second World Wars were, we must now realise, 'civil wars' within the European family of peoples. In the 1970s such facts as the existence of the European Economic Community and Germany's massive contribution to the International Monetary Fund Loan to Britain have endorsed this view of the double carnage of our century.

The blood-drenched fields of Paschendale and the Somme, of Gallipoli and Archangel, and then so soon after a restive lull, the stampede towards 'obliteration bombing', the searing of millions to death, the agonies of Rotterdam, Coventry, Coblentz, Lidice, Dresden, Hiroshima and Nagasaki, the bombing of babies - this catalogue of horrors has raised a great question. It has seemed to thoughtful people that we must redefine 'civilisation'. For those nations most confident of their superiority had turned their great treasures and rich talents, not to the attainment of world peace but to a frightful carnival of hatred, destruction and death.

As the dust of the second hateful war settled, great processes of reversal began that are still far from being finished. In the ebb-tide of 'the west', peoples long called 'backward' and 'inferior' began to let their voices be heard. With a growing number of allies in the 'metropolitan' countries of Europe, they called a halt to 'imperialism'. For to them that had been the climax of their humiliation when uninhibited exploitation had grabbed their hidden riches and shattered their social and political systems. "Never again", they were now saying with startling unanimity and setting their course towards national sovereignty and independence.

The great pendulum thus swept away from Europe the 'golden age of empire'. Kipling's glib talk of "lesser breeds without the law" was a voice of yesterday. The new 'outlaws', in the eyes of the rapidly growing United Nations Organisation, were the 'fascist' states of Southern Africa whose polity was founded on a doctrine of racial superiority. As the clamant voices of the 'new nations' called for the supreme sanctions of international justice against 'white supremacy' and imperialism, there inevitably followed a growing castigation of Christian 'foreign missions' as handmaids, however unwittingly, of those processes of annexation and subjugation that we associate in southern Africa with the name of Cecil Rhodes.

For Western Christianity this swing of the pendulum meant much heart-searching and agonising reappraisal. For the people responsible for the work of missionary societies and of the foreign mission committees of various churches, it meant the devising of new policies for their 'foreign fields'. Belatedly, as the political articulation of 'overseas dependencies' broke loose, those churches had to call on their Asian, African and Caribbean 'dependents' to assume executive roles in what were being spoken of now as 'indigenous churches'. In some cases, their 'overseas converts' looked at first askance at that invitation. "Why now?" they asked. "Why not before?"

The two great wars had gravely crippled the missionary enterprise of the protestant churches. They did not practise formal 'confession' and the flood-tide of evil in the world brought them nothing of the harvest of thank offerings for 'absolution' that the Roman Catholic Church was bound to reap. So, for western protestantism, the post-war years meant 'retrenchment'; and 're-trenchment', by its very nature bred a mood of disenchantment and dismay. The number of protestant missionaries began to fall markedly and the funds available to maintain those who remained were subject to severe restriction. The missionary who wrote a book on *Christian Missions and the Judgement of God* had trenchant thoughts to share in that time of often crippling disquiet.

When the tide of the great missionary movement of the latter nineteenth century was flowing, the ink flowed also from the pens of its chroniclers. There are still to be found in second-hand bookshops, some gripping books written by men and women in the front line of that great enterprise. The days of dull disenchantment have instead, however, sealed up peoples' hearts and little has been chronicled of the fortunes of missionary work in the mid-twentieth century. Just as many people in western countries have seen the end of the colonial era as an exhibition of ingratitude on the part of their backward beneficiaries, so there has been something of the chill of a winter's twilight about the withdrawal of missionary enterprise and initiative from the overseas churches.

It has been called 'the end of the missionary', this period of disengagement; and the word 'end' has something forlorn as well as something final about it. Forty years after I first went to Central Africa, however, I wrote an article entitled 'Hallelujah for the end of an age'. It had seemed to me, you see, that we were witnessing not a debacle but a watershed. Of course there were areas of friction, outbursts of recriminations, harsh judgments and a rash of misunderstandings. But what was happening, I had come to believe, was within, and certainly not outside, the 'gracious purposes of God'. As someone said in my hearing over twenty years earlier, the great missionary movement could be summed up rightly in the five simple and biblical words: "And it came to pass". In its passing, there was nothing ominous - not more so than there is ominousness in the evening as we pause to sleep in anticipation of tomorrow.

The last of the missionaries are thus to be seen, I am sure, not as funeral undertakers but as 'bridgemen'. For them the toil and tears of the pioneers opened the tillage and weeded it. The impressive insitutions that those pioneers created and the buildings in which they housed them, often so grandly, were perhaps not really more than bags for the seed and hoes for the fields. What mattered was 'bread for the world', the breaking and sharing of Christ's body in a fellowship whose quality makes nonsense of all ethnic and cultural differentials.

It was the lot of my generation of missionaries to be inspanned to overseas work in the hour of the bridgemen. It was a time of turmoil and radical change. But it was not a time to feel that a beloved cause was now being abandoned. Rather it was a time when the Spirit swept in on the wind. One of the fruits of the Spirit, we are told, is joy, yesterday, today and for ever. So may what I set down here be read as a testimony of experiences whose irrepressible obligato was this joy, coming and going 'with happy'.

Chapter 2
THE
MAGNETISM
OF MWANGONDE

When my father enrolled as a student of Edinburgh university in 1910, he met a man called Matthew Faulds. Faulds had the same name as his famous grandfather, the centenarian weaver of Fenwick in Ayrshire. My father's name was the same as his father's. My grandfather, Hector Macpherson, was widely known as the influential Liberal editor of the Edinburgh Evening News. Faulds and my father recognised each other's name as the class list was called on their enrolment day. Thus began a lifelong friendship.

As students, they often talked about the role of Christianity in the world. Faulds initially rejected 'foreign missions' as patronising interference in the life and culture of faraway peoples. My father believed like David Livingstone that mission was essential to the life of the church. But he declined a suggestion that he should go to Manchuria as a missionary. Scotland bound him with too strong a bond of love. Matthew Faulds, however, was drafted, as a YMCA chaplain in the First World War, to East Africa. On his return, he offered himself for missionary service. From then, until 1938, he was a missionary in Africa, first in southern Tanzania and then in northern Malawi.

From Karonga on the shore of Lake Malawi, then called Lake Nyasa, wonderful letters came to us from time to time from 'Uncle Matthew'. After each four year tour of service, he and Mrs Faulds came home 'on furlough'. As a boy, I fell under his spell. He did not speak of missionary work, as some did, in terms of little romantic tales of scantily clad converts. Instead, he foretold the 'awakening of the African giant'. He spoke of the scandal of the 'colour bar' in southern and central Africa. He pled that Christ's people in Scotland would wake up to the coming conflict and that Christ's servants, sent abroad, must witness to the reality of a healing fellowship that would transcend every barrier of suspicion, hatred and contempt.

Matthew Faulds traced a great question mark within the shape of Africa thus: "Whither Africa", he asked, and I caught the fire in his heart when he declared that 'the Cross' must face the menace of racism fearlessly and witness in life and in action to our common humanity in Christ; for "God made of one blood all nations of men". (Acts 17.26)

By the strange quirk of human character, one or two of his colleagues in Nyasaland (as Malawi was then called) who lived at the central institution of Livinstonia Mission, looked on Matthew Faulds and others like him as 'bush wallahs', mere infantry men, foot sloggers who allowed their 'bush work' for instance, to slow down their 'office' output. But Matthew Faulds, whose mind was richly stored with the treasures of English literature, whose wit was swift and incisive, whose laughter was boyish and infectious, was a giant among them in the way in which he combined ideally the roles of pastor and prophet.

In 1956, eighteen years after he had had to return to Scotland, thousands gathered, at very short notice, at Karonga to inter the ashes of his body. For me, that was the ultimate confirmation of the measure of his devotion. It is good to know that folk like him are, as the letter to the Hebrews says, in that 'cloud of witnesses' by whom we are surrounded, packing the grandstand, cheering us on and wishing us well as we, in our turn, strive to run the race that is set before us.

Matthew Faulds laid the kindling sticks and struck the match to give me my first warmth of Africa when I was still a boy. Moreover to what he wrote in his letters and what he told us when he was 'on furlough' he added a book-list, the best of the writings of the missionary pioneers. Among these was one priceless one: J.W. Jack's *Daybreak in Livingstonia*. "Have you sixpence?" Uncle Matthew asked me suddenly one day in Edinburgh. "No". "Why?" I asked. "Because I've a book I picked up in a second-hand bookshop and you might like to have it". When I told my father, the sixpence was provided and I became the owner of "Daybreak". "Good", said Uncle Matthew with a huge laugh, "I got it for four pence!".

In November 1936, having 'skipped' the Sunday evening service, I was reading by the fire, curled up in a wooden box that I had tried to convert into an arm-chair. My book was *Mary Slessor of Calabar*, the story of the mill-girl from Dundee who went to eastern Nigeria as a missionary in 1846. It was then that I became certain that I wanted to prepare myself to go to Africa. My envisioning of the great continent had to draw, for lack of more accurate material, on the pictures that appeared in missionary literature and on the descriptions given in books like *In Lionland* of the endless stretches of forest and high grass through which David Livingstone seemed to have pushed his way for years. It was thus to Matthew Faulds that I owed the beginnings of a deeper understanding of 'Africa emergent', the waking giant, the great question-mark of the coming decades, the area in which Christ's people must reckon with powerful forces of cruelty and exploitation that were using all the resources of modern technology to make sure that they would have and hold Africa in perpetuity, making her 'native' peoples hew wood and draw water for them in the name of 'white civilisation'. What I had learned from my father of the prophets of Israel, especially perhaps Amos, and what Matthew Faulds told me of Johannesburg, the Belgian Congo, Kenya, the Northern Rhodesian Copperbelt, and the crude realities of 'the colour bar', merged in my mind and helped me to see Jesus as, to use a modern phrase, 'the man for others', the one who, above all, shows that the denial of humanity and the rejection of the 'family of God' are the greatest human sins.

Years later I learned of the names by which Matthew and Doris Faulds were known among the Ngonde people of northern Malawi. His was 'Mwangonde', a royal title of great honour. She was 'Bangubosa', meaning: "All the people are my people". It was the magnetism of Mwangonde and Bangubosa first and then, when I was 15, that vivid biography of *Mary Slessor of Calabar* that kindled my heart to certainty that I must go to Africa.

The Coming of Kamuzu

When I was 18, Matthew Faulds, now home from Africa, introduced me to a medical doctor, born in Malawi and trained in America, called Hastings Kamuzu Banda. Banda had excellent degrees in history (BPh of Chicago) and in medicine (MD of Meharry in Tennessee). He had come to Scotland to take his triple qualification (LRCP, LRCS, LRFP & S) in order that he might practice medicine in the British Protectorate of Nyasaland.

We quickly became friends, though he was many years my senior. On park seats in the Meadows, behind Edinburgh Royal Infirmary, he gave me lessons in his mother tongue, the language called Chinyanja or Chichewa. My father, as minister of the Church of Scotland, ordained Dr Banda as an elder in 1941.

By dint of perseverance, my family and I persuaded Hastings Banda to tell us the story of his life. Dr Prentice of Kasungu Mission had been his early Christian teacher, he told us. In youth, he had become certain that he must learn the scientific medicine that people practised in Europe. But there were no funds, no profits from cocoa or coffee to pay his fees, as was the case with some of the people from West Africa who came to Scotland for university studies.

I was to meet Dr Prentice in Malawi in 1947, and he was able to recall Banda as a very intelligent pupil at Kasungu. All that he had had to carry him on his chosen pilgrimage was that quick mind and strong determination. The journey south had to be undertaken on foot. A low paid job as a hospital sweeper in Harare, then called Salisbury, enabled him to start saving a little each week. And so the time came when he was ready to move on, this time to Johannesburg, the city of gold in South Africa's Witwatersrand, Again, he was ready to accept any form of work, however hard and meanly rewarded. This time it was as a mine labourer, for whom hours of digging deep below the ground must have been physically wearing. But his studies claimed his constant attention until at last he was ready to apply for a place in Lovedale College at Alice in the Cape Province and had saved enough to meet the financial requirements of enrolment.

Suddenly however, his plans were changed. An Afro-American whom he met urged him to go instead to America and, finding that his money would just cover a sea fare, he set off for New York. There, in the United States, with the help of benefactors of whom he spoke with great appreciation, he completed secondary education and was admitted to university studies in Chicago leading to the degree of Bachelor of Philosophy, majoring in history. But this was not a departure from his dream of being a medical doctor. He resolved to take a degree in 'the humanities' first, he told us, because medical studies might, on their own, be too specialised and narrow. Only when he graduated from Chicago, did he go south to Meharry Medical College.

His objective there was, he told me, very clear: to go from America, after completing his medical course, to Scotland and enter his name for that 'triple qualification' required by doctors who wished to practise in British territories. For he was determined to go home and resolved to serve as a doctor in one of the Church of Scotland hospitals there if possible.

It was not long after his arrival in Scotland that I was introduced to him by Matthew Faulds. I remember Banda's sorrow, expressed with no hint of bitterness, when he told me that he had to lay aside his hope of working at the hospital at Livingstonia because, so he had heard, some of the mission staff had declared their unwillingness to work under a black doctor. "If that is how they feel", he said, "I am glad they have said so now and not later". Various other avenues were attempted in his search for an acceptable entry to medical practice in Nyasaland, but he met with blind alleys. He had correspondence, he told me, with the Colonial Office about an appointment in Zomba. But a brief communication arrived one day from London advising that, if so appointed, he must understand that he would not be allowed to seek social relations with white medical staff on a basis of equality. Once again, without any expression of bitterness, he said that it was better to know how things stood sooner rather than later. He then began to seek opportunities for general practice in Edinburgh. After some weeks of questing he suddenly announced his departure for Merseyside.

As I knew him in those days, Dr Banda was a man of perfect courtesy, reserved and punctilious in company, affectionate and generous in friendship and quick to respond in compassion to suffering or sorrow. When he undertook medical practice among poor people in Liverpool's dockland and elsewhere he often paid the rents of families under threat of eviction.

The Afro-Scottish Circle

At the same time a number of students from West Africa were at Edinburgh University, most of them studying medicine. For many of them it was their fathers' business as cocoa producers that provided the money for their studies. Theodore Shealtiel Clarke, an able student of architecture and town-planning, was the first of my friends in the 'Gold Coast Group'. Rufus Onyemelukwe was the first Nigerian to join us as we laid plans for what we called the Edinburgh Afro-Scottish Circle. The number of my African friends grew rapidly and we shared much laughter and fun.

The circle was formed partly because those friends of mine found the gatherings of the Edinburgh International Club too stiff and affected. It was at a meeting of one such Club that - so the story went - an elegant matron in a long evening gown and holding her Turkish cigarette in an ebony mouthpiece, met an African student from Oxford. "Tell me", she asked, "how many natives are there in your year?" "Well", he said, as he started counting on his fingers, "apart from a Ugandan, a man from Ceylon and a Jamaican, I think they are all natives". Those friendly, intelligent West Africans were not looking for patronage. Our common desire for something less stuffy set the Circle in motion.

The activities of the Afro-Scottish Circle were a happy mixture of sense and nonsense. I remember one party at which someone suggested community singing as a respite after strenuous and noisy frolics. A Scots law student who had a winsome proclivity for *le mot* not quite *juste* at once suggested "The Darkies' Sunday School", which was greeted by the black members of the Circle with a burst of hearty laughter. Thus were strong friendships forged. Most of the Gold Coast members of the Circle were to become leading citizens in the Republic of Ghana. From among the medical students then in Edinburgh some, like Ellis Djoleto and Emmanuel Evans-Anfom, were to make outstanding contributions to medical administration and scholarship. Dr Evans-Anfom was, for some years, Principal of the University College at Kumasi. I remember him as a faithful Sunday School teacher in the Edinburgh congregation of which my father was minister.

Meanwhile my reading on Africa went on apace, while Dr Banda's excellent elementary lessons in his mother tongue introduced me to a new world of not only grammar and syntax but also concepts, social philosophy and communal wisdom. For as Edwin Smith the great missionary and Africanist had said, language is, in Africa as elsewhere "the shrine of a people's soul".

I had not yet drunk of the waters of Africa at the fountainhead but people were passing me cupfuls of it from the bottles they carried themselves, as it were, and it was like no other water I'd known.

Towards the Springboard

Time seemed to accelerate after I received my formal appointment as a missionary. I had collected an Honours degree in history and completed three years' study for the ministry at New College Edinburgh. With the help of the Africa Secretary of the Church of Scotland Foreign Mission Committee, I had an introduction to the Edinburgh Education Department who used me as a temporary teacher during the weeks between the end of the New College session and the school year. I had squeezed in some lectures, etc, at Teacher Training College, but could not, of course, fulfil the requirements for a Teaching Certificate while studying theology. Those College classes, along with a very varied range of class teaching opportunities in a number of city schools, were undertaken with a view to deepening my experience before I plunged into the standard missionary involvement in education.

The war ended. The obscene outrage of Hiroshima and Nagasaki had marked its climax and the world seemed dazed and unbelieving. But the staffing needs of the missionary societies were acute and increasingly the Africa Secretary and I had come to believe that I should be sent to the Northern Rhodesian Copperbelt as the second ministerial appointment from the Church of Scotland to the United Missions team working there.

I wrote therefore to the Leader of that team, Revd Arthur Cross, not knowing that he had died suddenly in November 1945, nor able to guess that his elder daughter would become my wife only three years later. At long last, my letter to the Copperbelt was answered by Frank Bedford, the Methodist member of the team whom I was to be appointed to succeed. Thus spring and summer of 1946 passed and at last, in early October, after paying a brief visit to Dr Banda in London, I sailed from Southampton on the Winchester Castle, very much a bachelor.

A first sea voyage like that was bound to be unforgettable. It was made even more so by the fact that the liner was still rigged out as a troop ship; the beds were closely stacked hammocks in an increasingly hot and airless part of the ship; the food, though adequate, was monotonous; and the voyage lasted a full three weeks, taking us through the Mediterranean and down Suez to the Red Sea, then along the ancient Zanj-i-bar, the long coastline of Eastern Africa, and at last to Durban. One memory among scores flashes before me as I write: that of a loud-spoken woman passenger in sparkling white tropical wear, telling her friends and all around how she had 'beaten down' an Arab street seller in Port Said for a box of 'quite delicious dates'. "You must have one", she said, as she took the box from her bag and began to open it. Then her face fell, for, neatly and individually arranged in date-sized wrappings were two trays of pebbles.

Nor can I forget the sickness that seized scores of passengers as well as members of the crew as we steamed south from Suez. "Mass hysteria", the Captain was reported as saying as the ship's doctor pottered around with doses of bismuth for passengers doubled up in pain, some crying out and many vomiting. Then, said the grapevine, the Big Man had a sharp attack of mass hysteria alone in his solitary suite. My own experience of the sickness was very sharp but short. With buckling legs, I took up my sheet and joined two other lads who felt the same need for air at night. We found a secluded spot and were sucked at once into sleep, only to be rudely awakened around midnight by a lusty team of deck-swabbers who sent us scattering down below.

Daily Bible study, searching, frank and lively, in an outstandingly ecumenical group of around twenty, was a source of real stimulus under the equatorial sun. One of the group, a gifted poet, was a young Afrikaner in training for the ministry of the Dutch Reformed Church in South Africa, who confessed privately to deep disquiet about his Church's equation of Christianity with apartheid, yet saw no way out of his dilemma and so was in reality accepting it as a schizophrenic necessity.

The day we docked in Durban I was at the head of the queue waiting for permission to land. When, however, I reached the Immigration Desk, the rough young officer there said that my documents had not yet come from the ship. I must go back and get them. So up I went in vain, and down again, for another crack of his rough tongue and back up once more just as they were closing the ship. Six hours later, when everyone else was gone, the Officer picked up a paper that had been on his desk all day. "This is yours, I suppose", he said and began to drill me with questions, all of which I had answered on the form.

At last, weary, and parched, I found a taxi and was dropped at a luxury hotel. As I struggled up the sweeping stairs, clutching my baggage, dressed in khaki shorts and sticky with sweat, ladies in flowing gowns were gathering on the lawn in the cool of the evening, for the customary sundowner drink.

Next day I met up with two Scots women missionaries who had been on the Winchester Castle and were also heading north. A special settlers' train took us from Durban, through the Valley of a Thousand Hills and then across Southern Rhodesia to the Victoria Falls. David Livingstone discovered that mighty cataract in 1855, they tell us. But 'discovery' is a very relative term and often very parochial. For the Tonga and the Lozi people had known the Falls for many generations before the lonely missionary-explorer sighted them. The great river that runs from the watershed region where Angola and Zaire meet and curves southwest and then eastwards until it spills at last into the Indian Ocean is given different names by the different peoples who fish its waters - Yambeshi, Lyambayi, Gwembe, Zambezi and so forth. For them it belongs to the dawn of their corporate history in that vast region of middle Africa.

The rains had started as our train chugged through the Tonga plateau by Choma and Mazabuka on its way to Lusaka, the capital of the Protectorate. At its frequent stops, children from tiny scruffy villages nearby rushed out to greet the train. A few men followed with carved curios for sale. Women with flat baskets of bananas, nuts and big coarse home-baked buns did a brisk trade around the 'native' carriages. But it was to the 'European' section of the train that the children crowded, many of them in ragged clothes, some little boys without trousers, young teenage girls carrying a little sibling or nephew or even grand-nephew or niece on their backs. "Ceef me one penny, plees Bwana - o' bled, plees", they chanted as their bare feet skliffed in the sandy ground. "Plees, Meesees, bled. Am ve' hungly - o' penny plees". There was little response at first. The supplications grew perceptibly louder, till suddenly an anglers' rod lashed out from a carriage window, and the children scattered like chickens. As the train at long last juddered into slow motion, a few pennies - Rhodesian copper coins with holes in them - pattered on the ground and the children pounced on them, and tussled with one another like city sparrows. But white was white and black was black in the Protectorate, as I was to realise more each day, and never the twain would meet.

Before leaving Scotland, I had visited an old missionary in a cold corner of Peeblesshire, a man who had spent many years on the sun-soaked shore of Lake Malawi. He had, I noticed at once, the apple cheeks of a Scots school-boy on a keen winter morning; the more surprising after long exposure to the sallowing tropical sun. It is not however for his complexion that A.G. McAlpine appears here, but for a word he spoke when we met. "What a mistake we made", he said, "when we first went to Nyasaland! We forgot that of course God had been there before us, so we set about preparing to introduce him like a foreign visitor".

I arrived in Mufulira on 2nd November 1946. My pocket edition of Daily Light had as its caption, "Unto this are you called". Now, so many years later, I recall strongly the sense of benison over my days. As the old steam engine hauled us north from Kabwe to the Copperbelt, I scribbled these lines:

> He was here first. I see, I know it.
> Finger prints of a joyous grace
> Tell of Him. Love all unexpected
> Welcomes me. Christ has blessed this place.
>
> He's here still - so I am not lonely,
> Making friends for Himself and me.
> When His friends are my friends,
> Believe me, God reveals His eternity.
>
> He'll be here when I'm gone, my Master,
> Knowing where I have toiled and sought.
> His the planning, the grace, the keeping.
> Lord, empower me to live this thought.

Chapter 3
MUFULIRA

My reading of the etymology of this name of my first African sphere of work gives it a meaning similar to Bethlehem - a place of plenty. The part of it to which I was first taken was the 'non-Mine' section of the 'European township', the few streets sometimes called the government township. There the local District Commissioner lived in a large villa. There too lived the police officers, teachers, shopkeepers, bankers, railway staff and all other white people who were not employees of the Mufulira Copper Mine.

But whether Mine or non-Mine, the houses of the European township presented a colourful picture of plenty. For Mine employees, the free water allowance was so great that their gardens could be watered daily through the six dry months from April to October. The Mine also provided delightful sports facilities for white employees, including a swimming pool, though quite a few houses had their own family pools in their gardens. Each house had its quota of domestic and garden servants. This necessitated the existence of a one-roomed brick shack or 'kaya' at the bottom of the garden of each bungalow or villa. Between one row of such servants' quarters and the next ran the sanitary lane, from which bins of domestic refuse were removed by the cleansing department.

Life in the non-Mine part of the white township was a shade less lustrous but generous and expensive nonetheless. As a missionary, I had to live in this part. Water and light were supplied by the Mine and charged to such non-Mine householders. My monthly bill for these utilities was, I discovered to my horror, not much less than a third of my pay. But then only other missionaries were in that wage bracket.

This austerity, however, detracted in no way from the warmth of my welcome by the Revd Frank Bedford and his family. Thus for me began six weeks of 'familiarisation' before the Bedfords would set off for England. Bedford, who was of great stature, combined enormous energy and zest with periodic moments of

deflation as he strove to wind up his work and carry out a
satisfactory handover to me. Thus it was that, shortly before
Christmas, he called me to what was to be my office and placed
before me three tomes. "There you are", he said, "Your cash book,
your ledger and your journal". A cash-book I had operated in
Edinburgh for the expenses of the boys' club camps. The word
ledger had a faint sulphuric tang of Scrooge about it. David
Livingstone kept diaries. I had two volumes of his *Last Journals*
waiting to be unpacked from a tea-chest of books. This other
connotation was wholly strange to me. Learning how to use the
journal in harmony with ledger and cash-book and to round off
every such monthly harmonisation by making a bank reconciliation
was a discipline which had been overlooked in the bright tales of
missionary enterprise that had fed my earlier dreams in Edinburgh.

First Impressions - First Tasks

My work in Mufulira was, they told me, to be fourfold. As a
minister of religion I was to serve two wholly unrelated
congregations, one black, one white. I was to be honorary Manager
of the three African schools in the area; a lower primary and a
'middle school' in the 'government location' and a big upper
primary in the 'Mine compound'. Lastly, I was to be responsible
for all the financial transactions and book-keeping in Mufulira, as a
member of the United Missions in the Copperbelt. The Northern
Rhodesia Government was then applying an increasing number of
regulations, through its Provincial Education Officers, for the
administration of African schools. But apart from fixing the
amounts allowed for equipment and laying down the wages of
African staff, NRG left missionary Managers of Schools to 'run'
the schools without remuneration. I was later to discover that when
the territory was ruled by the British South Africa Company (1890-
1924) and for a considerable period thereafter, the total cost of
African education was borne by missionary societies which thereby
had to exact fees in cash or kind from time to time from the pupils'
families. I was to learn, much sooner, that my association with
'schools for munts' made my name 'stink' for a section of the white
population whose pathological hatred of black people has for so
long darkened southern Africa.

When the Bedfords left, I took over the mission house and at
once asked John Ngwele, their 'garden-boy' to stay with me and

look after things for me. Ngwele was about 16 years of age, short
of stature, but lithe and strong. He had planned to leave the
Copperbelt for his home on the upper reaches of the Zambezi, the
country of the Luvale People. Soon he would be looking for a
wife, he said. But he agreed to stay and I found him considerate and
companionable as well as competent. When I was tempted to skip
a meal because of an overloaded time-table, he would insist that I
relax and eat. Though he had never cooked our type of food, he
learned quickly what I knew and soon surpassed me. He had a
quick sense of fun. Only once, when I placed a three-legged
chameleon under a baking bowl and then suggested he should put
the bowl back on its shelf, did a joke misfire. Then stricken horror
showed on his face as he fled from the house. For the chameleon,
arch-deceiver, all colours to all creatures, was the incarnation of
Evil to his people, as was the snake in Eden.

   Life was non-stop in Mufulira. The work of the African schools
had me on the go by 7am and many nights it was after 10pm when
meetings or visits in the white township ended. For among members
of the 'European' church were many kindly people who thrived
on hymn-singing and Bible study and whose favourite hymns were
constantly being chosen. A spontaneous unaccountable parody of
one of them - "When the roll is called up yonder... I'll be standing
at the corner of the street" - tickled my fancy sorely and made it
excruciatingly difficult to sing the correct words without exploding
in mirth. So too the ditty: "If you've had a kindness shown, pass it
on", which goes on to observe, *a propos* of nothing it seems, that
"April beam, the little thing, comes to cheer the flowers of spring".
This piece of bathos evoked from our mission Leader, George
Fraser, a gloss hissed *sotto voce* through clamped teeth: "April beam,
the itsy-witsy, tootsy-wootsy little thing". Fraser, son of one of the
distinguished missionary pioneers in Nyasaland, Donald Fraser,
was a man of boyish, often impish fun, combined with selflessness
and relentless devotion to duty, all inspired by a vision of the love
of God shared with others who also lived out its amazing assertion:
"Unles you become like little children, you cannot see the
Kingdom".

A Racist Church

   That white congregation was drawn from a wide spectrum of
protestant denominations and sects, some of whom baptised adults

to a chorus of 'pentecostal' hallelujahs. But solid Scots were there too, with merry Methodists and big-hearted Baptists. They all wanted to share something of fellowship and prayer and praise. They sang with particular gusto the hymn that begins with the words "Sing we the King who is coming to reign" and goes on to declare that "races long severed his love shall unite". What they believed, individually in their inner hearts about race relations in Africa, it was hard to guess. But there would be few among them to reject explicitly the assertion of one of that congregation that "the only native who's allowed into this building is the cleaner and he's not allowed to pray".

Yet once I remember unexpectedly tapping a spring of compassion. We had been building a new house for Revd Gideon Chinula in Ndola's 'main location'. When it was all but ready for occupation, the thatcher swept up the loose straw on the ground and lit it. A capricious eddy in the breeze lifted a bunch of burning grass and blew it against the roof. As the breeze increased, the whole roof became an inferno and only valiant efforts with buckets drawn from a single tap saved the rest of the woodwork. That was on a Thursday. The Cottage Meeting of the Mufulira European Free Church was just starting when word of the fire reached me. I mentioned it as a simple statement of fact. Before I went home I had received cash and cheques totalling quite a lot more than the cost of a new roof. Yet it was sadly true that, if I had announced that Gideon Chinula would visit the next Cottage Meeting, many if not all would have stayed away. "I find", said Paul of Tarsus, "a war inside myself".

I have made these jottings about the white township of Mufulira, not because my relationship to it was the primary part of my life, but because, by the emphatic operation of what was indeed a totalitarian colour bar, if not by explicit 'law', I was obliged to live in that segregated township and would not have been allowed to reside in the so-called 'location' where by the same token, my senior colleague and beloved friend, Revd David Ramushu, had to live. The neighbouring compound, with its many thousands of inhabitants, was officially the private property of the Mine and residence there would have been unthinkable.

Our lives cannot but be influenced to some extent by where we sleep and clean our teeth. So, you see, it was understandably easy for a missionary, himself of European origin to be enfolded by the community of his ethnic 'kith and kin' and moulded by its *mores*. And because that community was noteworthy for its big-heartedness within the circle of 'whiteness', it offered by and large a pleasant environment. There was a genuinely sweet seductiveness about, say, an evening meal at the Nels' or the McAllisters' or the van der Westhuizens' - a cool dining room, dinner by candlelight and the quiet movement of the shoeless feet of the silent servants as they anticipated your wants at table, bringing food and removing dishes so rhythmically that table talk could flow uninterrupted. Thus it was fascinating if nonetheless frightening to see how people from a single-end in Port Glasgow, now owners of a private swimming pool could make the transition so smoothly and swiftly to served dinners and a feudal form of master-servant relations.

Effective African Leadership

Mufulira's total population was, I believe, about 47,000 in 1946. But only just around 4,000 were white. The majority, like that minority, came from a range of widely separated home areas. There were Nyakyusa from Tanzania, Mbundu from Angola, Shona and Sutu from south of the Zambezi as well as people of every 'tribe' in Zambia and Malawi. By an understandable fact of history, a group of Bemba men from the northern province had been large enough, in the first days of the copper mines, to establish their own Chi-Bemba language unwittingly as the *lingua franca* of the burgeoning bustling black communities of the Copperbelt.

Yet in the vibrant life of the young church that came to birth in those compounds and locations, especially notable leadership was provided by Malawians and eastern Zambians whose mother tongues were Chi-Tumbuka or Chi-Chewa. The 'African congregation' to which I was appointed in Mufulira had members from literally scores of different rural communities, and I found them thriving under the pastoral care of a Sutu whose origins were in the Transvaal and who had grown up in what is now Zimbabwe, David Mwankopane Ramushu. He was a glorious person, short of stature but with a soaring soul and an endless capacity for fun and frolic. He was, I imagine, about 12 years older than myself. My memories of him are legion, not least of his happy home life and his beds of deep red roses round the tiny house rented to the church for his use in a scruffy part of Mufulira's delapidated 'government location'.

I can see him standing on an ant-hill proclaiming the gospel to a milling crowd in the Mine compound on a Sunday afternoon while, well within earshot, a team of young tap-dancers in white tunics and red sashes pipe out their rhythm on raucous tin whistles. Suddenly a very drunk man shouts as Ramushu is speaking and confusion threatens to cut the message short. But the little minister commands the drunkard to be quiet with such authority that order is restored and the message is received.

I can see him 'dressing down' an elderly evangelist for slackness in his visitation of outlying contractors' compounds. I can see him going down into an open sewer to drag from it a drunkard who has ridden his bicycle off the track and plunged into the noisome creek. And I can see his genial smile when I introduce him to Ray Stuart, warm-hearted church member in the white township, who responds "Oh, so this is your minister boy? Pleased to meet you. Are you helping your new Bwana, eh?" For Ramushu knew as I knew, that the boy in the relationship was really myself; and for me, working under Ramushu's leadership was a great privilege.

I can see him again when suddenly our work is thrown into darkness by the spread of a slanderous tale that he has been interfering with other men's wives. For at first we could not find the source of the lie. Mary Ramushu's quiet word: "Don't fear for me. I know my David" made my task slightly less grim when at last I had to chair the meeting at which the mischief-maker was identified and condemned. David's Good Friday message, soon after, revealed a deepened insight into Gethsemane and Golgotha, though he made no mention in public of what he himself had been made to suffer.

I have two other indelible memories of David Ramushu. There was the time when he became convinced that many black folk were afraid to go to the Mine African Hospital because of the sadistic cruelty of the white South African male nurse in charge. The two of us collected convincing testimonies about the man's brutalities, which included the sawing-off of a gangrenous leg without anaesthetic. The more he heard, the hotter became Ramushu's anger. Then choosing his moment carefully, he strode one day to the hospital. The Superintendent, he was sure, would be in his office then; and so he was. So, without knocking, Ramushu entered, crossed the room quickly to stand at the man's back and shouted: "Listen to me". Pouring a torrential list of his malpractices upon him, he finished like this: "You may not fear my people's anger. But you will answer for this to God". Then, without waiting for the man to muster his response, David strode from the room.

Northern Rhodesia, despite the benevolence of the title 'Protectorate' was, in those days, a replica of South Africa. Ramushu had therefore taken a grave personal risk in denouncing the man to his face. Not long afterwards, however, on becoming aware of the possibility of a major popular demonstration against the nursing superintendent by African miners throughout the Copperbelt, the authorities, so we heard, terminated his appointment, though not without generous financial provision for travel, holiday, etc.

The last of these selected memories also relates to Ramushu's character as a committed Christian, in a racist situation. He had been to the Methodist Conference at Kafue. He was travelling north by train and being 'non-white' could not travel in comfort. I went to Ndola station by mission car to meet him and carry him the 43 miles back to Mufulira. The train, as usual, was very late. When he alighted, I saw at once that he was fevered. There were plenty of mosquitoes around Kafue. He was shivering, his teeth chattering and a cold sweat beaded his brow. He was wearing a clerical collar. "He needs somethimg warm", I decided and went to buy tea. Even the refreshment kiosks were segregated but I bought two cups and was about to carry them to where he was waiting when the European girl at the counter said: "Who's the second cup for?" "For my friend", I replied. "He's not allowed a cup", she retorted. "He's a kaffir. He's got to drink from a tin mug". At first I ignored this remark but as she became more strident, I said, "He's drinking from this cup. If it's against the law, I'm pleased to break it. That's the last word".

Such incidents leave you shaking a bit. After I had settled Ramushu into the car, wrapped him in a rug and driven off, I expressed sorrow over such a horrid encounter, especially when he was unwell. "How do you feel", I asked, "when such things happen?" "Such things do happen, Fergus", he said. "They've happened before and each time my first reaction is great anger. You know I get hot quickly. Then I remember that they crucified Jesus and this is nothing to that".

As a postscript to those few memories out of so many about David Ramushu, let me tell the story of his name as he told it to me, and as I then used it for translation into Bemba for my higher language exam. Mwankopane Masemula was a young Musutu whose father held some chiefly rank. The lad went on a visit to the big city, presumably Cape Town. As he wandered up and down, gazing at the strange life of city dwellers, he saw a crowd gathering round a man who was clearly going to address them. What that speaker said no one could recall. But it was a Christian message and it touched young Masemula's heart. "I am going to follow Jesus", he said, his doubts gone, and went off home to tell his family of his great experience. To his father, however, his good news was very bad news. "No son of mine", said he, "shall ever worship foreign gods. We have always prayed to the High God through the spirits of our forefathers. What has been good enough for us is good enough for our children. So drop this nonsense, my boy and never speak of it again."

But Mwankopane Masemula's heart had been entered by this Jesus and he could not close the door of his soul now. "Please don't be angry, father", he pled, "for this new thing is inside me now". That only increased his father's fury. "I shall give you one night", he roared, "till dawn tomorrow and no longer. By then, if you are still in your foreign madness, my soldiers will drive you from my kingdom for ever". And so it was. Jesus hadn't withdrawn from Masemula's heart by sunrise and so, filled with hot tears and great fears, he raced away on his long legs, carrying nothing with him, hoping against hope that he could reach the frontiers of his father's realm before the soldiers caught up with him. Terrible days followed: no food, no rest, just fleeing like a duiker from a pack of lions.

Not till he was far, far beyond the reach of his father's power did he dare to stop. He had come upon a village, but the people were all away, probably in their fields. Too tired to think, Mwankopane dropped down in the shade of a big tree and plunged into the deepest sleep of his life.

At last he awoke. The air was filled with chatter. "Who are you?" they began to ask him. "We've never seen you before. Where have you come from?" "Oh, please", he begged, "let me kneel before your king and let me be his slave if only he will allow me to stay here".

So they took him to their king and he told his tale of woe. "Of course you may stay", said the kind king, "but not as a slave. As a free man you shall live as one of my people, on one condition only: that you keep our good law of peace". Mwankopane, however, was afraid to tell his name, lest word of him should somehow be carried back to his old father. So they understood and they called him Ramushu for the big tree in whose shade they had found him sleeping. Thus I heard the story of my friend David's family name: and found with it a parable of the kingdom.

Living Christianity

Our congregation in the Mine compound was always singing. Sunday after Sunday so many people came that as many sat on the ground outside as found space to sit inside. And when you left the pulpit to receive the offering, you had to step over children packed close together around the communion table. Some high churchmen might have found it offensive: Jesus would have loved it. Sometimes during the service a little old man from some distant village would rise and tiptoe out, soon to tiptoe back again. It was some time before I discovered that the thirst for snuff could become so compelling that a brief absence was necessary for a quick packing of the nostrils. Snuff was not offensive. Its main immediate effect was an audible one: all the 'm's in hymns became 'b's until the nasal passages cleared again.

The giving of the offering was a great moment in the service. Instead of elders or deacons touring round the pews collecting peoples' gifts, the congregation would move up in long lines, women and girls first, men and boys behind, to place their offerings on the Table. Often a little woman would come up, stooping meekly, and extend a coin as she neared the table from her head-cloth or her waist-band. Money was scarce for most black people and a sixpence was more than she could spare. So she would lay down her sixpence and neatly flick five pennies from the table into her palm. There her gift would lie, under the eyes of the deacons, along with cobs of maize and little bowls of eggs, until the service ended. The eggs would be deftly tested in a basin of water for freshness and then sold and turned into the cash that the work of the church required.

Learning the Language

However busy my days were, I had to keep before me the urgency of grasping the local language. The Protectorate's all-pervasive 'colour bar' made it hard when black people spoke to white, to seek, let alone find, that ready, lightsome reciprocity that is the mark of true friendship. That fact, added to inherent courtesy, made a missionary's black associates reluctant to correct him if he made mistakes in their language. My first such experience came when I went one day to see Patrick Mkandawire, headmaster of the Mine School and found three of the women who supervised sewing classes waiting at his door. "How are you, mothers?" I asked. "Is there peace at your places?" - which is the literal translation of

"*Mwapoleni Bamayo. Bushe kuli umutende ku myenu?*" "Yes," they assured me, "we are well, if it is well with you". Then came my clanger: instead of saying correctly, "You'll be seeing the headmaster about housewifery matters?" I said what actually meant, "You'll be here to discuss your gynaecological affairs with the headmaster". But the ladies showed no sign of surprise, let alone resentment. It was a tiny doubt that started niggling inside me as I cycled home that led me to discover what I'd really said.

Nor could I comfort myself by remembering the tale of the dedicated, bustling, loquacious Anglican lady missionary who, on arriving in the country, sought to learn by heart the Bemba translation of this pious utterance: "I have come to be your friend" - "*Naisa ku kuba ichibusa chenu*". A word of perilously similar sound to '*chibusa*' was among the first words she naturally heard and identified. Affably, she moved around, smiling on all and sundry, protesting her pleasure in seeking to be their '*chimbusu*', which means 'outside toilet' or 'pit latrine'.

This comedy of errors must conclude with the story of a missionary, who very early in his career gained a well-earned reputation for outstanding linguistic ability. Decades after he left Africa I found people still remembering him as the man who truly spoke as if the language was his mother tongue.

The lake-shore prayer-house was packed and scores sat outside. The African minister was present. Kalimanjira they called him, plougher of the highway, because of his tireless travelling among his people. He expected of others the commitment he gave himself. His presence heightened the tension of the moment for the young missionary, as the people's whole-hearted praise uplifted his spirit. 'Righteousness' was the theme of his message, righteousness as a way of life, never a matter of lip service, but instead pervading the whole network of relationships that make up daily living. "In the home, between husband and wife, parents and children, let righteousness be expressed in thought, word and deed. In the market-place no less, where temptations are strong, let true righteousness be your only way of doing business. If misunderstanding is spoiling your dealings with someone, put practical righteousness into your words and deeds, so that peace may return". And so on he went, conscious of a real rapport between his hearers and himself.

The worship was over at last. Hundreds of hands shook his as the people spoke their thanks and good wishes. Back in the little vestry, the young man found Kalimanjira. "That was a great word", said the old saint. "Truly we have never had a *mzungu* here who could use our language as you do".

"*Ndagha, ndagha, mwalafyale* - Thank you so much, sir", said the young missionary, "But please, I want you to tell me about my mistakes". Kalimanjira hesitated but at last, in response to the lad's sincere entreaty, he spoke: "No," he said, "you did very, very well. The one mistake did not matter for they would all understand what you wanted to say. It was just this word" - and he quoted the key word of the message - "When you wanted really to say such and such, our word for righteousness". The meaning of the wrong word, so similar in sound, suddenly flashed into the young man's mind: it meant 'vomiting'. "In the market place, where temptations are strong, let real vomiting be your only way of doing business... In short, in your family life and no less in all your other relationships, vomit copiously and ceaselessly. This is the only way to obey the law of God". For a long time thereafter the thought of his monumental blunder was enough to turn the young man's stomach!

Nonetheless, in my first weeks I found the truth of the Bemba proverb - "*Uwa matwi, tawa ku nsala* - He who listens won't go hungry". For it was by constant, conscious listening that one could discover the riches, the short cuts, the innumerable nuances of what was often called 'the vernacular': and with them a host of insights into social philosophy and communal wisdom. The hunger was always there but so was the food to appease it. And one would have had to be really obtuse not to find fascination in the multifarious ways of saying hello and goodbye.

In my early teens, I overheard two church elders greeting each other on a raw, dank Sunday morning in Edinburgh. "Good morning, George", said Tom. "What's good about it?" answered George; confirming the pitiful devaluation of what had once been the benediction: "May God give you a good morning". A reciprocal concern for each other's welfare had thus been supplanted by a dreary, dejecting commentary on the meteorological condition of the moment. Central Africa, it has been said, has climate but little weather. But the absence of abrasive abuse of weather conditions reflects, I am sure, something more positive than the mere absence of weather like the weather of Scotland.

"Are you all at peace?" "Yes, we are in health if you too are well". This typical Zambian greeting surely bespeaks a deep conviction that, in John Donne's words, "No man is an island"; that indeed, health, like sickness, and peace, like the absence of it, are properties of neighbourhood. Having drunk of the waters of Africa, I cannot find such phrases as 'Cheerio' or ''Bye' other than banal when compared with "May you stay in peace" and "May you go and arrive in peace" which are in everyday use in Zambia.

My first months in Mufulira coincided with the rainy season. Towering cumulo-nimbus clouds built up more and more in early November until they burst in torrential rain, followed by scintillating blue skies and greatly sharpened visibility. More great clouds soon formed, however, and so the cycle was repeated. I found the storms of lightning and thunder glorious, especially after dark. The rainy season, *amainsa*, also brought release to a symphony of piquant perfumes long bottled up in the dry ground and in the leaves of the dust-coated forests. Sometimes I had a conscious longing for the tang of sea air. But I was finding undreamed-of spicy fragrances that belonged to the interplay of *lusuba* and *mainsa*, the semesters of dryness and rain that profoundly influenced life in the savannas of Zambia. *Umuloboko*, the first rain, uttered a sharp call to myriad creatures great and small to revel in the drenching and the resurgence of the sun-parched earth.

Children, stark naked, screaming with delight as they splashed in huge pools that had been dusty hollows only yesterday; frogs with eyes drooping with the exhaustion of an orgy of guzzling flying ants as they poured out of little holes in the earth in response to some mysterious but irrestible impulse; these and many other symbols never failed to delight me as each year revolved. And talking of rain, there is a truth that we ignore to our own hurt in the Zambian proverb: "*Apa kusangile imfula e pa bukulu bwa mpanga -* Where the rain finds you, there is the middle of the world". Pining for somewhere else can only debilitate you. At whatever point of place or time you are, in youth or age, in weal or woe, in cloud or in sunshine, take and spend the strength given to you, esteeming no place, for the present, more important than where you are. Take and use it as a farmer would take and use his hoe as the crusted earth yielded to the kneading fingers of most welcome rain.

Chapter 4
GOING UP
COUNTRY

The rains of the 1946-47 season were nearing their end when the United Missions agreed to give me a spell of intensive language study in the heartland of the Bemba people in the northern province. Understandably, the proposal was resisted by some colleagues who stressed that every team member was badly overworked, and no one could be expected to 'cover' for me. But the Committee in Edinburgh strongly stressed the importance of language study, and so I was allowed three months' absence from Mufulira.

Bound for Lubwa

Lubwa in the Chinsali district, east of the River Chambeshi, was my destination. A Scots missionary had been stationed there in 1913 when the centenary of David Livingstone's birth had evoked increased offerings for missionary work. Nine years earlier a vigorous pioneer programme in evangelism had been undertaken in Chinsali by David Julizya Kaunda, a Tonga from the shores of Lake Malawi. He had had his Christian education at Livingstonia. His nine years had yielded a striking harvest. His Bemba nickname of endearment, Chendaluta, was given in honour of his constant visitation of the little schools and congregations that were springing from the seeds he had sown. David Kaunda is commemorated still on the wall of the church building at Lubwa. Twenty-six years after his death, his youngest child, Kenneth David, was to become, in 1958, the chosen leader of Zambia's struggle for liberation from the ill-starred Central African Federation and for national sovereignty.

The journey from Mufulira to Lubwa was hazardous. In the hope that I could cross the Chambeshi by canoe, I was flown to Kasama in a tiny plane, piloted by a man who, I guessed, hadn't assuaged his thirst for monkey tricks in the air by the time the European war ended in 1945. He shouted at one point that we were above the Bangweulu swamps and it flashed on me that,

seventy four years earlier to the month, David Livingstone had
struggled through that hostile terrain, with Susi, Chuma and the
rest, on the way to Chipundu and his death there in the house of
Chief Chitambo. Weren't all of us, missionaries of the twentieth
century, in some way his heirs? Years later, I was to hear some of
the nicknames by which he had been known: *Chilezu* (Beardy),
was descriptive, but said little; *Ikulamubanga* was more perceptive
- He who could drag a *mubanga* tree, memorable for his sheer
compulsive vitality; but perhaps *Chilele-pa-maba* tells us most - He
who would sleep in the marshes if need be. For Livingstone was
known and loved for his innate humanity. For him 'our race' was
the human race, not the *herrenvolk* of apartheid's fascist philosophy.
So he'd be content to stop and sleep wherever his companions might
find a spot, even (by poetic licence) in the swamps.

It was an agent of the African Lakes Corporation who met me
off the plane. I wonder if I was visibly spinning as I felt I was when
the little plane spilled me onto the rough grassy runway. The
Corporation was called Mandala throughout Nyasaland and
Northern Rhodesia, in commemoration of its founder. John Moir,
whose spectacles reflected the *mandala* of the sun. The Kasama
agent, who had married a missionary, was 'too fond of the bottle'
and had a leg in plaster in consequence. There was no possibility,
he told me, of crossing the Chambeshi at Mulema by canoe. The
great river was in dangerous spate. However, his senior colleague,
a stout and breathless man with a kind heart, more than one African
wife and a considerable progeny, dreamed up a trip for his freight
lorry to Mupika on the Great North Road. Somehow he managed
to arrange for me to be met there by missionaries going from
Chitambo to Lubwa for a meeting of the Mission Council. My
seemingly hopeless problem was thus swiftly and efficiently resolved
and I was soon hammering along the 140 miles of earth road in a
huge vehicle carrying far less than a payload of Tom-tom cigarettes,
tins of corned beef, bags of salt, four gallon 'debbies' of paraffin
and a variety of other goods for Mandala's little shop at Mupika. I
was carried free. *"Apo Lesa anayila, tapafuka chushi"* say the wise
ones of the Bemba - "Where God cooks your food, there's no
smoke".

Kaunda and Kapoli

I kept a diary in those days. Many of its entries were minimal. But for April 1947 there were these jottings: "Chat with teachers, Kenneth Kaunda and others"; and then "Another chat with K. Kaunda - singing together". On arrival at Lubwa, I had found the mission staff busied with the meetings of the Council. I was glad of the chance to meet the local community and had to ask for help at once in planning how best to use my twelve weeks in language study. It was then that I met Kaunda. As I look back over the fifty years and remember the many other mission stations that I would come to know, I am sure my memory is correct: Lubwa, despite the pleasantness of the company of missionaries together and, on the other side, the ready laughter of village people, had something heavy in its atmosphere. In subsequent years, the small and outwardly decaying mission station, far away in the 'bush' was to gain fame on account of the international stature of Zambia's first president and also alas! from the tribulations associated with the 'Lumpa Movement' of Alice Lenshina. Thus Lubwa has been the subject of scholarly research; and it has been suggested that, as it struck me in 1947, Lubwa lived for a long time under the sombre shadow of its first Scottish missionary.

He was an old man when I met him at Lubwa in the month of the harvest moon. We had corresponded before I left Scotland. His letters had a deep solemnity in them, so different from those merry epistles that we had received as children from 'Uncle Matthew' in northern Nyasaland. A printer by trade, the old man had joined the team led by Dr Robert Laws in the Livingstonia field of the Free Church of Scotland. A meticulous interest in African languages had marked the whole of his career, with a record of some translation work in the Tonga language of Malawi and in both Mwanga and Bemba in Zambia. His exceptional dedication to church affairs led to his being 'ordained on the field' and so he was 'the reverend' when he was sent to Chinsali in 1913. In his early days there, he clashed on a number of occasions with Rhodes's British South Africa Company which had seized and subjugated the territory in the 1890s. The conquest was driven home by ruthless tax collectors and by coercive labour recruitment. Lubwa's first foreign missionary is remembered still for his stern reaction to the excesses of these tax collectors. But he built the mission station on lines of visible segregation and, perhaps most sadly, set special seats in the transepts of the church for people of European stock. The young Kaunda and his fellow teachers spoke bitterly to me about those 'white seats' soon after we first met. "Will there be different sections in heaven?" they asked.

Gravitas does not readily assimilate with joy; and the particularly stern manner that distinguished the old missionary unwittingly equated virtue in an African associate with submissiveness, and placed confidence in people of humble obedience rather than in those of questing intelligence and critical minds. Inevitably sap that was needed for the nourishment of the young church was channelled away from its roots and they, in turn, did not go deep enough to support mature growth in the local soil. It was at the time of my first visit to Lubwa that I became aware of two books by an Anglican missionary and missiologist, Roland Allen, significantly entitled *The Spontaneous Expansion of the Church* and *Missionary Methods: St Paul's or Ours?* I became conscious also of how complex was the challenge of history to the missionary churches of the post-Livingstone period. For they exported their agents and their doctrines in sharply and sometimes bitterly denominational packages; and they did so at a time when, in the interests of convenience as well as in simple secular faith in the imperialist outreach, they found it easy if not natural to regard the rapacious colonialist conquerors of central Africa as 'powers that be' who were 'ordained of God'. As I pondered these crucial issues, I had reason to be even more grateful for the radical insights of Mwangonde Faulds.

It was Kenneth Kaunda, as headmaster of the local school, who selected a tutor in Bemba for me. One day, as I sat at the desk in my room in a big house on the hill behind the mission station, attempting to translate a passage of Matthew's Gospel in Bemba, I heard a muffled cough on the verandah outside. Then, after a moment's silence, a voice said "*Odi*", a handy little word announcing one's arrival and to which the correct reply is "*Odini*". I rose and went to the door, where there stood a lad, glistening with freshness and life, his hair very neatly combed and parted, his white teeth gleaming, and clad in a khaki shirt and a brief pair of khaki shorts, very carefully ironed.

"*Nine, mukwai*", he said. "It is I". "And who are you?" "Myself? Oh, I am (let us call him) Jonas". "Jonas who?" "Oh, it is Kapoli, my name. It means to say wild pig", he replied and could not contain his mirth. "He can't be more than 14", I thought but I said: "*Ni shani, Ba Kapoli*", meaning "Can I help you, Mr Kapoli?" "But myself I am helping you", he said now laughing freely. "If you are Bwana Makfason, the new European from Mufulira, it is myself your teacher in Bemba."

An Unexpected Journey

Thus began a very happy relationship made more so by the sudden notion of a senior missionary from the southern station that I should accompany him on a farewell odyssey to all the Scottish mission stations in Northern Rhodesia and the northern part of Nyasaland. I couldn't go, I protested, since the UMCB had sent me on a brief and intensive language study course. But I was overborne not only by the man who planned the 1800 mile tour but by other missionaries. "You're getting on fine with the language", they said. "Take a Bemba with you and you'll manage to learn a lot on the way. My conscience was in a spin. I sensed, though he would not say so, that the master of the odyssey really wanted a co-driver. He seemed old and tired and I was under pressure to help him in this way. But what would my fellow members of the Copperbelt team say when they heard that I was gallivanting round the world?"

I do not dispute Shakespeare's assertion that "there is a tide in the affairs of men which, taken at the flood, leads on to fortune". All I knew in that last week of April was that a strong tide was bearing me where I'd never dreamt of going. In retrospect perhaps I have rationalised it in terms of a verse I wrote once in parody of Omar Khayam:

> The moving finger works, and having wrought
> Moves on. Yet from each ravelling, each knot
> Stands forth a tapestry of grace, and hope
> That Love, so proved, has all the future fraught.

For that totally unscheduled escapade was to prove of great interest to my future life.

The Ford International 15-cwt vanette in which we were to make the grand tour was ramshackle but roadworthy. The missionary from Chitambo was a wizard at motor mechanics and was, moreover, giving lessons in driving and car maintenance, at a fee of five shillings a month, to his personal house-servant who accompanied us. So, along with a clumsy load of baggage, car tools, etc, plus two forty-four gallon drums of petrol, off we went, first

as far south as Lusaka and then eastwards, through the Luangwa
escarpment, by Fort Jameson (now Chipata), named after Leander
Starr Jameson, Rhodes' henchman whose armed raid on the
Transvaal Republic had ignited the Boer War in 1895. From there
we drove into Malawi.

Once again, hundreds of memories clamour for inclusion - but
only a very few can be admitted here. The first is of our night at
Kapiri Mposhi, 40 miles north of Kabwe and 120 north of Lusaka.
The hotel there was for 'Europeans only' as were all the hotels of
the Protectorate. So who was being protected from whom? This
meant that the domestic servant-cum-learner mechanic and young
Jonas Kapoli had to sleep elsewhere. It was not till the morning
that I found where in fact they had slept: a broken-down, lousy
shed by the roadside which was the only provision for black
travellers. I inspected it with Jonas. There was no caretaker to look
after it. My Bemba teacher had had to keep his little wallet inside
his trousers and sleep clothed, for fear of *bakabwalala*, the prowling
pick-pockets who did nocturnal business in such places.

As we climbed into the mountains of the Luangwa escarpment,
the road became very rough. The missionary was a fast driver
himself, but competent. When he suddenly decided to let his servant
take the wheel and sit beside him barking instructions, Jonas and I
had to lie on lumpy baggage in the truck behind and carry on our
language lessons horizontally. The canvas canopy of the vanette
was old and full of holes. Dust swirled all the time, especially when
we ploughed through sand drifts. Meanwhile the petrol drums
waltzed an erratic twosome, sometimes bowing to us ominously
and straining the ropes that were meant to keep them steady.

"Say now: I shall see him tomorrow". "*Nde-mu-mona mailo*".
"No, please, sorry. It changes for tomorrow". "Oh, I remember:
Nka-mu-mona mailo. Is that right?" "Yes, please. *Nde-mu-mona* is
of today, not of tomorrow."

So we went on, and it was very enjoyable. Mercifully I did not
then realise that we were working with a language in which one
can list around thirty verb tenses. "Africans have no sense of time",
I often heard white folk say. Superficially perhaps they were right.
Peasant people go by the sun, especially in a sunny land. But I was
discovering a most precise sense of the relation of event to event,
of the completion or extension of action, and of gradations of
pastness and futurity which are made explicit in this long list of

tenses. Mobile mongrel languages like English, for all the virtues of
versatility that enable them to be instantly at the service of every
new technological phenomenon or extension of theoretical science,
have, on their negative side a certain vulgarity and a patent deficiency
in the leisured expression of sympathetic greetings. Thus, for
example, Scottish church elders do not have, readily to hand, a
practised vocabulary of pastoral therapy when there is a row in the
choir or Bill McSporran is threatening to break up his marriage
and go off with another man's wife; at least, not that gift for
articulating corporate healing that I have often witnessed in Zambia
and Malawi.

It was at Nyimba that we stopped for a night's rest. The
caretaker of the senescent government rest-house bustled about
preparing a room for us two white men. As he dusted the sheets, I
am sure he did not know that the net that he spread like a bell-tent
above my bed would keep in, and not out, an emaciated mosquito
ravenous for human blood. I heard its little piping voice but could
not hope to track it down. Dog-tired, I fell asleep at once; and, as
was to be confirmed two weeks later, *mung'wing'wi* went briskly
to work on my blood-stream.

As we drove eastwards we stopped at Chasefu, a mission station
founded from Nyasaland but geographically in Northern Rhodesia.
There, for some reason or other, the missionary from Chitambo
had some managerial authority over the district schools. Indeed,
he was anxious to see the local teachers and evangelists before taking
his farewell. Our stop at Chasefu resulted in my recruiting a team
of 'evangelists' for service in the Copperbelt.

The district served by each mission station was huge. Chasefu's
district included the *marambo*, a thinly populated region full of
wild beasts, that stretches from the Zambia-Malawi border to the
River Luangwa. Village schools and churches on the western side
of the river were supervised by Chitambo, whose district covered
more than 20,000 square miles. It was probably because of this
common boundary along the Luangwa that the School Manager at
Chitambo had been involved in a remote and largely nominal
supervisory relationship with the marambo. The downright, short-
tempered old man who had planned our round trip wasted no time
in 'winding up' his managerial task and handing over responsibility
for supervision of Chasefu's network of village schools to a senior
teacher and church elder, Harry Nyirenda.

Segregation Painful

Loudon Mission at Embangweni was our first stop in Nyasaland. It was late in the afternoon when we arrived at the house of the missionary-in-charge. A couple of servants appeared instantly and carried the bags of us two missionaries into the house. A zinc bath was put into our bedroom and filled by buckets of warm water. Night swooped down and as throughout most of the year, the temperature dropped sharply making a crackling log fire most welcome in the sitting-room. The local missionary's family were all away in Scotland. His servants however were quietly efficient and we were soon well fed. But I was now anxious about my young tutor. The learner-driver from Chitambo was an experienced traveller, but Jonas had never been away from home and we were now over a thousand miles from Lubwa. The local language, Tumbuka, was unknown to him, and so I was not reassured by my senior companion's irritable remark: "Forget it. Don't mollycoddle the boy. They know how to fix themselves up". I was by now familiar with this kind of comment from white people about anything that concerned the welfare of their black associates.

After coffee, therefore, I made an occasion for excusing myself. Outside, the air was now cold and the clear sky above was ablaze with the light of millions of stars. Orion, as always in the southern hemisphere, was standing on his head. The place was strange to me, but at last I heard Jonas's voice in response to my soft calling of his name. Had he found somewhere to sleep? I asked. No, he was just moving up and down to keep himself warm. "What about food?" "Mukwai, where could I find it? I am a stranger here". "Where is Chisembo the driver?" "Katwishi, mukwai. I don't know, I think he has been here before. Perhaps he knows someone". I decided then to look for the senior servant of the house, a dour man called Moses. Earlier I had heard his master playfully shouting for him, with a lisp, "Mozez, where's Mozez? I'll shoot the bootz off him". But Moses was clearly in charge of his own domain and respected for his capability.

Jonas was apprehensive about my approach to the old *major domo*. "Perhaps he is not happy feeding servants of white visitors", he said. But I could find no other solution. Moses, when I found him, was far from cooperative. At last he reluctantly agreed to allow Jonas to sleep on the ground in an open shelter beside a dying fire. But he offered no food. Then I remembered a half packet of pretty tasteless biscuits which I had left in the vanette. I don't know how many of them my tutor consumed before lying down, under a thin blanket, beside the embers of a fire. I was now feeling miserable. There was no way, short of making a real fuss in this house of strangers, that I could procure a decent meal for the lad. Nor did I want to express to him how I felt about the situation, which I now knew to be the pattern of behaviour in almost every place in central Africa where black and white had occasion to 'rub shoulders', so to speak, in proximity but without community.

"Goodnight, Jonas", I said. "I hope you will be able to sleep". "But we haven't said our prayers, mukwai", he replied. "Let us pray, please, before you go". I had no words myself and so asked him to pray. It was such a night as to make almost audible the declaration by the heavens of the glory of God. "*Natufukame*", said Jonas. "Let us kneel", and in his prayer he specially named my parents, my brother and my sisters in Scotland, asking God to keep them in happiness and health and peace.

Just as foreseeing is seeing beyond the normal range of sight, so surely forgiving is giving beyond giving. Somehow, though refreshed by a warm bath and well-fed, I had felt the physical discomfort of my guilt, as the 32nd Psalm describes the psychosomatic evidence of the shame we each have in what Paul called 'this body of death'. Young Jonas, on an empty stomach and chilly to the bone, gave me something then that went beyond the range of ordinary giving, all unaware that he was thus, as Francis of Assisi put it, an instrument of God's peace.

We spent a Sunday at that mission station. Again, as at Lubwa, seating in the 'house of prayer' was segregated, only instead of in the transepts it was what one would think of as choir chairs round a raised chancel that accommodated white people; a position of even more embarrassing prominence. Years later, I came across a comment made in the 1890s, in the news-sheet of the Blantyre Mission, to the effect that such divisive elements must not be allowed to spoil the transcendent fellowship that was of the essence of true Christianity, especially in situations of racial stress. My researches in central African history also brought to my notice the advice of a director of the British South Africa Company to white church people in the Zambian town of Livingstone that standards of social hygiene must not be endangered by admitting black people to

'white' churches. How wisely then the architect of the great church
at Blantyre in southern Malawi, had chosen the text for the wall of
the chancel: "My house shall be called of all nations the house of
prayer." How perceptive too is the root meaning of the Tumbuka
word for fellowship *wene-na-wene*: namely, one life and its concerns
and another life and its concerns, bound together. Any lesser
concept would be mere word play.

It is just because the classical texts of the Christian faith offer
some of the sublimest visions of living as 'members of one another'
in the rough and tumble of real life, that behaviour by Christians
which contradicts those visions becomes, however unwittingly, a
cause of stumbling and of scandal.

Livingstonia

There will be reason to speak later on about the enterprise of
Scottish missionaries that culminated in the establishment, in 1894,
on a high plateau called Khondowe, over 3000 feet above the Lake,
of a great centre of education, health and evangelism, whose founder
willed it to become 'the university of central Africa'.

The name Livingstonia commended itself at once to the band
of men and women of the Free Church of Scotland who planned
and brought to birth this project in Northern Nyasaland, only
two years after Livingstone's death in 1873 in the heart of Zambia.
The whole new field of evangelism was named after him but
increasingly the word Livingstonia was used specifically for the
mission estate on Khondowe.

Now, at last, I was to see Livingstonia and far sooner in my
career in Africa than I could have dared to hope. We had paid a
visit to Ekwendeni on the way north from Loudon, to Khondowe,
I still have a glowing memory of that visit and of the kind welcome
of the Revd Patrick Mzembe who introduced me to many of the
church members, the teachers and pupils of the upper primary
school and the staff of the hospital. Twenty-one years later, and
three years after Dr Hastings Banda had become first President of
the Republic of Malawi, I presented myself at a Malawian
immigration post, seeking entry from Zambia so that I could do
local research on the lake-shore about David Kaunda for my
biography of his son, the President of Zambia. But I had no triptique
for my vehicle. They'd assured me in Lusaka that no such document
would be required. The junior immigration officer, by the light of

a guttering candle, was telling me courteously but firmly that I could not be granted entry. Then the door squeaked open: the wind jumped in like an importunate child and all but snuffed the teetering candle. "*Kasi mu na suzgo kuno?*" said the burly senior officer, in white shirt and shorts, to the wee man at the desk: "So you've trouble here, have you?" Knowing the Tumbuka language, I jumped in: "*Nadi, Fumu, ti na suzgo likuru* - Yes, indeed, sir, we've a big problem" and I started to explain it from my point of view as supplicant. The big man lowered his head and stared at me in the flecked light and shadow of the official candle. I said my piece: a short silence followed. Then, rolling the 'r' gloriously, he said "Mac-a-ferrson?" "That's my name, yes", I said. "How do you know me?" "Ah, you can't remember me", he replied, "but I remember you. I was a pupil in school when you visited Ekwendeni in 1947 and Revd Patrick Mzembe introduced you to us all. You taught us a song. I have never forgotten that day". Then turning to his assistant, "Let him into Malawi", he ordered. A deep chuckle of gratification rumbled in his ample paunch and he clapped his hands and laughed: "Never venture", he exclaimed, "never win". Perhaps we underestimate the role of music in the more delicate areas of international diplomacy.

Ekwendeni was always to be a special place for me, not least because of the birth there in 1958 of our fifth child, Alison Mary. In 1947 it was the last stop before my first sighting of Khondowe. When I was taken on a conducted tour of the extensive estate, built on expansive lines through the benefaction of wealthy friends of the Free Church mission, a phrase from Genesis popped into my consciousness: "There were giants in those days". And there, as elsewhere, lines from a well-known hymn seemed to gain a sharper focus for me: "Brothers, we are treading where the saints have trod". Historians of central Africa and of Malawi in particular, acknowledge the Livingstonia Mission's outstanding contribution not only to the spread of basic education on the European model but also to the broadening of horizons. For that was so necessary an attribute of those men and women who were to begin, however, hesitantly at first, to articulate the deep and widespread African condemnation of the imperialists and to give expression to their people's determination to win liberation from the burdensome yoke of the foreign masters and the grievous humiliations of the colour bar. "Don't ever overlook this, my son", said old Donald Siwale of

Mwenzo, to me in 1975. "Without Livingstonia, Zambia perhaps might not yet be independent".

The polytechnic college, in modern parlance, which Robert Laws founded at Khondowe, was called the Overtoun Institution, in honour of James White, Lord Overtoun, one of its principal benefactors. His name was also used, more specifically, for the watercourse that the mission engineers laid down along a mountainside to carry water from a great catchment area in the hills above to supplement the waters of the Manchewe River below for the driving of a turbine. For his lordship's money had enabled Laws to instal in 1902 what was reputedly the first hydro-electric plant in the southern hemisphere. The institution was to provide basic education in 'the 3 rs' on the Scottish model, which would lead into specialist training for teachers, ministers, nurses and clerical workers, and also to five-year apprenticeships in building, carpentry and engineering. Because he envisaged its development into a full university, Laws arranged for its governing council to be called 'the Senatus'. The ultimate vision was not to be realised, but from the outset, the Institution produced an impressive number of skilled people whose studies had included the history of Greece and Rome, Israel and the birth and growth of Christianity, and an introduction to European philosophy.

The plateau was accessible only by ascending and descending perilous roads both from the Henga valley to the south and northwards to Karonga along the lake-shore. This latter road involved a descent of over 3000 feet from Khondowe to the Lake by way of 22 hair-pin bends. But the altitude of the estate removed the dangers of malaria and secured a site of breath-taking grandeur. Standing at the stone house, built for Laws himself as Principal, the eye can swing from the lake below to the slopes of Nyamkowa, 4000 feet above, thus spanning over 7000 feet.

Mosquitoes may have failed to make the ascent but the plateau offered no hindrance to monkeys. On that first visit in May 1947, I was invited by one of the Scots missionaries to join him in an early morning assault on a family of vervets who were making havoc of his mango tree, and pandemonium withal. His weapon was an old air-gun with a weak spring. As we approached, all the monkeys but one scuttled to cover behind the tree's thick branches, reducing their screeching to a timorous twitter. The one who didn't hide perched himself on an open branch and picked nonchalantly at the salty flakes on the skin of his abdomen. My companion emitted a growl of anger at this dumb insolence, loaded a slug into the gun and prepared to fire. The vervet waited, enjoying the view. As the slug was fired, he deftly caught it in his leathery palm and tittered. "I'll teach you", said the missionary and loaded in another slug. The monkey, unperturbed, stretched and waited. The gun went off, a direct aim. But he side-stepped the slug and caught it as easily as the first, with a derisive chuckle. Uttering a fierce imprecation, my companion turned on his heel and made for the house. As I followed him, the sotto voce titters from the heart of the tree began to swell again to the wonted piercing cacophany with which monkeys seem to delight to make mockery of men.

One very bright memory of that first visit to Khondowe is of tea and warm scones at Chihoro Castle, the home-made house of William C. Mkandawire, the Institution's accountant, and his wife Nyalubanga. His middle name Chiswakhata meant: he who cut through the thicket. For this is what he had done, in figurative speech, when he, a Phoka, sought a wife among the lake-shore Tonga; thus breaking through the barrier of social sanction or, in Scots idiom, loupin' the dyke.

It is not much less than 300 miles from Khondowe to Mwenzo, where the most northerly of the Scottish mission stations in the territory now called Zambia was founded, as a westward extension of the Livingstonia field, by Alexander Dewar in 1894. The road between those two settlements was rough and tortuous, climbing through great hills and crossing rickety bridges of palm logs over innumerable streams. The retiring missionary from Chitambo was thus completing his farewells and planned to drop me at Lubwa, 140 miles south of Mwenzo, so that I could return to my language study. I did not guess then that some day we would live and work in the Mwenzo district. Our overnight stop at the mission was brief. I recall a gracious afternoon tea party on the upper veranda of 'the big house', with beautiful crockery, lace tea-cloths and a big polished silver teapot. At the hospital I was shown the ward built by the local community in memory of *umukundwe sing'anga*, the beloved doctor James Chisholm who had served there as minister and doctor from 1902 to 1936. When he was dying, they told me, a refresher course for teachers and evangelists, from all over the 15000 square miles of the district, was being conducted at Mwenzo. People did not know his illness was fatal and he was expected to be well enough to address the gathering before they dispersed. Irene Pearce, the missionary in charge of the Girls' School, went to ask him if he had any message for them and he said: "Just say this: '*Mutazimyu mulilo* - Don't let the fire go out'." But this was a word of farewell used in the Mwanga language by anyone going on a long journey. Its meaning was quickly grasped. The doctor was dying. His instruction, couched in negative form, was heard as a call to positive action: revive the work of the Gospel. A striking movement of revitalisation swept through the whole region. I believe its influence can still be felt in Mwenzo's far-flung parish.

Chinsali again
After the odyssey, I had just over two months for intensive Bemba study. A tour of village schools by bicycle was planned, on which I was to accompany a missionary not long arrived in the area. An old bike was found for me and we set off by way of the mission settlement of the Roman Catholic White Fathers at Ilondola, 18 miles west of Lubwa. On our third day out, I felt suddenly tired. My head began to spin and I crashed against a tree. My colleague was ahead on the narrow forest path and soon out of earshot. I remounted, started to pedal, wobbled for some yards and crashed again. My strength was now gone. When Bill came back to look for me, he quickly realised that I was sick. "You're green", he said. Somehow, miserably, I staggered on behind him to a tiny village where I was offered shelter. Kind and curious people came while I tried to sleep. Bill sent a runner back to Lubwa and all we could do was wait. Meanwhile gifts of eggs were laid solemnly at the door of the little house. At long last they came to say that a car was as near as it could come to the village and I was assisted to stagger towards it. The Teacher Training School's Scots principal had come in his own car, accompanied by Sister Margaret from the hospital. The car had stuck in a stream that they needed to ford and had had to be heaved out by a score of willing helpers. In we piled, my body now racked and nauseated. "It's malaria", said the Sister. That *mung'wing'wi* in the rest-house at Nyimba, two weeks earlier, had injected a strong dose of his dreaded malady into me and I must just wait till the fever would leave me. I had not noticed that the Sister had filled her tunic pockets with some of the eggs given to me and apparently forgotten they were there. The pressure

of three bodies in the back of a small Austin saloon made a gooey mess of her tunic as the eggs were silently scrambled.

Jonas Kapoli was the youngest son in the big family of a mission teacher who had fallen prey to leprosy. The old man, though eventually cured, could not work again. So he decided to plead with me to take his son back to Mufulira and help him to go further with his education than he could at home. It was a difficult proposition. I would have to declare the boy to be under my personal guardianship if he were to be admitted to an urban school. I knew too that his family could make no financial provision for him. My earnings as a missionary were very small, less than a twentieth of the wages of a young and untrained white employee of the Mine. But I would have to clothe the lad and feed him and give him accommodation in my house. That in itself would be enough to earn me the censure, if not the open opposition, of neighbours in Mufulira European township.

Yet I felt indebted to Jonas not only for his faithful, careful and intelligent lessons in Bemba, but also for his most pleasant companionship. So, ignoring the problems, I said yes to his parents' plea. In due course at the end of June, we set off for the Copperbelt. A crowd of teachers and school-boys came to the road end, fifteen miles east of Lubwa, to see us safely into the bus.

The 'bus', however, was a lorry, its front two passenger seats reserved for white people and all its black 'passengers' huddled in the open, seat-less truck behind for the 400 mile journey to the point, at Kapiri Mposhi, where the Great North Road, so-called, met the main road from Lusaka to the copper-mining towns near the Zaire border. The driver was a man of mixed race. His father was 'Chirupula' Stephenson, who had come to the territory originally as an employee of Rhodes's Company. He had later become proprietor of a large estate with citrus orchards. He had a number of African concubines, one of whom was mother of our driver. 'Chirupula' means 'the great flogger'.

I asked young Stephenson at once to let Jonas sit with me in the front, but he said no. The white hotel keepers would report him, he explained, and he'd be sacked. However, after a few miles he allowed my young tutor to come in front on condition that he'd go back again well before we reached the first hotel at Mupika. I wondered what the other travellers in the truck would feel, but sensed that they approved my plea. As we thundered down what was then called Danger Hill, the engine made ominous noises, threatening to back fire. "Shouldn't you stop?" I asked Stephenson. "No", he said. "Not here. Did you see in the paper in March about the man who shot a man-eating lion at point-blank range near Mupika?" "Yes", I said. "Well, that was me", said the driver. "I was having engine trouble just here on this hill. I got out to check it. Suddenly I heard a rushing sound and turned to see a huge *inkalamo* racing towards me from out of the forest. My gun was on the seat, and loaded. I seized it and fired right at the beast just as it was about to leap on me. Sorry, we'll just have to go on and hope for the best."

So the long journey passed. At Kapiri I was glad that Jonas did not have to pass another night in that hateful verminous shed. But we still had to face the train journey on which accommodation was totally segregated. Jonas begged me not to worry on his behalf, but the tedious 100 miles to Mufulira had no joy for me. We got out and chatted together at each stop on the way and I was able to ensure that he had food and liquid. But I felt ashamed that he had to see now so many vulgar manifestations of racism. When at last we reached my cool house in Mufulira, John Ngwele welcomed Jonas as kindly as he welcomed me and we agreed that the little room next to my office should be Kapoli's study-bedroom. He was delighted. But I was aware at once that if a white visitor came to the house as Jonas was emerging from the bathroom, the fat could be in the fire. I hadn't had time to find many truly kindred spirits in the local white community.

Chapter 5
QUESTIONS ON THE CHURCH'S CREDIBILITY

I was plunged back at once, however, into a whirling programme of work, which included a journey to the London Missionary Society's station at Kawimbe above Lake Tanganyika, where the annual meeting of Presbytery was to be held and where a special three-man commission from the Church of Scotland would meet with church leaders from all over the area served by the Church of Central Africa in Rhodesia (CCAR). An initially fragile union of the churches founded by the LMS and the C of S along with the Union Church of the Copperbelt, was the start of a long process of unification of protestant denominations in Zambia, begun in 1945 and completed 20 years later. "I can understand Christians quarrelling and splitting in their own country", said David Ramushu once, "but you have no right to export your divisions to this country". Yet the process had a very brittle beginning and we sometimes wondered if the original union had the strength to survive. Blessedly, it had.

That meeting at Kawimbe focussed afresh the sore problem of fellowship, in its deep radical Christian meaning. Presbytery met for an afternoon session on our day of arrival and was 'duly constituted'. At the end, a local missionary rose and announced accommodation arrangements, beginning with white delegates. They were all to find beds in missionary houses. "African members", he then said, "are in the school dormitories, men in the boys' one and women in the girls'. I hope you've all brought your blankets and mats. Food will be served at the school boarders' dining shelter since they're all away on holiday. If you've any problems, see Mr Kampanda our Boarding Master. Timothy, stand up and let them all see you. There he is, the man who's going to look after you all."

My host and his wife made us very welcome with simple, homely fare and comfortable chairs in a cosy lounge. But it was

difficult not to feel restive for this was my first attendance at the
'supreme court' of a recently united African Church. So, after coffee,
I excused myself and, taking a torch stumbled towards the boys'
dormitory. There, on reed mats on the bare floor, I found the
bakalamba seated, the only light being provided by a couple of
home-made lamps, Vaseline jars with paraffin in them and pieces
of string stuck through holes in the lids to serve as wicks. When
they saw who I was, someone said *"Mwaiseni* - Welcome" and I
caught a whisper: *"Yangu, mulumendo Musungu wa ku Mufulira,
umupya* - Goodness, it's the European lad from Mufulira, the new
one". We all then sat down on the mats and slowly conversation started.

"How do you like this union of the churches?" I asked. "We
don't know. We were not involved. It was made by some
missionaries." "But surely it is good to be united? There is one
Jesus, so there should be one *chilonganino* (the common Bemba
word for church, literally meaning 'the assembling together')."
Silence, for a while, then someone spoke from the darkness, "We
have not really assembled together in true fellowship." "How do
you mean?" I asked. Again a long pause. "Well, look, the black
ministers from the Church of Scotland are better paid than we of
the LMS. How can they speak of one church when there is not one
and the same reward for all?" "But it is surely for the united church
to make things right in such matters now." "Perhaps. But he who
has more won't accept less. And we who have less are told by our
missionaries that we cannot have more, since some of our *chilambu*
comes from England."

There was unhappiness and disappointment in their faces, a
heaviness made heavier by the stygian darkness of the chilly
dormitory. For there was no glass in the window spaces and July is
the time of *mwela*, the cold air that comes after the end of the
rains.

Conversation went on stickily and I failed to dispel this
heaviness. At last I rose to go, bidding them sleep in peace. "One
more thing", someone said. "There is no real fellowship. On Sunday
we'll sit all together for *umulalilo* (the sacrament of communion).
We will take little pieces of the bread of you Europeans. So with
the cup. But there is no fellowship of white and black for food. In
this dormitory we are all black. Speaking is one thing: doing is
another."

What could I say? The hospitality arrangements had not been made for inimical reasons. "The Africans will be happiest by themselves" was a sentiment spoken sincerely and not unkindly. But it missed the creative magic of 'the grace of the Lord Jesus Christ and the love of God and the fellowship of the Holy Spirit'.

As we drove south at the end of Presbytery we stopped at Luwingu, 'place of flame' where there was a government administrative post or *boma*. We sensed that the officers were shocked by something and then one of them told us what had just happened. The senior Messenger had gone off the previous evening by bicycle to visit a polygamous wife. He had not reported for duty in the morning. A search had found his bicycle by the side of a forest path, shreds of his uniform, his whitened bones and the footprints of a very big cat.

Back in Mufulira, I learned of the trouble at one of the schools. A smartly dressed young teacher - let's call him Hubert Chilasha - had misbehaved with a school girl and the headmaster wanted his immediate suspension. As School Manager, I had to look into the matter and so went to visit Chilasha. His house was open but he was not at home. I caught sight of a large photograph on his wall - Adolf Hitler in uniform. Leaving a note requesting him to call at my office, I went away. The next day, Saturday, he arrived early. "You have called me", he said, and so I had to tell him what I had heard. He was a good-looking fellow. As he listened, he drew a gold cigarette case from his pocket, flicked it open and, as I finished speaking, said, "Smoke?" "No, thank you." "Mind if I do?" he replied and lit up, puffing smoke rings. He offered no contradiction of the headmaster's report of his mis-conduct. "So be it", he said philosophically as I made it clear that he was suspended pending dismissal unless he could disprove the charge. "I understand", he said and moved towards the door. "Just one point", he added. "I don't want you to think that what you are doing will drive me from Christ. I'll find my own Christ. Not your dirty white Christ." What could I say. Then I remembered the picture on his wall. "I see you have Hitler's picture in your house. I wondered why?" "Ah, yes. That's right. Why not? He knew how to deal with men."

Looking to a New Relationship

The headmaster of the middle primary school in the Location was a man with a stoop. He was a faithful church elder whose home village was near Mwenzo. He seemed to feel obliged to report to me everything that happened in his school. One such report was of the arrival of an angry visitor. "Where is my wife?" he had shouted. "She's not cooked for me". Then storming from the school office he had marched into each classroom till at last he shouted "There she is! Come here, you useless mushroom", rushed in among the pupils, seized a teenage girl by the arm and dragged her out. The teachers had failed to secure her return to the classroom. The man was in his forties.

Another day, Mr Sintoyi arrived at my office, looking burdened. When, he wanted to know, was I going to inspect the teachers' houses. I had been in Mufulira since November. Of course I had been away in Lubwa and other places but the houses needed inspection. "You mean the teachers' own houses where they live with their families?" "Yes", he said. "The School Manager inspected them every Saturday. Why not now?" My protestations that I could not thus invade the homes of adults did not seem to impress him. "But what if their houses are not kept well? There is one careless teacher I know who does not always spread his bed in the morning. He should be warned by you." "Not by me, my friend", I said, sure in my own mind that such practices should not be revived.

But there were to be other evidences now and then of an acceptance of inferiority which left a bad taste in my mouth. When John Ngwele was away in his home village negotiating his betrothal, I had the temporary help of an older house servant. One day as I mounted my bike, I remembered to ask him to set two places at table for lunch. Mr Ramushu was coming for an afternooon's work and we would lunch together as we often did. But the old minion demurred. "Myself, I not serve food to black man", he said.

Feeling the Pinch

At the end of my first year the cost of living was beginning to worry me. The quarterly cheque paid in advance, came to less than £50. My worries were not eased by a chat with a young white miner who wanted to arrange a church wedding. Slim and blue-eyed, he had the mould of a young Viking. In neat brief shorts, hung lightly on his narrow waist, well-squared shoulders and 5-inch socks at the bottom of long straight honey-tanned legs, he was a delight to the eye.

"What brought you to Mufulira?" I asked. "Well, my old man has a farm in the Orange Free State. Farming's not my line. Not that I've ever done manual work. Our kaffirs do that, of course. But the fields and the dust and the smell of cattle everywhere bored me. Then one day I saw an advert in the local paper for young white men wanted for the mines here. Nothing about qualifications. So I wrote away and sure enough, I landed lucky." "What about training?" "Well, they apparently needed rock-breakers, and so they ran a short course. I said OK but of course wanted something different. Rock-breaking scares me a bit." "How do you cope, then, when you have to do it every day?" "Well, gosh, man, on my own I'd be sunk. But there's Petros, you see. He's my boss-boy. He's great. Knows it like the back of his hand." Here my Adonis warmed up: "You should see Petros. He picks the spot for drilling; then he sets the charge, won't let anyone else touch it. Then when all's set, he clears us all, me and the boys, out of the line of blast. So he's the only one out of shelter when he ignites. Boy, does he jump for safety when he sees the big bang coming! Been at it for around twenty-five years." "What age is this Petros?" "Gosh, I don't know. Couldn't really reckon one boy's age from another. Say perhaps around 50. I know he's got grown-up kids." "What does he earn?" Around £10 a month. He has to be listed unskilled of course, being a kaffir." "And you? How are you doing financially?" "Oh boy, I've landed on my feet. £180 a month plus copper bonus. That's pound for pound. Makes a nice packet, and tax is just peanuts. How's that for a start, eh?" he asked, rubbing his hands and beaming. "A bit more than Petros?" He suddenly looked solemn and sad. "Well", he said, "I know I can tell you in confidence that I have sometimes wondered about it. Couldn't breathe this in the Mine Mess of course. Then I remember the girl-friend and our plan for a wedding. I really want to give her a decent down-sitting. That helps me to forget Petros."

In Loco Parentis

Yes, the cost of living was grim, so worrying that I began to wonder if I should look for some other sphere in which I could work for what I believed in. The Government Gazette had recently advertised a junior lectureship in History at Makerere University College in Uganda. My degree should make me eligible. It was now January 1948. I'd been in Africa over a year. Applications had to be in by March. So I filed away the Uganda notion for further thought. Yet I felt it shameful, somehow, even to think of resigning from something I'd been preparing for for over ten years.

My life was very full, far too full in fact. I found hardly a moment for relaxation. If it hadn't been for Jonas Kapoli, I'd perhaps not have paused at all. He was working well at the Mine School but sometimes waylaid me for a chat.

One glorious night, I vividly remember, we went for a walk in the forest some miles from the town. Chat flowed easily as we swung along. That night there was a good-sized moon in the sky behind us, but a blanket of cirro-cumulus cloud covered it. The floor of the forest was springy to our tread after weeks of wondrous rain. *Chilala*, the mid-season pause in the rains, had now come and the weather was at its sweetest.

Suddenly the cloud left the moon and, at the instant, a million leaves in front of us shone silver. The glory stopped us in our tracks and we both gasped at the wonder of it. "God is an artist", said Jonas.

But he was not always poetic. Sometimes he was persistent to the point of being pestilential. He hated the school latrines. The old school rule, strongly supported by Mkandawire the Headmaster, forbade pupils to wear shoes. Jonas dreamed of shoes, day and night and launched a subtle propaganda offensive in the interests of hygiene. His argument was incontrovertible. But the law was the law and my soundings had confirmed the Headmaster's adamant refusal to change it - though he wore polished brown shoes himself. He set his face against anything that would stratify his pupils economically and pressure from me as School Manager for something keenly desired by my personal ward would have inevitably embarrassed his authority.

It was 'skin shoes' of which Jonas was dreaming, and this gave me an escape hatch. I couldn't afford them! "Then canvas will do", he replied, smiling sweetly in expectancy of victory. And so it was: I bought the canvas shoes on condition that he wore them only on going to the latrine and that at all other times, they were to be carried in a bag. On weekends, of course, he could wear them round the clock.

The End of Singleness

The Principal of Chalimbana Teacher Training College, east of Lusaka, had been a Church of Scotland missionary at Lubwa. Hearing of my appointment to Northern Rhodesia, he had at once invited me to visit the College and conduct worship there. But the UMCB could not allow me time for such a trip. Now, in February 1948, he had renewed his invitation with added warmth and so I was reluctantly granted four days' absence, a Thursday to a Sunday.

It was a short break after sixteen months, but "a bird in the hand...". So I planned to go by night train right down to the Victoria Falls, spend the Friday there, travel to Lusaka on the Saturday, go straight to Chalimbana and then back to Lusaka on the Sunday evening in time for the night train to Mufulira. The Zambezi surpassed all imaginings. I walked about thirty miles to and fro on its southern bank, met the stares of a band of big baboons and saw a lunar rainbow after dark on the spray above the Falls.

Chalimbana was most welcoming. Principal David Maxwell-Robertson - nick-named 'Chifunga' on account of the kilt that he wore as a pioneer of the Boy Scout movement in the country - was founder as well as head of the College. On my return to Lusaka, my host for an evening meal was the Revd Edward Nightingale, Superintendent of the Methodist Mission. It was he who dropped me at the railway station for the night journey home.

And there I met the widow of the first leader of the United Missions, Mrs Frieda Cross. She and her older son had visited me a year earlier in Mufulira. On this occasion her older daughter and younger son were with her, seeing off some Brethren missionaries. And the Lord said to his unworthy servant: "See that lassie? Well, she's to be your wife". It was as clear as that and so I had to hatch a plan for another visit to Lusaka to take the matter further. That meeting, lasting about twenty minutes, was on February 29th. Not till 11th May did I manage that second visit, but we were engaged five days later. On November 8th we were married in Lusaka by Revds Edward Nightingale, David Ramushu and our UMCB Team Leader, George Fraser.

Myra had been born in Ndola. After a few years of schooling in Kitwe, she was sent to Johannesburg for secondary education. Her arrival in Mufulira delighted many who had known her father and honoured his memory. John Ngwele stayed in our employ

and young Jonas remained until, having been refused a place in the
territory's only secondary school for black boys, he went to Adams
School with all his expenses paid, at my request, by Dr Hastings
Banda.

A Gulf too Wide for Bridging?

Two events, perhaps more related than I guessed at the time,
happened in 1948 to remind us of the totalitarian pressure of the
'colour bar' on the country's life. In mid-1948 and most
unexpectedly, I was asked by the European Mine Debating Society,
to give a talk on 'the work of the mission'. About 15 white
employees were present. The atmosphere was tinged with
apprehension and, as I began by reminding them that the way to
learn about the work we were doing was to come a short walk and
visit it, one man rose and left the room. The others, however, gave
me a courteous hearing. In question time it was clear that old racist
prejudices confounded the thinking of many of them: eg "How
many native pupils have you?" "About 480." "How can you teach
them all?" "Oh, but we have about 25 teachers." "Who are they?"
"Blacks of course." "Gosh, who'd have thought that? Kaffir
teachers!" Then the chairman asked me to help them to find a way
of meeting Africans "without this kitchen kaffir business, master
and servant stuff". "Why don't you invite some Africans to your
meeting?" I asked. "Utterly impossible. The Mine would forbid it,
for fear of an outcry."

They were right. But the desire for an informal inter-racial
meeting was excellent and so I offered my house as a venue for it. If
they would guarantee 12 from their Society, I would invite the
same number of black people. So it was agreed and thus was born
the Afro-European Friendship Group. It had two meetings before
I went south for our wedding. At one of them, Kenneth Kaunda,
who had joined the Mine School staff, was present. He spoke little
but listened intently. The atmosphere was relaxed. At the end one
of the Central School teachers expressed appreciation. "But", he
said, "when a *musungu* lady came to offer me a scone I was
speechless, that such a thing could ever happen in this country". It
was marvellous. The Group continued after we were married,
sometimes spending a happy evening playing games. We overheard,
however, that some white ladies in the town had warned their

friends to have nothing to do with us, for "Mrs Macpherson has kaffirs drinking from her tea-cups".

Incidentally, one member of our inter-racial group was Mrs Madeleine Robertson who met 'KK' (as President Kaunda was popularly called in later years) for the first time in our house. After Zambia became a sovereign republic in 1964, Mrs Robertson was nominated by the President as a Member of the National Assembly.

At the end of our honeymoon, I met an Anglican priest in Lusaka who was secretary of the Christian Council. 1949 was to be the year for a meeting of what was called the General Missionary Conference. "But I can't find anywhere for it to meet", he said, "so maybe it'll have to be postponed". "What about Mufulira?" I asked in all innocence. And so it was agreed. The Conference would meet in the European Free Church and a sort of marquee would be erected in our garden for meals. There certainly would be no rain in June.

When Myra and I reached Mufulira in December 1948, we found that our house had been decorated and our bedroom furnished, without the knowledge of the UMCB, by the European Church Council, It was a lovely surprise. Then in January, the Church Council met and I passed to them a letter requesting the use of the church for the GMC in June. "That would be OK", said somebody and then another member spoke. "I've a question. Who's coming to this Conference?" "I've never attended one," I answered. "But I imagine it'll be ministers, teachers, nurses and others from all over the country." "Any natives?" "Yes, I'm sure there will be some African ministers and Christian teachers." "Then, chairman, I move that we throw this letter back where it came from, for it's an insult. No native will ever enter this building as far as I am concerned."

He was quickly supported. "Chairman, we've nothing against you personally, but we don't like your association with the mission business. When we ask people for money for our new Sunday School extension, they ask us which church. When we tell them, they reply 'Macpherson's church? Not on your life. He's the chap that works among the munts'."

Similar comments followed and then one man stood and said: "I've got a simple solution. Let's put a big notice on the front door

- 'This Church is reserved for Europeans only'. That should put things right and let everyone know where we stand."

"Let me ask two questions", I said, for I'd waited in vain for someone to argue with these speakers. "Supposing an Indian Christian came to Mufulira as a teacher, a man who spoke English of course but, like many of you, knew no African language; and supposing he saw this building and came to worship next Sunday, what would you say?"

"He'd have to leave. Sorry, but that's the position."

"Second, supposing that an African house servant had been assaulted by his white employer when she had a hangover after a late-night party; supposing he was a Christian" - at which point someone barely suppressed a guffaw - "and so as he passed down this road and saw this house of prayer he came in and knelt to ask for strength not to feel hatred but instead to act according to Christ's teaching, if you found him here, what would you do?"

"Put him out. And send him packing with a flea in his ear." "Because", chipped in another voice, "listen: only one kaffir's allowed into this church, the guy, what's his name? the cleaner - and he's not allowed to pray."

I was 27 and felt the loneliness of that evening very heavy. I made the point that people could set up a racial club but never a racial church, since Christ was the Church's Head. I then said that as a servant of the Church of Scotland, as a member of the United Missions in the Copperbelt and as a believer in Jesus, I could never accept racist rules to mould the church's work and witness.

"We must then look for a new minister - and it shouldn't be too difficult - who'll respect the feelings of this community", said one councillor as quickly and courteously as he could. "There are lots of good ministers down south." That was it. I walked away from the council room into the starlight, trying to think how to tell my bride of the sorrows of the night.

In the weeks that followed, the rest of my work went on. But a succession of lay preachers conducted the services in the European Church and we saw very little of the people who, so recently, had been so friendly and kind when we returned from our honeymoon. Then one day, the front veranda door was pushed open and in came Ray Stuart, the burly breathless foreman in the Mine concentrator and a member of the Church Council.

"Padre", he said. "I want to speak. Gertie and I are sick at heart about what's happened in the church, eh. We are South Africans from longer ago than I could tell, generations, man. As a lad, I had my own 'native boy' from when I was a toddler. I kicked off my 'jamas in the morning. He folded them and put them under the pillow. If I got into trouble playing round the farm, he got the blame because they said he was in charge of me. If I blamed him to the old folks, he got another row. It seemed OK to me then. Never gave it a thought. It's not that I went out of my way to be cruel to natives. Just that I was there" - and he raised his hand to shoulder-level - "and they were there" - and now he pointed to the floor. "It was our way of life, how God had made us, so I was taught. But Padre, you've made us see that Jesus is in this thing and we're going to stand with Jesus." As quickly as he had entered, he rose, gave me a double hand-shake and left.

Myra and I had decided that it would be wrong to absent ourselves from the evening worship in the white township, even though I had been effectively discharged. It was a hard decision for it seemed as though anyone with a bee in his bonnet could occupy the pulpit. One night we squirmed under the clotted nonsense of British Israel and, the next week, a tirade from an ex-Salvation Army officer who took great pride in his notion of racial superiority. It was all the more painful because, on the wall of the building, a copper plaque commemorated Myra's late father:

> Remember Arthur James Cross - First Leader of the United Missions in the Copperbelt, 1936-1945 - 'He was a very parfait gentil knight'.

A letter came in soon after, signed by the Church Treasurer who had assumed the Council chairmanship. In 1948, the year of the electoral victory in South Africa of Dr Malan's Afrikaner Nationalist Party, he had said to me one day: "If it's a choice between South Africa and some people's idea of Christianity, I choose South Africa." He was a neat little man, with jet black wavy hair, burnished with Brylcream; he was friendly and courteous, But John Khonje, elder of the CCAR congregation, once asked me if I preached the same message to white as to black. When I said that I thought I did, Khonje said simply: "I doubt". "Why?" I asked. "Because I work under a boss who is your treasurer. If you spoke the same message, it would have to make some difference to him. But he does not change."

The letter called me to attend a general congregational meeting whose agenda was given thus:

a) Statement by the Chairman
b) Statement by Padre Macpherson
c) Arrangements for appointing a Minister
d) Any other competent business.

The Meeting was to take place in ten days' time. Myra and I couldn't help remarking how strange it was to be sleeping through these waiting nights in the bed presented so generously by the same Church Council a few weeks earlier.

Meanwhile, and unexpectedly, Dr John Arthur, distinguished doyen of the Church of Scotland Mission in Kenya, who was touring southern and eastern Africa, came to spend a weekend with us. As he heard our account of what was called 'the Free Church Crisis', he said he'd like to accompany us to the general meeting which was to follow the evening service, and so along we all went. The building was generally quite well filled but that night we could hardly find a seat. Looking round, I noticed at once that some well-known drunks from the Mine Club were present. They could not conceal their awkwardness in a building in which they were total strangers. But all the regular church members were also there.

The Chairman's statement was competent and restrained, but he confirmed that the Council rejected the proposal to hold a Conference in their building with 'natives' present. In my statement I summarised the questions I had put to the Council. In the discussion that followed, someone said that I must not think there was any animosity against myself. It was just 'the stigma of the United Missions' that bothered them. "Is that a stigma?" I retorted, pointing to the memorial plaque for Myra's father, and my sharpness clearly saddened the faces of some who remembered him with personal gratitude. Then a kindly octogenarian Major of the Salvation Army rose. "Our minister and I are very good friends", he said, "and I admire the work of the mission. I'd just like to ask him to remember that when God made black and white, he meant them to be separate." I was finding it difficult to respond calmly. "If that is what my friend believes", I said, "why has he joined me on several occasions at services in the African church?" The old man's eyes filled with tears but he said nothing.

"We have the motion of the Council before the meeting", the Chairman said. "It is probably time we took a vote." Some of the fat boys from the Bar began to fidget, hoping for an early release. But Ray Stuart rose: "Chairman, I move that we erase the Council's action from our minutes, that we try to forget this ever happened, that we pray God's forgiveness and that we ask our minister to stay with us." His words drained him utterly and he slumped to his seat, his dentures rattling audibly. "I second that", said a little woman from Durban. "And I want to say", called out another very South African woman, "that I'd be glad to serve tea to black ministers the same as to white, and I hope the Conference takes place here." "I agree." "So do I." "That's right. Why not?" said various voices, and the Chairman called for order. "Let us now vote", he said firmly.

"One point", I said. "I ask the Chairman to rule that no one can vote who does not support the church by either worship or service or offering of money." To my surprise, this met with audible approval from many of the members present and the Chairman had to rule accordingly. The specially dragooned drunks looked bitter and some of them rose and left. The voting took only a moment, showing a strong majority in support of Ray Stuart.

Thus it came about that the General Missionary Conference took place in Mufulira in June 1949, attended by a number of African delegates along with missionaries from all over the territory. We ate together, laughed together, sang together. But inevitably the Free Church saw no more of some old members, and notably a Scots couple from Aberdeen, who were 'scunnered at the Church's surrender' on the 'native question'. "I've worked with natives for forty years. I know all there is to know about them." "You can never know anyone", I replied, "until you can exchange thought and understanding with him". But the couple were not impressed. She had been shocked, she said, when I had mentioned an open-air campaign by the African Church in a prayer one evening: "We're sick of being deeved at about the kaffirs". On their coffee table lay a copy of the anthem book of the United Free Church of Scotland. She had been a choir member for many years.

Chapter 6
A BRIDGE
TOO BRITTLE

Colonial government operated in the rural areas through District Commissioners (DCs) and District Officers (DOs). However, the rapid growth of towns in the 1930s and the influx of some thousands of so-called Europeans from various parts of Europe and also from South Africa, had created the need for special forms of municipal administration. The Mines managed both their compounds for African employees and the townships for white miners. But Management Boards were established for the non-mine townships and the so-called government locations. These Boards ran beer-halls in the locations and attempted to cover their staff salaries and other administrative expenses from beer-hall profits. There were also urban DCs whose position was somewhat parlous. I knew some colonial officers who dreaded nothing more than an urban posting.

The DC at the time of our marriage was a huge man with a tiny wife. I gave him some tuition for a Lower Bemba examination which he had to pass for incremental purposes, somewhat late in his career, having failed to pass a Higher exam in his first language, Lozi. He was a hearty fellow with what was sometimes called a typical Oxford accent. One day, he asked me to see him for a private talk. "We're planning a sort of get-together here at the Boma for some of our senior Africans; open-air do, you know, tea and buns, with some Europeans and their wives who can be relied on to play ball. I'd be so glad if you and your lady would join us."

We went, of course, but found it comic to the point of farce. Seating was totally segregated; white people on deck chairs, black people on backless benches. There were coffee tables for the Europeans with tea-cloths, a pleasant selection of scones and cakes and waiter service, on the ratio of about one waiter to six guests. A couple of waiters were put in charge of the African guests, and carried round trays of the kind of fat, coarse buns that were sold to travellers at the local bus terminus. One waiter approached a black woman and held out the tray, which she took from him and placed on her knees. An amiable altercation ensued with various people telling her that she was to take only one bun. Meanwhile the chatter went on in the two areas pleasantly enough. In inter-racial terms it was a fantastic non-event. When it was over, the DC thanked us for our presence. "Nice, jolly get-together, what?" he said heartily, at which we could only smile.

Racism's Rough Reality

Just then a young Welshman appeared in the town, a lad whose voice would have caught the attention of Caruso: mellifluous, light, vibrant and true. We saw a lot of each other. He dropped in for brief chats at our house. He went everywhere on a racing bike. Then one day he appeared with a question: "I've just heard that you've something to do with the African schools in the compound." "That's right." "Well, can you help me? I want to meet some Africans for an ordinary human sort of chat. In the Mine, it's impossible. Kitchen Kaffir's not for conversation - *Buya lapa, hamba lapa, faka lo* so-and-so, *bwisa lo* such-and-such. It's all orders, and they're all rough. So I thought, if I could meet some African teachers, I might begin to enjoy life here a bit better. I've been very disappointed. Here I am in Africa and the one thing I can't do is meet an African for a decent chat. Trouble is I don't know a word of African. So if I could meet some teachers, we could always speak English."

I wasted no time, took him one day to the Central School where Gibson Bwalya was teaching and after introductions, I left them together. Gibson had some friends at his house. The next Sunday, the Welshman spoke to me after evening worship. "It was great", he said. "What a grand bunch of lads! And here, we'd not been chatting for long when Gibson mentioned that he was trying to start simple art lessons in his school. So happens that I've done quite a bit of painting, in an amateurish sort of way, of course. But I've had the great advantage of being able to get the right materials, back home in Cardiff, and also to attend night classes. So, anyway, the upshot is that we've fixed up to meet weekly and just work away together with paints."

His happiness was perfect, and I soon heard from Bwalya and his friends that they were equally delighted. So it went on for three or four weeks. Then one day, when stock-taking with the Central School teachers, Gibson Bwalya said, "Oh, by the way, how is our friend from Wales?" It struck me that I hadn't seen him for some time and I said so. "But I thought you were seeing him every week yourselves?" "We were, but for two weeks he hasn't come."

Life was very busy and it must have been about a month later when I suddenly saw the sweet singer parking his bike outside Barclays Bank and put my hand on his shoulder. His face, as he turned, clouded at once with sadness. He tried at first to sound casual but I pressed the question about the art group and said that they were all very anxious to keep it going. "I'll not be back", he said and his eyes moistened. "I can't." "Why not? It was your own idea and going gloriously."

Leading me from the main stream of pedestrians and then signalling that we cross to the quiet side of the road, he looked at me, his blue eyes full of truth and sorrow. "I'd better spill the beans", he said. "I loved that Thursday group more than I can say, but on a couple of occasions I stayed so long that I missed dinner at the Mess. Then the next week as I rushed in sweating just before they'd stop serving, I noticed a group of lads watching me. Anyway, I ate my grub and went for a shower. I was dog-tired, so I decided to turn in. Well, I hadn't been in bed long when there was a sharp knock on my door. It was hot and I'd no pyjamas so I had to wrap a towel on and see who was there. 'We want to see you, Taffy', said one of the group who pushed in as I opened the door. I've only the one chair, so I went onto my bed and said, 'Yes, what is it?' I'd seen most of them around the Mess but didn't know any of them well.

"'We'll come straight to the point', said one of them, a tall chap, very tanned, with a deep voice. 'We've a question for you, Taffy. Before deciding to ask you, we checked up on one or two points. So here goes. Why are you often late for dinner on Thursdays? Where have you been that you have to come rushing in late for skoff?' I told them I'd things to do and that it was my business. 'Oh, no it's not', said one of them and at that they began to close in on me. They stood with hands on hips, all looking down at me in my towel. 'Come clean, Taffy', someone said from behind my head. 'Don't think we're clueless. Tell us all about it'."

"Well, I started. It seemed better to tell them about the art group than to try to make up a story. They'd got to hear of it somehow, that was clear. After I'd spoken for a bit and they'd asked how I got to meet Gibson and the others and I'd told them about knowing you, one of them cut in roughly. They'd heard enough, he said. It was now my turn to do the listening. Then the leader, the guy who'd pushed in first through the door, he started speaking, very slowly. If I didn't cut it out at once, he said, if I tried even once again what he called 'this nigger-loving stuff', they would teach me a lesson. I was sick with fear when they at last left my room."

"Don't be too afraid", I said. "People like that find it easy to talk that way. But they'd probably not do anything serious." Yet, as I said these words I wondered. For the climate of the town gave substance to his fears.

"I haven't the guts. That's the trouble", he said and a great sorrow covered him. Then, glancing at his watch he told me that he was late and must rush off now. "See you soon", I said, but we were never to see each other again. Like a duiker scenting leopards, he'd gone to cover and a blossom of hope and happiness had shrivelled and died before our eyes. It was hard to explain this to Bwalya and his friends. "*Twaumfwa, mukwai*", was all they could say: "We understand, sir."

Ministerial Moves

David Ramushu was no longer in Mufulira. In his place had come the Revd Ewen Siwale, son of a famous worthy from Mwenzo, Donald, who had been a fellow-student of David Julizya Kaunda at Livingstonia at the turn of the century. The reason for the transfer of Ramushu was that the congregations in the Nkana-Kitwe-Mindolo area presented problems that called for his quality of leadership. The man who had been there had been failing to fulfil his pastorate and in consequence the congregation at Wusakili had been threatening to hive off on its own. Most of its members were Tumbuka-speakers from northern Malawi and eastern Zambia. It was from among their groups in the various towns that there had come many of the pioneers of what had been called the Union Church of the Copperbelt. That grass-roots church had welcomed people of many different languages and had, in 1945, been formally united, as I mentioned earlier, to the churches that had grown out of the mission work of the LMS and the Church of Scotland in the northern parts of the country. But pressure to make Bemba the language of all the congregations, as it was becoming a *lingua franca* for the whole Copperbelt, was resisted by the Tumbuka. Despite

Ramushu's efforts, the secessionist urges continued, to the detriment of all.

Siwale was a quieter personality but, like Ramushu, tireless in pastoral care. His use of English was charming if often not exactly idiomatic. In a letter to a missionary, he mentioned other missionaries thus: "You will have pleasure to know that the So-and-Sos have been blessed with the gift of a kid."

A Moment of Dread and Delight

A missionary tour of service in the Copperbelt was expected to be 3½ years followed by around six months' home leave. For Myra and me the last months of 1949 and the beginning of 1950 were filled with expectations of our first baby. All went well as the refreshing rainy months passed. The due date came and passed, however, and Myra still waited. Then at last, on 4th April, the last lap was reached and I took her to hospital. But the hours went by, many more than desirable and when I at last went to bed, there was still no news. I placed my bed under the telephone but was none-the-less startled by the call, with the news that a baby girl, 8lbs 10zs, was safely delivered. I raced to the hospital, glimpsed the baby and looked in to see Myra, deeply asleep under anaesthetic. "Ring us at 6 in the morning", said the nurse. "She needs a good sleep now." On the way home I passed the word, as promised to Ray Stuart and his wife and then found John Ngwele waiting for me at our house. With joy he shook my hand like a pump handle.

Sleep engulfed me at once. But at 5.45 am I wakened sharply. I was about to dial the hospital when I was suddenly sure that I must go in person to see how my lasses were. It was a beautiful quiet dawn as I cycled through the town. Tip-toeing along the hospital corridors I could find no staff around, so I pushed open the door of the labour ward and realised at once that something was badly wrong. Myra's lips and finger nails were black and her skin a ghastly grey. I could barely hear her breathing. Pressing the bell-push hard, I waited and then heard someone racing towards the ward. It was Sister herself, a plump Scots girl. At one look, she raced away to bring a doctor. The senior Sister, aptly nicknamed the 'Battleaxe', trundled in and together, the Doctor and the two Sisters started resuscitation. But there seemed little or no response. The Battleaxe's face advised my withdrawal and so, after pacing up and down, I went to consult the Superintendent, a man well-known

for his fierce anti-missionary outlook. He was head of a strong
team of doctors and sisters in this hospital built to serve the 4,000
white people of Mufulira. The African hospital, surrounded by
over 40,000 people, was under the direction of a male nurse, the
successor of the man whom Ramushu had once denounced to his
face for sadistic cruelty. There was no resident doctor there and
most of the 'nursing' staff were African orderlies, minimally trained
and miserably paid.

The Superintendent was curt as I entered his office. He and
another man were smoking together. "Shall I call my wife's
mother?" I asked. "Not worth it", he answered. "It's too late". So,
debarred from the scene of the struggle being waged in the labour
ward, I cycled home, told John Ngwele that 'Mama' was very,
very ill and then rang Ray Stuart. The hours dragged and I had no
idea that Ngwele had wakened a number of servants of neighbouring
houses and called them to his tiny house for prayer; or that Ray
Stuart had raced round the white township by car, summoning a
number of fellow-members of the Free Church to meet in their
church building to intercede for Myra.

It was about 9.30 when I stood again at the door of the labour
ward. I could see that the tension in the room had lessened but the
doctor and two sisters were all still there. Baby Catherine was in
the cot, with her eyes open. The blackness of Myra's lips and nails
had faded. Then suddenly at 9.40 she opened her eyes. "Where's
my baby?" she said and the plump Sister went at once to bring
Catherine to her. I stayed for a while, knowing the Sister was near,
but promised not to weary Myra. Her skin colour was now normal,
her breathing regular and sound. The danger was past.

It must have been mid-morning when I stopped at the Stuarts'
with the good news. "I'm so glad", said Gertie, kissing me kindly.
"You know it was not till twenty-to-ten that we stopped our
prayers." Half-an-hour later I was at home, and Johnnie and I danced
together with delight after a phone call to the hospital had assured
me that everything was now splendid. "We prayed, *mukwai*. We
prayed a long, long time. When one man from somewhere had to
go to his work, he sent someone else to join us." "Did you know
these fellows well, Johnnie?" "No, some, but not all. I called them
because we had to pray. We prayed in my house until twenty to ten."

It has been a delight that Catherine, the first of our big family,
is a medical graduate of the University of Zambia.

Chapter 7
FIRST FURLOUGH - THEN TO MWENZO

We were on leave from May 1950 to January 1951. After a short stay in the Andrew Murray Missionary Home in Cape Town and a leisurely voyage to Southampton, we spent seven months in Scotland and I had my first experiences of visiting numerous congregations, Woman's Guilds, youth groups, etc, and speaking to them about the why and how of the Church's overseas missionary work. On such visits, I was kindly welcomed and generally overfed. There were, however, occasions on which it was hard to keep a straight face.

One such was a week-night 'missionary meeting' in a town in the north-east. The minister who chaired it had formerly been, I believe, a policeman. He constituted the assembly by clapping his great square hands resoundingly and continued throughout to handle his audience with the finesse of a professional cheer-leader; heartiness from start to finish. The programme, he said, included talks by four missionaries (myself the last) with music between. From our vantage point on the high platform, I noticed three things at once:
(a) that few of the folk in the well-filled hall were under 65;
(b) that many of them were stout and motherly - there was only a token sprinkling of father figures in attendance; and
(c) that peppermints and other confections were passed quietly from person to person as the first speaker was introduced. That first speaker who worked somewhere in India, set out to describe a typical day in his life, in a leisurely monotone. As he finished, the ex-policeman called for applause and a few desultory hand-claps responded.

"And now we'll have a song from our very own Dougie McTavish. Dougie, what are you going to sing to us?" Dougie rose, an incredibly slender young man, with, I vividly recall an exceptionally long neck, providing scope for the acrobatics of an exceptionally prominent Adam's apple. He looked very shy, especially as cheers of delight hailed his rising. Then, as the clapping subsided, he announced reedily, from the back of his throat: "Bless this House". If you know that pop song of a bygone age, you'll remember that it finishes on a high note. Dougie approached the finale strenuously, dropping a demi-semitone per note. But the mothers and grannies lifted the roof.

The second speaker had spent some years in India among the Santals. He was earnest and had a message to share. But again, only a few limp hand-claps were heard as he sat down. "Now, Dougie, what's next on the menu?" asked the chairman. "Because", said the young tenor, the frog in his throat nicely bedded down by now. That song also soars to a climax in a grand assault on the heartstrings. Once again the last note was lower than what the score required. But the piano was also well off concert pitch and so the discord was diffused.

A man from the Scots mission in Manchuria, in China, spoke next. He was profoundly concerned about the swing to communism in that great land. "Don't think it's far away, ladies", he suddenly said. "It could be here, right here in your midst any day", at which a brief stir took place as though someone had whispered that there was a mouse in the hall. Then, suddenly, leaving his far eastern theme, the speaker said this: "I have a friend who has a little grandson called Tommy. One day Tommy was playing quietly in my friend's study and as his grandad was working he was singing softly as he played. 'What's that you're singing, Tommy?' asked Grandad. 'Let me hear it'. So Tommy sang:

Put a little penny in
To the missionary tin
If you want a shilling out
You've had it, had it, had it.

The tune was a well-known hit of the day. The audience came briefly alive, the sweetie papers rustled and there were audible clicks as peppermints were popped in behind dentures.

Dougie's last item was another great missionary song: "I'll walk beside you"; and he was faithful, in the closing crescendo, to his penchant for dropped tones. But the response was only short of a standing ovation.

After my talk and a hymn, as we dispersed into the chilly air, I wondered just what had happened that evening and how it related to the purposes for which the kirk sent people like myself abroad.

'Deputation work', as we called it, took missionaries over large tracts of Scotland and I was glad of the chance of hearing something of the life of rural areas which I had never seen in the years before my departure for Africa.

Back to the Savanna

Sea-sickness in the Bay of Biscay made us green but left us quickly, as our liner steamed south in January 1951. Before leaving Edinburgh, we had heard that the Mission Council had decided to 'post' us to Mwenzo on our return. We had hoped for a spell in a rural district but had expected to go to Chitambo, the nearest 'station' to the Copperbelt. Instead, it was to be the farthest, about 650 miles from Mufulira and in a different language area.

The founding of Mwenzo in 1895 had been part of a westward movement from the Livingstonia field, related both to the growth of the LMS field at the southern end of Lake Tanganyika and to the plan for a road to run from Karonga to Mbala, linking the Lakes. The capital for that road was to be largely provided by a gift from James Stevenson, who was a member of the Foreign Mission Committee of the Free Church of Scotland. The commercial expansion of the African Lakes Corporation - 'Mandala' - was an added incentive to a Scottish enterprise of road-engineering.

Moving into the hills above the station at Karonga, a group of missionaries had settled earlier at Chirenje in Ibanda. But disease had taken a heavy toll and so Alexander Dewar's caravan sought a higher, healthier site at Mwenzo, very close to the Anglo-German frontier separating Rhodes's annexations from German Tanganyika. The development from 1890 by the RC White Fathers of a network of strategically sited stations in the northern parts of Northern Rhodesia greatly troubled the Protestants of both the LMS and the Scots mission, and gave a further compelling motive for the founding of Mwenzo. It was a hazardous sally as Bemba raiders, in collusion with African agents of the Swahili Arab traders, were terrifying the Mwanga people and their Mambwe and Nyika neighbours. Local memory round Mwenzo still recalls how Bemba raiders welcomed Dewar to his chosen site by decorating the trees along his path with skulls of the local victims.

Mwenzo means 'the heart' but can also mean, as an adverb, 'of one's own free will'. It carries the implicit challenge 'who can hinder me?' The Mwanga people trace the appearance of a significant form of political centralisation in their history to the arrival, many generations ago, of a Bisa iron-smith from the south who brought with him not only his skill in working metals but also some seeds of red millet, *amalezi*, in his hair. Having found the original loosely knit kinship groups of Sichalwe, Simwanza and Sikaonga living near the sacred lake Mwanga, he moved east in search of a site for his capital and, finding it between the Kalulu and Matipa streams, he built his *isano* there and declared: "*Nazenga umwenzo* - I have built of my own free will". A fine grove of trees close to Mwenzo shelters his grave, according to local tradition. Local historians say that it was under Musyani's rule that a system of local government officers was established and that those *awalasi* were links between the ruler and the scores of villages which made up the Mwanga state.

Our welcome to Mwenzo was very kind. As I began to travel around the district, usually by bicycle, I found the same open-hearted kindness everywhere. When I visited a school or a village congregation for the second time, I was often greeted by an embrace and by the word *kuku*, hands on each other's shoulders, left cheek to left cheek, right to right, less effusive than a French or Yugoslav greeting but essentially similar. I was hardly ever called bwana in the Mwenzo district. Instead I was often addressed as we *mulasi witu*, *umulasi* being the singular of *awalasi* mentioned above. In Mufulira, I had had to persist in resisting the title bwana as a one-way form, reserved for white men. Though used in the area influenced by Swahili as a term of respect, bwana had been appropriated to Europeans in the racially defined situation of the Copperbelt. I therefore worked - and it had to be done explicitly - for the use of the highly useful reciprocally respectful Bemba word *mukwai*.

But Mwenzo was outwith the Bemba area of influence and *mukwai* was rarely heard. I did not find *umulasi* undesirable. Though it denoted my work in the community as 'missionary-in-charge', it was a familiar local term and had been given to the late Dr James Chisholm in affection as well as respect. Indeed it was not possible to be unaware of the legacy of *ichikuku*, of graciousness and goodness, that Chisholm had left at his death fifteen years earlier.

It was always true, I am sure, that missionary work, from the birth of the church to our century, manifested the aptness of Paul's assertion that "we have this treasure in earthen vessels". "Clay water pots" is how that has been rightly translated into African languages. Missionaries are people subject to inner and outward strains and liable, in an alien land, to feel the heat and burden of the day. There can be cracks in the clay pots. Some of the precious refreshment that they carry from the Fountain of Living Water may be spilled and lost. But the treasure in these pots is of God and to him alone be the glory.

There must, however, have been very few cracks in James Chisholm. He had clashed at the start of his career with Mwenzo's pioneer, Alexander Dewar. But the years had refined and strengthened him and his wise heart had learned the lessons of the way. His nickname *Lindalinda* caught the essence of his charisma. You could translate it into Scots as 'Wait a wee bittie'. It meant 'I'll be with you now' for he always made time for the folk, hale and sick alike, who came for help or counsel. "The man who wants to see me", he often said, "is the man I want to see". He was once chided by a harrassed colleague for his incurable patience.

Chisholm's mark was still upon Mwenzo when we arrived. It lived strongly in the dynamic translation of the New Testament into Mwanga. The frequent use, in that translation of *umukwasi* (the parent, the begetter) for 'father' when applied to God transcended the general differentiation of 'father' from 'mother' which makes the image of God masculine and can deprive it of tenderness. Maybe Chisholm had been, as I was, surprised and delighted by some of the prayers of Mwenzo believers: "*We Leza we tata swinya we mayo* - O God, our father and mother" was the salutation of one such prayer. "*We nyina-nkoko* - O mother of chickens" was another, recalling Christ's cry of sorrow over Jerusalem's rejection of his gospel: "How often would I have gathered you as a hen gathers her chickens and you would not have it!" (Matt 23.37)

An Unforgiven Trespass

The grave of Musyani was, as I mentioned earlier, within a grove of closely-packed tall trees on the edge of Kasichila's village beside the mission station. Its custodians were members of the Simwanza clan. So, when Kenan Simwanza, church elder and retired teacher, invited me to visit the grove with him, I was delighted. It was a short walk from his house and we were near where the narrow path entered the shade of the trees when suddenly a man leapt from behind some tall grass and commanded us to stop. He did not know that I understood the Mwanga language and turned his sharp anger on old Kenan. "He shall not enter", he said. "Have you forgotten what the *Wazungu* (white men) did to Robin Kula?" That was what my ears heard without comprehension. But clearly it would outrage the man's feelings if we were to insist on proceeding, and so I asked Simwanza to turn back with me. "Who was Robin

Kula?" I asked. "The King of the Ndebele in Rhodesia", he replied,
"the one whom the white men killed". It was Lobengula, I realised,
and indeed there was a widespread belief that had clearly travelled
over a thousand miles north of 'Matabeleland' that the grave of the
defeated king had been desecrated by some of Cecil Rhodes's
brigands. The passion in the eyes of the man who turned us back
from Musyani's grave testified to smouldering anger at such an
outrage and his determination to allow no member of the
conquering race to commit such trespass there.

Scripture Translation - Choosing the Right Words

Soon afterwards, I was looking through the drawers of the
office desk when I came upon the record of a decision of the Mission
Council of a few years back approving the preparation of a
translation of the book of Psalms into Mwanga. In over 50 years of
Christian presence there, the people had only the New Testament.
The idea of such an undertaking fascinated me at once and so I
began looking for someone with a good knowledge of English who
could work with me. It was the time of the school holidays and
lads who were in the senior primary classes at Lubwa, lads in the
middle and upper teens, had come home for two months. One of
them, a son of the senior hospital orderly, was the first I found.
"Would you like to put this into China-Mwanga?" I asked, and
passed him the 121st Psalm. He produced a translation after some
time, accurate enough but with the vibrancy of rice pudding, good
solid stuff.

Then his friend appeared, looking for him. He was taller and
slimmer and obviously outgrowing his clothes. He would be about
sixteen. As was generally the case with village lads who managed to
find a place in upper primary school, he wore no shoes. His shorts
were too small and over a fraying shirt, he wore a brief blue
waistcoat. My first lad had left our house before Caleb arrived.
"Would you like to turn this into your language?" I asked him and
put the same Psalm into his hands. I left him in my study, and after
a while looked in to see how he was faring. It was a translation
that, even to my foreigner's eye and ear, was mysteriously yet
emphatically different from his friend's offering. It moved like a
bird above a lake, full of music:

> "Nkapunamila aminso yane ku myamba. A kwi nye kuno
> kungafuma ukwavwa kwane?"

So began a happy partnership producing first '*Amalumbo* - the Praises or Psalms' and a few years later '*Ilayano kali*', a book of Old Testament selections from Genesis to Malachi. Others worked with us and we constantly checked the acceptability of our work to people of different generations. But the poet in the team was always Caleb Simpamba.

An Agent of Darkness

My working day at Mwenzo began about 6am. After a cup of tea, I cycled down to the office and came back for breakfast at 8 with Myra and our baby Catherine. We ate on the veranda with a lovely view to the hills on the Malawi border. On one such fresh morning, our head builder was waiting for me at the office at 6am. He looked worried. "You should see this", he said and put a bunch of papers into my hand. "I've been taking them off the trees before sunrise", he went on. "I've been doing this for some time. You are a new man and this is a big trouble. But I must now show them to you." I started to read. My China-Mwanga was adequate enough to let me know that those letters were full of hate, curses and threats. In most of them someone in the employ of the Mission was named. I noticed that the handwriting was awkwardly altered in some of them but that they were all clearly the work of one person. "This started before you came", said Silumba. "It was reported to the European at the Nakonde Police Post. But all he said was to discharge from work anyone named in such letters, to protect him from attack." "And was that done?" "Yes, at first two were sent home. This made me collect the letters secretly, because discharging people was no good." "And who can be the writer?" "Mulasi, I do not know."

Silumba and I agreed that we must involve some other senior members of the community, in confidence, in the search for the anonymous 'son of darkness'; knowing of course that rumours were flitting through the whole district like bats, spreading fear. A day or two later the builder told me that the headman of the nearest village was patrolling the station by night with his gun on his shoulder. The old rascal was usually maudlin from constant beer-drinking; now he had left the beer pots and his head was clear. "We must cleanse our place", he told Silumba. But the malevolent one was still afoot. Seedling lettuces in the garden of the Scots sister were uprooted and trampled roughly. Filth was laid on her doorstep one night, and we agreed that there was a marked increase in such acts and in the virulence of the letters that were still being pinned to the trees.

Then suddenly, clues began to appear. There was a medical orderly who had been a school pupil in Mufulira when we were there. He was regarded as a favourite of the Sister. Something in one of the letters seemed to link him with their authorship. "Call him to see you at your house", Silumba suggested to me. "You could be wanting to talk about the times when you knew each other on the Copperbelt." It was a good idea and I acted on it at once. The young man duly arrived and we chatted lightly. I had to watch for a chance of checking our suspicion. So, as casually as possible, I quoted *verbatim* an innocuous sentence from a letter which Silumba had collected the previous night, which no one else would have seen. The orderly's eyes suddenly glazed over and then he regained composure. But he had clearly been caught off guard.

Events moved swiftly now. It was useless to refer the matter to the young Police Officer. He simply had no idea of how to investigate such a type of crime. There was nothing for it, said our senior friends, but to set up a sort of *ad hoc* people's court; and I was impressed to find how quickly and unanimously they chose the probationer minister to act as chairman of it. He was a senior teacher who had recently been trained for the ministry at Livingstonia.

I was profoundly aware firstly of my own lack of knowledge and experience in such a situation and secondly of the urgency which the 'court' placed upon the need to 'cleanse our place'. The chairman was obviously a man of wisdom and determination. Just before the court was due to meet, he called on me to say that another orderly, whose name had figured in recent very menacing letters, would be hidden in the hospital chapel, where the court would convene, and then be revealed at the right moment. "*Ukuwa a ca nkama coo* - But of course this is a dead secret", he added.

The charge against our suspect, Silungwe, had been stated to him and he had heard it without comment. On the afternoon appointed for the trial he duly appeared and was placed in a passable replica of a dock. Most of the examination was conducted by the minister, and at first the accused seemed to be coping ably with his rejection of the charges *in toto*. Then subtly, step by step, the chairman led him to make statements that revealed a frightening depth of malevolence involving the concealed witness. "Situnga, stand up", said the chairman suddenly, interrupting Silungwe's tirade. At the sight of his fellow orderly, the accused visibly crumpled. "You have heard", the minister said to the tall young man who had spent the first hour crouching behind the solid wooden lectern. "What do you say?" But there was no need for an answer. The face of the accused announced his surrender. Did he now admit his guilt, he was asked, and in a faint voice, he said, "Yes". "Then, my friend", said the chairman, "we shall ask our chieftainess Wayitwika to banish you from her realm, for you have brought defilement and fear and the danger of death."

So it was done. Silungwe walked with us to the *isano* of the comely lady who was recognised by the colonial government as the local 'native authority', a chieftainess who, by the constitution of the Mwanga kingdom was answerable to the Paramount Chief Mkoma, who however lived some miles away, beyond the Tanzanian border. Wayitwika accepted the words of the minister without question and pronounced judgment of banishment upon the sick young pervert who meekly accepted her verdict and speedily left for the Copperbelt again. The change in the atmosphere at Mwenzo was miraculous. In the hospital especially, where so many of the staff had been personally cursed and threatened, there was a mood of immeasurable relief. Meanwhile the old headman hung his shotgun from the smoke-blackened roof of his delapidated house and shuffled back to the beer pots.

Mwenzo's District - over 15,000 square miles

When we had come to Mwenzo, we had not known how long we would stay there. But in fact it was for only five months. They were a time of pleasantness in so many ways, during which I had opportunities of visiting the thirty little schools of which I was Manager. There were hills and valleys, sparkling streams and green and grassy plains to be traversed, mainly by bicycle. On one such journey, Myra joined me; Catherine, now just one year old, being carried in a contraption like an old-fashioned meat-safe, a light wooden frame with mosquito-proof wire mesh covering the sides. On that occasion, we took a couple of station workers as porters, who bore along our baby in her cage while we cycled slowly beside them. The veteran minister, Revd Jonathan Mukwasa went with us, riding an ancient bicycle, and wearing a black felt hat. He fell off his bike two or three times, chuckled as he dusted down his old black suit and mounted again amidst the cheers of the rest of us. At Nachipeta, where we were given the school office to sleep in, our bed was straw with a mosquito net extended over it. In the coldest hour of the night I woke to a sharp pain, to find that a field rat had taken a bite at my scalp through the net. And in the morning a fat frog somehow managed to push his way into bed beside us.

A Sudden Transfer south

The factors that foreshortened our first spell at Mwenzo were two. The first had developed from my discovery while in Mufulira, that the text accepted by the British and Foreign Bible Society for the full translation of the Bible into Chi-Bemba was too archaic in vocabulary and abstruse in grammar and syntax to win the widespread welcome that was vital to a rendering into the language which, as I mentioned earlier, had become the *lingua franca* of the teeming townships of the Copperbelt.

At Lubwa, in 1947, I had been given 40 copies of the New Testament in the pedantic text, to pass as gifts to 'deserving cases'. The Copperbelt congregations used a looser and sometimes inaccurate translation which had been the work of LMS missionaries in the Luunda area of Kazembe. Whenever stocks of *Chipingo Chipya na Masalmo* - The New Testament and Psalms - arrived in the Copperbelt, they sold like hot cakes. But there was a dearth of this edition in June 1947 when I returned to Mufulira with my free gifts of the version from Lubwa. Very courteously, the people to whom I offered them said, "Thank you very much. But sorry, I cannot understand this Bemba".

Then unexpectedly, 150 copies of the LMS text arrived one Saturday evening. At church next morning, I asked Simon Mutambo to take charge of the books and it was announced that they could be purchased after worship. As soon as the benediction was spoken, the congregation became a surging mob. Fifteen minutes later Mutambo staggered into the vestry, his pockets bulging with coins, his hair tousled and his jacket dishevelled, looking like a man who had been at the bottom of a rugby scrum. "Did they go well?" I asked and his answer was to pass the fingers of his left hand briskly across his closed lips, releasing a puff of breath as he did so, a familiar non-verbal way of saying "Completely finished".

Shortly afterwards a Brethren missionary who had, as a kindness, been typing the MSS of the new Lubwa translation, told me of his fears that the Bible would not sell. "It may feed the white ants in our bookstores", he said sadly. I was very worried, and so enquired discreetly, of as many ministers and church members as I could, how they felt about the Lubwa text that the Bible Society had accepted for publication. They all gave the same answer; it was not going to be comprehensible to the people of the Copperbelt.

Something had to be done, I was now sure; and so, as we stopped in London on our way back to Africa in January 1951, I visited the Translations Secretary of the BFBS and told him how the matter stood. A quick decision, on the part of that far-sighted man and involving, I believe, an initial extra outlay of some thousands of pounds, led to the setting up of a three-man committee to 'recast the text'. After some negotiation, its members were chosen thus: the African minister at Lubwa; the missionary who had helped in typing the now discarded MSS, and who worked among the western Bemba; and myself. This meant that we had to prepare to leave Mwenzo and take up residence at Lubwa.

The other factor was that I fell victim in June 1951 to a miserable combination of what a doctor called 'gastric malaria' and pneumonia. I was Moderator of the CCAR for the year 1951-52 and chaired the Presbytery meeting at Mindolo near Kitwe. As Moderator I was appointed to go to the western province, then called Barotseland, with my dear old friend David Ramushu, to discuss plans for uniting our church with the Church of Barotseland that had grown out of the enterprise of the Paris Evangelical Missionary Society. That enterprise had been pioneered by Francois Coillard in 1885.

After a most interesting few days at the PEMS station at Sefula, during which Ramushu and I presented our plea for organic union to our somewhat hesitant hosts, I was suddenly assaulted by violent sickness and a thundering headache. The trip back to Lusaka was to be by light aircraft. I have never felt so miserable as on that jerky flight. Myra, who was staying in Lusaka with Mrs Cross, met me at the airport and I was rushed to the European hospital, pressing cotton wool against my nose as it bled profusely. As Myra was going to stay in Lusaka until the birth of our second child, due in October, she was not to return to Mwenzo; and my return was delayed for at least six weeks because of what a wee Scots nurse described as my 'r-r-r-right r-r-roaring' attack of 'malarial pneumonia'.

A kind of delirium engulfed me as they laid me in my hospital bed. I am not sure how long it lasted. When it left me, as it had come, swiftly, I was aware of profound, almost ethereal, physical fragility coupled with wondrous lucidity as my mind, that had slept through days of unconsciousness, awoke to the world again. Naturally I found it difficult to sleep, for I had slept enough to last me about ten days. And so it was that I was to experience an incident in that ward which I later incorporated into my second novel *One Finger* (1974) with, of course fictitious characters involved.

The hospital was very quiet around midnight. I was wide awake and opposite me there glowed the cigarettes of the only other patients, a farmer who hailed from New Zealand and a young football player from South Africa. Their chat was intermittent but it was clear that the older man was anxious to get the young fellow talking. "This government of ours", he asserted, "is communist. Soon this'll be no country for white men. These weeds in government are bending over backwards to curry favour with the natives and it shows in the cheek we get from our boys on the farm now. How do you manage down south? I bet you've got things under better control there." "Sure", said the footballer. "We stand no nonsense." "How come?" "Well, take my old man's farm. We give in a return of Kaffir labour in round figures. That suits us and it suits the Labour Officer. Easier to work with, and it gives us some come and go. So if we find a cheeky kaffir or some boy that's too fond of his beer, we can fix him there and then." "How? I mean, that's my question. Here, they can walk over us." "Not so down our way. If we catch one of the kaffirs causing trouble, we send him out on some faked-up job or other to the edge of the farm, digging a pit or some such stunt, away from all the rest. After a while we ride out and pitch into him. If he kicks up rough, we can always do him in there and then and bury him. And no one's the wiser. But somehow the word gets around in the kaffir compound and you usually get a spell of better behaviour as a result."

The crickets were strumming their unremitting *kleine nachts musik*. I heard a cock crow, out of turn, away in the distance. The New Zealander was getting fidgety and reached for his bell-push. As the black orderly skliffed in on shoeless feet, he bawled something about the water. The orderly went out and then came with a glass. But it was the bottle that was wanted and the old farmer let fly with a mouthful of obscene abuse, lurching as though to strike the orderly, who at once made for the door. I had had enough and called over to the old man to stop the noise. He and the footballer muttered something angry and silence fell.

Next day the Sister moved me to a single room. As I lay reading, the door opened and in came the New Zealander, in his dressing gown. "What bit you last night", he asked. "And who are you anyway?" But his tone was amiable and I was able to tell him how I reacted to such outbursts of abuse from white to black which were so common in those days. "You wouldn't believe it", he said, "but when I was a youngster back home I wanted to be a minister. Things didn't work out that way and after drifting around I landed here and made quite a good thing of farming." Before he left, he told me that the South African footballer was in for eye treatment but had not told the doctor the real cause of his troubles: a tin of mustard powder thrown at him in self-defence by the black man in charge of a late-night hot-dog stall which the footballer and his mates tried to 'take over' after a heavy night's drinking at the end of their tour of play.

"Come Back Soon"

Convalescence was slow and I was to feel a pain near the bruised lung for a long while after. There was so much work waiting at Mwenzo but I was not allowed to return quickly because the only means of travel was for me to drive the old Dodge vanette nearly 700 miles myself. Moreover I had to go via the Copperbelt, the Luapula river pontoon, and Mansa so that I could visit the Brethren missionary, who was joining the new Bemba Bible translation team, and lay plans with him for joint action. The enforced rest was however a chance to delay my goodbyes to Myra, Catherine and my mother-in-law. But letters from Irene Pearce, the girls' school headmistress at Mwenzo, reminded me that my daily work was being carried by already over-burdened colleagues who hoped I would return as soon as possible. It was not easy to explain to them by letter, without hypochondriac overtones, that the synchronised assault of two powerful diseases had knocked the stuffing out of me.

Chapter 8
BACK INTO HARNESS

Lusaka was to remind us sharply during that period of the continuing vulgarities of the colour bar. We went into town one day and, after shopping, dropped into a cool cafe for ice-creams. As we sat with Catherine in her push chair, the door opened and a black man came in, laying a parcel on the ground as he approached the counter. The white woman assistant immediately shouted, "What do you want here?" "Please, I want bled, missis", he replied pointing to a loaf on the shelf. "Get out", she said. "*Hamba lapa manje* - now, now, get out". "But please, just bled for my childrens." The second assistant had now appeared and together, without further ado, the two of them rushed at the man, opened the door and pushed him out, and one of them kicked his parcel into the traffic. It was the old dilemma again for us: do you pretend you haven't seen such disgraceful behaviour, or do you make some form of protest with its unavoidable psychosomatic recoil on yourself, leaving you spent and shaking? For unless you've a zest for confrontation, it cannot be otherwise.

We rose to leave. As I paid the bill, I said, as quietly and coolly as I could, to the assistant: "You may not realise it, but the law of assault could be applied to what we saw you do just now." But before she could answer, a burly white policeman came in, followed by their banished black customer, and his face told us that he intended to speak severely to the woman. It was one of the few signs, in the early fifties, that NRG - as the Government was called - was feeling obliged to take some cognizance of such incidents and of the real possibility of a concerted African reaction one day.

No such burly officer was around, however, alas, when, a few days later, I had occasion to go to the Railway Parcels Office. There were no other customers when I entered and the tall white woman behind the counter dealt promptly and courteously with my business. I was still in the office, putting some papers into my wallet, when a black man came in, with a large parcel under his arm. By his dress and bearing, I guessed he was recently arrived from some rural area. He hesitated at the unfamiliarity of his surroundings and then moved to the counter. But the order to get out was delivered before he had reached it. He started to try to say something in his minimal broken English which served only to fuel the woman's virulent abuse. The man said no more but turned and moved towards the door. Knowing his language, I greeted him quietly and asked what he had wanted to do. He began to tell me and I realised that, in fact, he would have to send his parcel by bus as its destination was far from the line of rail.

Now the office was a large building and, at a right angle to the counter, there was a smaller room occupied by the Manager. He, I remember, was a Scot. The door of his room was open and I had seen he was busy with papers at his desk. He did not look round but his ears must have caught what he would probably have called 'native gibberish', and that was enough to open the sluices of his fury. As he let fly, he turned and our eyes met. The black man stood still beside me. The Scotsman's face registered shocked surprise to find that one of the 'natives' was white. "Are you speaking to us?" I asked, but he made no reply. "We were talking quietly", I went on, "so we weren't disturbing you, I hope. But perhaps I should tell you why we were talking together". I then described the incident and the behaviour of his woman assistant. "I cannot guess the reason for her abusive behaviour to this gentleman", I said. "There can surely be no cause of offence to you in our quiet discussion and my attempt to give him the help he should have received from this lady." But there was no reply at all. As we left, the Manager was still at his desk, staring blankly at us. Behind all bullying, surely, lies chronic cowardice.

My weeks of convalescence gave me the opportunity to meet the lively congregations of the Methodist Church in Lusaka. The General Superintendent, Revd Edward Nightingale, was a born teacher and services led by him were always nourishing. Revd Matthew Lucheya who as pastor of the black congregation - for alas! the 'middle wall of partition' was still in evidence - was a tall, burly, big-hearted saint, well-suited to the task of building fruitful fellowship in a congregation drawn from many parts of the land.

I had to get back to Mwenzo, however; and so when the old Dodge had been checked at a garage, I at last set off, in mid-August for the far north via the Zaire Pedicle and the crossing of the great river Luapula. I had the company of a man from Mwenzo who had a driving licence but whose driving lacked confidence and who seemed to enjoy the passenger's seat. Though still feeling flabby, I preferred to drive than to sit apprehensively beside my inexperienced companion. The Dodge was old but the garage had assured me that it had been fully serviced, and so off we went.

When on our third day we reached the Chambeshi river, it was already dark. The water was low, for we were in the fourth month of the dry season. But we had to get across, so I tooted the horn and in a few minutes I could see the pontoon men with their storm lanterns mustering on the other side. As the pontoon, driven by the manual hauling of a steel hawser, was reaching our side, I lowered the vanette down the steep slope ready to drive on board and applied the hand brake tightly. There was much pleasant laughter as we all joined in pulling the pontoon back to the east bank, and then, after farewells, we set off through the hills to Isoka.

The night air was sweet and the engine was frisky as I drove up the twisting earth road, and Tembo and I were singing. Suddenly the lights failed and I instantly reached for the hand-brake, only to find that it had completely collapsed. Somehow, thus benighted, we stottered to a standstill by rapid downward gear changes and then stalling the engine. The extinguishing of lights, I found, was because so shoddy a switch had been fitted that it had put itself off as we rattled over the rough surface. The brakes, however, were totally dead. Driving on corrugated earth roads was a shuddering experience under about 40 mph. But I could not now risk such a speed along unlit tracks, without brakes. It was just after dawn when we at last arrived at Mwenzo.

Tremors of Unrest

My welcome home was full of warmth, not least from John Ngwele our faithful house servant. But the Sister and Miss Pearce could not wait to tell me about the visit of the Governor and his Lady, accompanied by their son and the aide-de-camp, for which the ladies had had to take full responsibility. The local folk, in those days were not expected to share in such ceremonial hospitality. Their role was that of silent spectators. But the gubernatorial party had had to spend a night at Mwenzo and so, by some unspoken protocol, His Excellency and his Lady had been received by Na-Mwenzo, Mother of Mwenzo, as Miss Pearce was affectionately called; and the Sister being junior in service, had played hostess to the two young men.

It was the Sister who told me, with radical blushes and almost uncontrollable giggles, about what had happened on that visit. The Mission houses were all ageing and needing repair and on discovering that she must host the son of the King's representative, she had decided that some redecoration was necessary, particularly of the little building in her back garden which housed the *chimbuzu* and which in bygone times in Britain would have been called 'the privy'. There were general dealers' stores just over the border at Tunduma and the Asian businessmen there supplied most household needs. But the only paint the Sister could find was scarlet. Like many folk, she thought she could do the decorating job herself and proceeded to deck all the woodwork in the little house in flaming red. The visitors would be there in a couple of days and so she used the paint liberally since there was not time for a second coat.

Her visitors duly came and made themselves at home. It escaped her notice at the time that the Governor's son was absent for quite a while from the sitting room in the evening. When they left next morning, however, she visited the little house and was stricken to find that the gleaming skin of red paint had broken, releasing oozing splurges all over the seat. A few days later, she met the wife of the District Commissioner from Isoka boma, 70 miles to the south, who told her that the gubernatorial visit there had been somewhat overshadowed by her Ladyship's insistence that they procure turpentine, or at least something equivalent, before the party resumed its journey southwards.

It was not till much later that I learned of what had taken place when HE's party reached Chinsali district and visited Lubwa. Local feeling was running high against Roy Welensky's plan to have the two Rhodesias and Nyasaland federated. For the 'indigenous peoples' of the three territories that could only mean the extension of the entrenched 'white supremacy' that dominated the region south of the Zambezi even more grimly than the north. The Chinsali branch of the African National Congress decided therefore to demonstrate in some visible way to the avowedly pro-federation Governor that they opposed the plan wholly. The secretary, Kenneth Kaunda, and his fellow-teacher Robert Makasa, joined the party welcoming the Governor to the district wearing *chilundu*, skirts of bark cloth. Mortified by such action by his employees, the missionary-in-charge of the school work instantly dismissed the two teachers and announced a ban on ANC meetings on the mission estate. The offenders' protestation, that traditional kilts had been worn at the Lozi court for the visit of King George VI in 1947, was rejected out of hand. Kaunda and Makasa were now free, in consequence, to devote their energies, full-time, to building up the Congress movement in the northern province.

At the time, I knew nothing of those significant happenings which I would have occasion to study in detail twenty years later while preparing my biography of President Kaunda for the Oxford University Press. The busyness of life at Mwenzo, with accumulated arrears of office work, engulfed me and consumed all my diminished energies. There were visits to schools to be undertaken and the book-keeping was amazingly complicated when educational and medical work, repairs, food supplies, fuel and transport all had to be accounted for week by week. Yet, knowing that my time in Mwanga country was running out, I wanted to make the most of the dry weather for visiting out-lying congregations.

The elders had decided that an old headman called Chulu should receive baptism and asked me to go to his village and give him this 'sign and seal of the covenant of grace'. As we approached the tiny family settlement, an ancient man came to meet us, leaning heavily on a staff. In the manner of his generation, he knelt down and clapped his hands softly in solemn salutation. He is very old, I thought. It was impossible to guess his age. As we walked together slowly towards the houses, I spoke of the church's pleasure that after a long life he had asked for baptism. "You must excuse me", he replied. "It is not I whom you will baptise. It is my father". Sure enough there he was, the most ancient of all, crouched on a reed mat in the shade of a little tree. By comparison, his son looked boyish. People from all the neighbouring villages came for the baptism, and as I wondered often, I wondered then at the happy rejoicing on the part of people who were not on the church's roll of members, for the celebration of so distinctively Christian an ordinance. It reminded me of Loudon Church in Malawi in 1947, when, after three or four hundred members had shared the sacrament of communion, around three thousand came together for the great open-air festival of thanksgiving.

It was during these last crowded weeks of our first Mwenzo spell that I was able to share in one of the genuine 'fruits of the spirit' that were a strong feature of the life of 'the body of Christ' in that area. In the village of Kaombwe about 50 miles to the east, there were one or two widows in the local congregation and an old blind couple. Their houses were badly in need of repair and so a team of us church members went to the village to build new houses for them. It was an occasion of carefree happiness and singing as we cleared the ground, cut the poles, mixed and trampled the clay plaster, soaked and twisted together strips of selected tree barks for rope, and cut and bundled tall dry grasses for thatching. My total lack of skill with the axe and the smarting of my bony shoulder under the weight of great bundles of tree poles caused much laughter. And when, in search of a lighter chore, I thought I could help by stripping down some barks for rope, the mirth was uncontrollable. For I was stripping trees whose bark a five-year-old would know to be quite useless for *ulukasa*, as the rope was called that bound all the poles of frame and roof together. Those houses had not a nail in them. Then at the end of a day of hard labour and profuse sweating, we gathered round the bowls of steaming maize *inshima* and its necessary accompaniment of *inyani* of chicken, brown beans and leaves, like spinach, cooked in oil. The church in Zambia and Malawi was not in danger of transferring its title from the people to the building. As in the New Testament, the word church meant the fellowship of Christ's companions. And *agape* was certainly in the feast we shared at the end of that day of the new houses in Kaombwe.

Seeking a new Relating of the Local Church and the Mission

In 1948 the Foreign Mission Committee of the Church of Scotland had approved the setting-up of a Central African Regional Committee to co-ordinate the activities of its agents in the Livingstonia and Blantyre fields in Malawi, in the northern and central provinces of Zambia and in the Copperbelt, with special reference to the process known as 'the integration of church and mission'. The time had come - some of us felt it was well overdue - to move positively towards the goal of indigenous responsibility for the direction of Christian enterprise in the region. Our Mission Council appointed the Nursing Sister at Lubwa and myself to attend the meeting of the Council in Blantyre at the end of September.

A lorry came over from Malawi to pick us up and take us, via the Overtoun Institution at Khondowe, to Blantyre in the south. As a boy I had read with fascination of the magnificent church building at Blantyre, conceived and executed by David Clement Scott. It fully lived up to my expectations, though its interior furnishings seemed fussy and more suited to Scotland than to Africa. Round the wall of the chancel ran words of special significance for a continent racked by racism: "My house shall be called of all nations the house of prayer".

I left the Regional Committee, to whose discussions I had contributed little, with a sharpened awareness of the need to move swiftly with 'the integration of church and mission' but also aware of two impeding factors: the slowness of some missionaries to recognise that their 'mission' had essentially 'come to pass' and must not perpetuate itself by default; and the strange lack of explicit pressure from African Christians for such a 'hand-over' of responsibility. This second factor worried me because I was sure that many black church members found the white domination of church organisations and of the administration of mission stations irksome. Their silence on the matter was not, I felt certain, the silence of willing consent to such a system but belonged rather to the existence of a 'middle wall of partition' between white and black. Healthy, bilateral discussion was very rare. The missions had arrived around the time when Cecil Rhodes's Company was subjugating the region at the turn of the century. All too easily missionaries came to be regarded as a special variety of 'bwanas' and 'donas'. A 'good African churchman' would therefore be a docile person who said "Yes" to what he was told by his bwanas and hid his own thoughts.

Around the meetings of the Central African Regional Committee there had been many opportunities for happy fellowship. At Loudon, on my way north from Blantyre, I attended a great service of the church in which body had to squeeze against body as we rose to sing and sat again. The singing of a rendering of the 103rd Psalm by Peter Z Thole, *Muwonge, mzimu wane, Yehova Ciuta*, filled the air with a vibrancy we rarely find in Scotland and I am sure I detected six or eight different parts being sung. Only a few of the huge congregation had hymn books but everyone knew all the words. Even the pressure of people in the building could not restrain the rhythmic swinging of bodies in tune with the pulsing pace of the song. After the service, some of the elders took me to visit the graves of Donald Fraser, the great father of our United Missions Leader, and of Jonathan Chirwa, the sweet singer (*ng'ombwa*) whose hymn *Ine, umoyo wane ni Yesu* is known over a vast area of central and southern Africa. I translated it thus:

For me, my life is Jesus my Saviour;
He died for me upon the Cross
And cancelled all my transgression
          Jesus, Jesus.

For me, my Well of Life is in Jesus:
My cleansing is His blood for aye
My sinful evil is ended.
          Jesus, Jesus.

For me, Thou art my Strength, O Lord Jesus.
If Thou forsake me, I shall die:
O leave me not, else I perish.
          Jesus, Jesus.

For me, my soul rejoices in Jesus:
Thou art my Saviour, Thou alone.
O stay beside me for ever.
          Jesus, Jesus

It was Mwangonde Faulds who had first sung that hymn to me, in Kya-Ngonde, long before I left Scotland. This second visit to Malawi only served to deepen my longing to hear more of these *sumu* whose words and music were the work of black Christians. Missionaries had often feared to allow the use of indigenous music for Christian praise for the reason that, as some of them said, such tunes might have witchcraft associations. The alternative was to translate hymns from European languages. In a number of cases this was well done. The 23rd Pslam in Chi-Bemba is a notable example and some of the simple hymns of the Moody and Sankey collection were readily translated into many languages. But sometimes the results were tragi-comic, as in one case I heard of where a hymn of, say, five rhyming English verses was rendered into five rhyming Bemba verses - like trying to 'squeeze a right-hand foot into a left-hand shoe', as Lewis Carroll put it. Worse perhaps was the damage done to the message by uninspired translators. 'Meaty' hymns like "Immortal, invisible God only wise" called for great care, finesse and a sense of poetry from their translators. They told me in Malawi that it was Donald Fraser who broke through the inhibiting fears of some of his colleagues in the conviction that the Holy Spirit would, as it were, 'baptise' such African tunes into Christian worship. The *Sumu Za Ukristu* of the Malawian church is a glorious vindication of that belief. But more of this anon.

No Paltry Poultry these!

As some of the Regional Committee lived at Khondowe, we from Zambia were taken there for a night or two and I renewed some of the contacts I had made at Livingstonia in 1947, notably with Chiswakhata Mkandawire and the Revd Stephen Kauta. While having tea at the house of a lady missionary, soon to retire, I heard that she was looking for good homes for her white hens and their handsome husbands. Myra and I had thought of keeping hens for eggs at Mwenzo and so I offered to buy them from the lady. "Please come for them just before you go so that I can keep them as long as possible and say goodbye to each of them properly", she said. "And I'll then give you their diet sheet." I shuddered and prayed for grace to respond fittingly to what promised to be a heart-wrung entreaty for the kindest treatment of her feathered friends. Next day, she kept her promise: a neatly written sheet bore instructions for their various meals per day which included raisins, cereals and lettuce; the times for water; their bedding; tonics, and indeed everything short of toothpaste. They were then loaded on the lorry under her eye and I was sure that she waved to them rather than to me as we drove off.

I was not long back at Mwenzo when, sooner than expected, a telegram from my mother-in-law suggested that I should go south at once if I wanted to be in Lusaka for our new baby's arrival. John Ngwele and I set to at once, packing tea chests and cleaning the house for whoever would be occupying it. Financial stringency dictated that all our possessions must travel in a 15-cwt vanette. I was worried about the excess weight's effect on the springs of an ageing vehicle, especially since, in October, the roads were heavily corrugated in parts. The crate of white poultry was too large to fit under the canopy and so was tied on the roof. Everything went well till we were about 25 miles from Lubwa, when suddenly I was aware of the juddering drag of the wheels that meant a puncture. We were in a bare stretch of country and the noonday sun was blazing as we stopped and found not one but two very flat tyres. Someone had to run to the nearest village and borrow a bicycle to race to Lubwa for help. The nearest commercial garage, going south, was about 500 miles away! We had not prepared for such a calamity and could do nothing but await the arrival of the Lubwa mission truck, if it was not else-where. As we waited, all my bonnie white birds in the crate on the roof perished from dehydration. "What would she say if she were ever to hear how they died?" I thought.

Somehow we reached Lubwa after sunset. The tubes of our tyres were so ripped that they could not be repaired, and there were no spares at Lubwa. So everything was emptied from the old vanette and in the middle of the night, with a 44-gallon drum and John Ngwele as companion, I set off again, this time driving the 10-horse power Austin Countryman that the Lubwa doctor had recently sold to the mission. With doors at the back, the Countryman sucked in an incredible amount of dust and we had no way of protecting ourselves from it. When we needed petrol, we found that the tools we carried could not budge the stopper of our 44-gallon drum and so we had to call in at Chitambo Mission, 240 miles south of Lubwa. It was just beginning to dawn when we rolled in, wakened the Sister there, gladly gobbled the porridge she cooked for us and, with the help of the mission driver, opened our drum, filled up and roared off.

It was late afternoon when at last we reached Dingley Dell, the thatched cottage allocated to my mother-in-law as a government secretary. Mrs Cross herself came to the door in response to my knock, stared at me and said "Who are you?" And I could not blame her, for the coating of red dust had made me all but unrecognisable. Then our 18-month old baby Catherine toddled out, looked at me for a moment and said "Daddy", and all was well. But we were late: Jamie had come into the world some hours before our arrival. Myra was fine. The wee lad weighed over eight pounds and our happiness was unclouded. A few days later, Myra and Jamie were discharged from hospital and we started to prepare for our return journey. We have often wondered since how the little Countryman carried all it had to: three adults, two babies, the essential petrol drum, all our luggage including the inevitable extras for a new-born baby, Catherine's 'meat-safe' carry-cot, and a crate of hens that a friend gave us on hearing of the doleful demise of the bonnie white birds from Khondowe. Jamie, who had been baptised by Edward Nightingale, was eleven days old when we began the 550 mile trek back to Lubwa. 420 of the miles were a heavily corrugated earth road on which the shuddering was bearable only when travelling at over 40 miles an hour. At 50 mph we moved like a speedboat on a choppy sea. We have happy memories of that journey, picnics on the way, and Catherine's delight in her baby brother.

The Danger of Private Finance

Our house at Lubwa was on a ledge along the hillside behind the mission station. The normal approach to the hill houses of the missionaries was by what they called the goat paths, precipitous tracks over and between rocks. Dr David Brown had lived in the house allocated to us, for twenty years from the date of its building in 1927. The bigger house in the middle of the ledge had originally been occupied by the first missionary to the district who had been sent to Chinsali in 1913, the centenary year of Livingstone's birth to a field of evangelistic and educational enterprise pioneered, as mentioned earlier, by David Julizya Kaunda. When we reached Lubwa in late October, the very new doctor, David Livingstone Wilson, great grandson of Livingstone, was living in it with his young wife. Though our transfer to Lubwa had been made so that I could take a full part in the Bible translation 'recasting' work, I was immediately asked to become 'Head of Station' and to take responsibility for the book-keeping and maintenance of buildings, etc that that task involved.

It became apparent right away that the congregations spread thinly throughout our 15,000 sq mile district were still troubled by the recent discharge of 100 of the 115 paid agents called 'evangelists'. It had fallen to Bill, with whom I had made my first tour of the villages four years earlier, to effect this drastic pruning. But he had had no choice. The benevolent doctor who had served Lubwa for 20 years had operated an evangelism account in the ledger on unorthodox lines. The large team of lowly paid agents had had their wages debited to an account which was cleared from time to time by personal donations from friends of the doctor in Scotland. When he died, suddenly, those sources dried up. The Foreign Mission Committee in Edinburgh could not allow the inclusion of such amounts in the shoe-string budget approved for Lubwa in those austere post-war years. The local church had never been involved in contributing payments and could not possibly have found the money. So, because there had been no participation of the local church in the financial administration of Lubwa and the other mission districts, Bill had to act, as it seemed, unilaterally in announcing that only 15 of that 'noble army of martyrs' could continue in service.

The crisis served to underline the urgency of involving the local community in the deliberative and administrative processes by which our evangelistic, educational and medical work was carried on. For the local church, the sudden termination of those evangelists' services resulted at first in a period of relative debility. For the missionaries, it was a pity that the current proposals for the establishment of 'station management committees', with African members, appeared to have been motivated by a financial crisis. For me, it meant immediate involvement in visitation of the 36 little congregations, some of which declared they were 'dying of hunger' - *tulefwa insala* - for lack of the Sacraments. Since the Revd Paul Mushindo was a key member of the Bible translation team, I undertook an intensive programme of visitation to these little congregations, which involved the administration of the Sacrament of Communion 72 times a year.

"Since you're visiting the congregations", said the Training School Principal, "why don't you also visit the district schools? It will save money and I'm over the ears anyway here at Lubwa." When money was so short for travel and not a penny was provided by NRG, his words made sense. But there were less than 300 miles of motor road in the district and so my travelling was to be done mainly by bicycle. As I plunged into this programme, my balloon tyred Raleigh and I observed an amiable *modus operandi* for some of the toughest tracks: we each carried the other 50% of the way! Money for district touring was very scarce and increasingly we were to find our itineration grant from Edinburgh spent before the driest and hottest period of the year.

My appointment as School Manager involved me right away in a sad task. Because the government limited the number of schools according to the amounts provided for the cost of teachers' wages and school equipment, there were hundreds of children who were denied even elementary schooling. The Church of Scotland, along with other missionary agencies, had provided some funds for the maintenance of what were called 'sub-schools'. With the help of parents and others, simple buildings had been erected, including tiny houses for teachers, and nominal fees were charged as contribution to the monthly bill for the wages of the teachers who were not funded by the Department of Education. In 1951, NRG ordered the closure of all 'non-grant-aided' schools, and it fell to me to explain this to the grieving village communities whose children, having just started school, were now excluded. Their chances of admission to any of the existing grant-aided schools were very slim, if not nil. More and more NRG's control on the schools was being tightened, though increases in government expenditure on African education were barely noticeable. At that time, I received the following equipment grants for primary school pupils, for a year: Sub A and Sub B - 2/6d (12p); Standard VI (the top class) - 6/9d (approximately 34p). The annual grant for the education of a white child in a day school was then £27.

Chapter 9
DARKENING CLOUDS

One Sunday in November 1951, as I was leaving the house of prayer (*ing'anda ya mapepo*), I found a group of well-known members of the Lubwa community waiting for me. Their greeting was very pleasant. Then one of them, a church elder said: "We want to ask what is your opinion about the African National Congress." It was an unexpected question just then, but after a moment's thought, I replied: "I am sure that there has to be an organisation like Congress in the country nowadays." "Why?" another man asked. "Because", I said, "there has to be a body which can express the people's feelings without being supervised like the African Representative Council, by government officials." "Thank you. That is good", was the response to my statement and a brief silence followed.

"If that is what you believe", said another of the group, "we wonder why you banned the Congress from meeting here in the school hall". This was a bolt from the blue, and so I answered with a question: "Is the Congress banned?" - for that was the first time I was to hear of what had happened following the bark cloth incident at the time of the Governor's visit. "And who said I made the ban? I am new here. Tell me more of this." The men seemed reluctant, however, to say much about the August crisis. Instead someone asked: "Would you, as missionary in charge, have banned Congress?" "No", I replied, and added that such action, in my view, could never rest on one person's decision. "One finger cannot pick up a louse", I said in Bemba, using the well-known proverb - *umunwe umo tausala nda*. "Should any political meeting be banned?" someone then added, and again I had to think for a moment. My reply came like this: "We are now in a dangerous time in the political affairs of Northern Rhodesia. Personally I dislike very much the words being spoken by Roy Welensky. Indeed, I am opposed to his plan to federate the three territories. I would not want to have him saying such things here, though I'm sure he would not come to Lubwa. He is speaking only to white people. But if he applied to use our buildings here, the matter would have to go before the Station Management Committee." "It is dead", someone said sharply. "Then it must be brought to life again. For any decisions about our life together here must be made by a body that can speak for the local people." "That is good, if it is true", one man said, smiling.

But I was now troubled. "Why have you thought that I had something to do with that ban?" I asked. "I wasn't here. I was actually at that time ill in Lusaka, waiting to go back to Mwenzo. How could I have been involved?" It saddened me sharply to think of the experiences we had had in Mufulira and the enmity of some white people against myself for being 'a nigger lover' or a 'white munt', as they said. "We believed the ban came from you", said the first speaker, "because we had just been told by Dr Todd that when you came, you would be missionary-in-charge. Then we heard about the ban from the Principal. So it seemed that you knew about the quarrel of the Principal and the Congress and had decided to ban ANC before you came." "No, my friends, you have been completely mistaken. I had no knowledge at all of the trouble here, and, as I have said, I would never act single-handed in any such matter. But what you have said makes it most important for us to revive the Station Management Committee." "We shall see. Anyway, we thank you. Go in peace", said the leader of the group and we parted. Climbing up the goat path to our house on the hill, I was conscious of heaviness of heart.

As a result of our move from Mwenzo, work on the Mwanga translations of Psalms had not been completed. I wrote about this to the National Bible Society of Scotland who were to publish the book as they had been publishers of the New Testament years before. The NBSS promised a small grant to enable Caleb Simpamba, who was still a pupil at Lubwa, to work with me at weekends and during school holidays. Using some of the grant, we had a little 'wattle and daub' house built close to ours which he called 'Psalms Lodge'. He was a very kind young fellow and often came in to amuse little Catherine. Myra typed the MS as we produced it and the work went on apace. Meanwhile a young western Bemba man was sent to Lubwa by the Brethren missionary who was in the 'recasting' team with Paul Mushindo and myself. He was to read the Bemba MSS with me so that we could check it for readability over a wide area of the country. When he was at Lubwa, he also was part of our extended family. He amused

Catherine by keeping the nail of the little finger of his left hand very long. Increasingly, however, my local tasks were making it difficult for me to play that full part in the Bemba Bible work for which we had come to Lubwa.

Healing and Hygiene

Dr David Wilson was keen to visit the district. Work at the hospital kept him very busy but we made a plan together for an early tour of the section of the district known as Ichilinda. Near a school in that part was a huge grove of trees, guarded by a royal priest called Shimwalule, where the kings of the Bemba were buried. David was a delightful colleague and we both looked forward keenly to our medical, educational and evangelistic tour in January 1952. On the Sunday before we set off, I took as a text the words from 1st John, "Try the spirits to see if they are of God", along with Christ's words in John 5.25, "The hour is coming... when the dead shall hear the voice of the Son of Man and those who hear shall live". Conscious of the growing stridency in Welensky's federation campaign, I listed various voices that were bidding for people's attention and included Welensky's among them. "This voice", I said, "is not a voice of peace. If the South African system is extended here, we will move into greater darkness." Then I added that, likewise, if his belligerence were answered in a similar tone, that could only worsen a bad situation. "We, as Christians", I said, "must instead test every spirit. For we are able to do so. We have Christ as our teacher and our example. Any spirit that counters the spirit of the Prince of Peace is unacceptable for Christ's people."

The rains had been steady for some weeks. The air was fresh and sweet. It promised to be a perfect time for travelling, and so, on the Monday morning, off went David and I, in the vanette with a load of school supplies, medical supplies, bedding etc, and the cup and plate for Communion. Word had been sent ahead to Ichilinda so that people could be sure to meet the doctor's team at the larger village centres where he would set up his portable dispensary.

Our travelling took us through a Roman Catholic mission where we stopped and were offered tea. It was one of the stations of the White Fathers in which the priests lived at a very basic level. A huge horny-handed brother cooked for them and it was cakes from his oven that were served to us. They must have been weeks old and were terribly hard. We laughed about them as we travelled on, rock buns made of pure river sand. We were glad we were not celibates and that our wives were such good cooks. Two years later at a visit to that same White Fathers' place, I arrived at the time of their mid-day meal. As we chewed our way through terribly tough meat, I noticed the horny-handed brother with his grimy nails, picking at a large bowl of straw-berries. They were to be our dessert and so I decided to decline them with the universal fabrication that I had done very well and was fully satisfied. "But then you must have cheese and bread", said the senior priest. "Brother, get the cheese". The huge man shuffled across the room, wiping strawberry juice on his tunic. As he opened the door of a wall cupboard which served as their pantry, legions of bloated blue-bottles zoomed out and whirled round our heads. I had the greatest difficulty in assuring my hosts that I was truly replete and could not take another bite. As I protested my gratitude nonetheless, a hunk of dark yellow cheese was placed on the table, its cracked crust varnished by longevity, and I had to swallow back my revulsion. "You must come again, any time", said my host as I mounted my bike and rode off in search of some shady spot where I could attack a packet of Myra's glorious gingernuts that I usually carried on tour. For I was famished.

In one of the villages David was shown a lad in his teens, terribly emaciated, who, said his parents, had not walked for years. He moved himself by shuffling along the ground, using his hands as a second pair of feet, his knees permanently bent. David began an exhaustive examination. "His reflexes are weak", he said to me. "But they are not dead". We explained this to his parents who stared back unbelieving. "But he cannot walk", said his father. "Yes, he can walk again", said David and then promised to have a walking aid made by the carpenter at Lubwa and sent to the village. He organised this as soon as he was back at the hospital. On the first opportunity a medical orderly took the walker out to the village and instructed the boy and his parents in its use. But it lay under a tree till the white ants had devoured it, for the people were sure that the doctor was wrong and looked for no betterment. You can take a horse to the water, but you can't make him drink. "*Cha bulanda nganshi* - Very sad, very sad", said the orderly when he learned of the total failure of that mission of mercy.

New and Old Approaches to Marriage
We spent a night on the way back at Mundu School, which took pupils through six years of schooling from sub-standard A to

Standard 4. The headmaster there was the son of an evangelist who had given notable service in Kitwe on the Copperbelt and whose grave was close to that of Myra's father at Mindolo. Charles Pambalu was the evangelist's name and his son, a church elder, was always known as Ason Charles. Mundu School ran well under his wise guidance, and the school gardens were exceptionally fine. A night at Mundu was always pleasant and the head and his staff chatted with us by firelight about many things.

One subject that came up was marriage and on this Ason Charles spoke gravely. He was very troubled by the new lax forms of marriage which were gaining popularity at the time. "These young people think this is how people marry in Europe, that if a young man likes a girl, thinks she is beautiful, he should marry her by his own decision. This is killing our country. They may call those arrangements marriages of love but this is foolish talk. Our old way is very much better." "Tell us why", I replied, though I was familiar with the widespread concern of older people about what was happening in the country. "Well", he said, "you see, in our society, a young man's fathers guided his choice of a bride" - those 'fathers' being of course his male begetter and all the brothers of that begetter, whom we would call paternal uncles. "His fathers would not force the lad to marry a girl he disliked but they would prepare him carefully to understand that their advice was for his own good. So too, with the girl. Her mothers had to share from her birth in all important matters of her growth. So when they had taught her about the duties of a wife and mother, they could then guide her in the finding of a good husband. The lad's family and the girl's family would talk together, so that they would be agreed before the wedding could be celebrated. This meant", he said, "that while the young couple were learning to know each other and perhaps feeling afraid or even uneasy with one another, the two families were nearby to surround them and help them. Divorces today are horrible. The two quarrel and break their marriage as carelessly as they made it. This should not be. How can children of such marriages grow well? With us, if the husband and wife quarrelled and perhaps she ran away weeping, her family and his would have to work to bring these two to understanding. Surely this is good." Communalism may stultify, I have often thought, but individualism makes people terribly lonely. Divorce in the western world is a sad commentary on societies that 'leave it to the individual'.

A Grievous Misunderstanding

As we stopped at Chinsali on our way back to Lubwa, we met the Scots Principal at the Post Office. "There's a letter for you at Lubwa", he told me. "It's a stinker. I'll say nothing till you've read it yourself." All he would tell me was that copies of it had been sent to such persons as the Secretary-General of the ANC and the NR Governor as well as to Dr Hastings Banda in London and the Foreign Mission Secretary in Edinburgh. "Anyway", said my colleague, "once you've dealt with these so-and-sos I'll have something to say to them myself."

When I reached home, sure enough there was the letter. It had upset Myra very much. It was a lengthy document and bore the signatures of Kenneth Kaunda as Branch Secretary of the Congress, and other committee members. As Kaunda had not been at Lubwa for some time, he must have agreed to sign it on hearsay. For it was based on the assertion that, in a recent sermon, I had attacked the ANC and was therefore an agent of the imperialists. There was a quotation in it from Bernard Shaw's *Man of Destiny*, with this vivid passage:

> When he (the Englishman) wants a new market for his adulterated Manchester goods, he sends a missionary to teach the natives the Gospel of Peace. The natives kill the missionary; he flies in arms to the defence of Christianity, fights for it, conquers for it; and takes the market as a reward from heaven.

There was no intention to take action against me, said the letter, but I must be warned. I was sure, however, that I must answer it in such a manner that the way would be open for removing this serious misunderstanding. At first it was difficult not to feel resentment against those men who had actually heard my sermon that day. I was not aware that Harry Nkumbula, recently elected President of the ANC, had spoken of answering Welensky now in his own coin. But again, I was to realise that local feeling against white domination and the new and very real threat of Welensky's federation was deep and passionate.

Black friends had spoken to me years earlier in Mufulira of their despair in a situation in which all the power was in white hands. "We can do nothing", they had said. I knew too that Kenneth Kaunda had a strong conviction that, as he had told me at Lubwa in 1947, "this terrible burden of inhumanity" must be lifted from Africa but that "the situation must be changed without violence".

I regarded him, rightly I was sure, as a Christian-Ghandian. I had lent him a book about Ghandi while he was teaching at Mufulira in 1949 and we had both been members of the Afro-European Friendship Group there. But bitterness was increasing in direct proportion to the campaign of Roy Welensky and Godfrey Huggins to impose their federation on the voteless, voiceless black majority of the three territories. I had felt from our first meeting a kinship of understanding with Kenneth Kaunda. This blow was therefore all the more painful. Yet I was sure, when my missionary colleague told me that he was now going to "sack the lot", that this must not be done. Our fellowship might be fragile but it must be repaired urgently.

I have never been able to interpret 'fellowship in the Spirit' in any other way than as an embracing, forbearing and forgiving community in the context of the realities of life in this world. Pietism that wears blinkers and turns its back on the conflicts and agonies of the world makes nonsense for me of the 'good news' that 'the Word was made flesh'. The faith is either all or nothing. So that moment in Central African history was no occasion for acts of discipline upon 'cheeky' employees of the mission. I was grateful to my colleague for respecting my plea to take no such action. Most of the signatories of the letter were on the staff of the Training School of which he was Principal.

There is some reference to that sad episode in my biography of President Kaunda. It proved difficult to persuade him as local ANC Secretary to agree to an informal meeting at our house or even in the small hall beside the church. It would have to be on neutral territory. Moreover he chided me for addressing him as Mr Kaunda, under his official title as Branch Secretary. For a moment we seemed to be on the verge of a hair-splitting, time-wasting debate about how 'official' letters should be written. No such meeting as I had requested took place, however, because the crisis in Central Africa was escalating steadily. Some of the letter's signatories continued to be pleasant when we met in the course of life and work on the station and in the district. But one teacher staged and sustained his personal boycott. When I saw him and greeted him, he would turn his head away and walk on without reply. He was an able and conscientious man and a leader of the Boy Scouts. But he was not going to countenance social relations with any *musungu*. His people had endured enough.

Chapter 10
MORE SNAPSHOTS
FROM CHINSALI

My periods of work at Lubwa were meanwhile more and more interrupted by the need to strengthen contacts with the district schools and congregations. Many of those journeys, mainly by bicycle, were very memorable. I called, one time, for instance, at Lupande school. After my inspection, the two teachers and I were standing chatting near the headmaster's house. Suddenly from behind our backs we heard 'a rushing mighty wind' and looking round, saw the gigantic spiral of a dust-devil - *kankungwe* - advancing upon the classroom block for Sub A and Sub B. As it struck, it lifted a great stretch of the thatched roof off and threw it all over the place. Tired, but by no means spent, it then switched course slightly and, as it were, strode across the clearing between classrooms and houses where the children played their games. Its funnel picked up paper as it came in our direction, moving now towards the second teacher's house. Once again, with a roar of power, it stripped off the thatch, raised it thirty or forty feet up in the air and bore it off over the tree tops, scattering bundles of it all the way.

I decided to send a full report at once to the Provincial Education Officer and to ask for an immediate emergency grant, knowing that such a report from the headmaster would probably be filed away and forgotten. Village people were expected to take responsibility for the maintenance of those schools and the current grant of £180 for a new brick school, with a 3-classroom block and two teacher's houses was enough only for the cost of cement for the ant-proof foundations and a small contribution to thatchers' wages. The bricks were pounded, moulded and burned as voluntary service from the community.

As we left Lupande, we had to ride over a long ramp across an area that was swampy in the wet season. Such a raised track was called *ngalandi* because some white man had said that that was how they crossed marshes in England! As we crossed it that day, the clay of the *ngalandi* was dry and very hard. We were battering along, Caleb Simpamba and I, when all of a sudden I was thrown off my bike and rolled over on the hard ground, shaken by the fall and the more amazed because it was wide open country we were traversing. Caleb dismounted at once and came to see if I was hurt. Then we looked at my bike, but at first could see nothing to explain its sudden stop. "Look", said Caleb, "see that balloon", and sure enough there was a huge balloon which had come out of my front tube and was over a foot in diameter. There must have been a little hole in the cover and the pressure inside had blown out that amazing bag of rubber so stretched as to be grey in colour. As the balloon had met the front fork it had caused my sudden stop at high speed. Caleb went forward. "I'll open the valve", he said, but before he could touch the tyre, the balloon exploded with a terrific noise that went ringing over the plain: 'wang-wang-wamg-ng-ng'. Back we went to Lupande to tell our tale of woe. "That's all right", said the head teacher, "I've a balloon tyred wheel on my bike. Take mine and you can send it back when you have sorted your own bicycle". That sort of kindness was shown very often when, in the course of extended travels, by bike or motor vehicle, I needed some form of help. One was never stuck alone in Zambia or Malawi.

The Church as Fellowship in the Spirit

Almost 28 miles from Lubwa by the back road by way of Fonkofonko at the crossing of the Lubu river, there was a school at a village whose name meant 'the great place of pigs', Chinkumba. I liked cycling by that back road, firstly because, being rarely used by motor vehicles, it had a much less corrugated surface; and secondly because it passed close to Chipoma, the place of the fine waterfalls on the great rocky river Chimanabubwe. Chipoma had almost been chosen in 1913 by the first Scots missionary as his site until he spotted a tsetse fly. At Chipoma it would have been simple to run electricity from a turbine. Instead, at Lubwa, it was for long quite difficult to obtain enough water for the needs of the 1000 people who made up the Mission community. At Chipoma I was in the habit of resting and bathing in the glorious lukewarm water as it rushed over the rocks into its ravine below.

On one such visit to Chinkumba, I combined a school visit with the sacrament of communion for the people there and from surrounding villages. The offering was being given in the usual manner, women first and then men, coming to the table singing, to lay their coins or eggs or grain there. I suddenly became aware that a girl of about 15 was coming up to the table alone, the rest of the women and girls hanging back until she laid her *susu*, as sixpence was called, and returned to her place. A *susu* was a large offering for that place at that time. When the elders and I met together after the service, I asked why that girl had come up to the table alone. "This always happens", they told me, "always since she first was big enough to walk". "But why?" I asked. "No one else came up alone." "It was like this", said one of the men. "When she was a very small baby she was dying. Indeed the women had started to wail and everyone believed death had come. But then Ba Mulenga came, he is this one here, our local elder, and when he saw what was happening he said, 'What is this? Why wailing? You have not prayed'. Then he stood up and called the young boys who were near. '*Balumendo*', he commanded, 'go now, at once, to all the villages and call the Christians. Quickly. Go now'. And those young boys raced away on their slim, shoeless legs. Soon the people began to come from everywhere, men, women and children and they all gathered around the parents' house where the baby was. You never saw so many people, outside and inside the house, squeezing on each other. For inside was Ba Mulenga and as he prayed aloud, he held the little one in his arms, people pressing on him from all sides. Then God heard him and the little cold body warmed again. So, to say thanks to God, every year at Communion her parents make their special gift, herself their young girl taking it to the table. Everyone must then wait for it is a great thanksgiving. That is why."

Companions in Ministry

West of Lubwa and beyond the big White Fathers' mission at Ilondola lay the section of the district called Ichingo. Two of the fifteen survivors of the once great band of evangelists worked in Ichingo: Mateyo Chilufya, a light little man with slightly squint eyes and a fascinating lisp, and Thomas Nkamba usually known as Shikulu Kabuswe, grandfather of Kabuswe. We travelled together on one visitation of Mwenge, Kabanda, Malekani and Lapukeni, a pocket of Bisa people in that Bemba area. We were all on bicycles, but the evangelists moved slowly. Frequently the little man had to stop to take a sniff of snuff. When mounted, he placed the middle of his feet on the bars of the pedals which had long since lost their rubbers and were bent. In this way he greatly reduced his thrust. Nkamba who was quite tall and sturdily built moved very little faster because his saddle was low enough for a child so that his legs were not really driving the pedals. As the evening wore on and the mosquitoes thronged around in welcome, I felt the need to accelerate. I always cycled with a high saddle to maximise my thrust and my bike, though well travelled, was much healthier than theirs. When therefore I reached our destination, there was neither sight nor sound of my companions. Compunction gripped me and so I decided to wait for them before entering the village. Ages later I heard the squeak-squeak of Chilufya's unoiled pedals and the crack-tum-crack hiccough of someone's loose cotter pin. The saints, I saw at once, were out of breath and sweating. "You have done wrong", said Shikulu Kabuswe. "You should have waited and we should have travelled together. *Abeni ni nkwa, bakakilwa pamo.* Strangers are like bark-cloth, knitted together." Duly chastened, I nevertheless appreciated the old man's mode of rebuke; for he knew I loved to hear and use the pithy *mapinda* of his language that so neatly encapsulated living truth. Another such proverb thus seemed to suit him perfectly: *Mwi bumba lya mukulu tamubula kambala inkokoto* - In an older person's pouch there is always a little something to eat - i.e. listen to the wisdom of experience.

Those villages in Chinsali district were sad in some ways. The balance of the sexes was all wrong. From the time of the subjugation of the territory by Rhodes's rapacious Company until my time, a dangerously high percentage of the able-bodied men were away in search of wages to pay their taxes and clothe their families. In an economy in which you ate what you could grow or gather, the women and the old men were hard put to it to scratch enough food from the unresponsive soil to feed their children and themselves. In the absence of the husbands, the whole upbringing of those children fell upon their mothers, many of whom lived with the nagging fear that their men might fall prey to the prostitutes of the distant mining compounds, those women of the night who somehow were able to escape the rough surveillance of the police and hide by day. Yet, for all their woes, the folk were quick to laugh and a village concert by the light of a huge bonfire was an uproarious event, at which young singers and dancers and actors performed to the delight of the neighbourhood. Two schoolboys, one on the other's shoulders, masquerading as one tall man, with sacks for short trousers and a carton for a sun-helmet, stalking around, hands on hips, imitating to a tee a District Commissioner's plosive Bemba *à la* Oxbridge, had the mothers and grandparents rolling on the ground and slapping each other's backs with mirth.

In the south-eastern part of our huge 'parish', on the other side of the great north road, lay the chiefdoms of Chibesakunda, Mukwikile and Mukungule, spread out and thinly populated, sometimes together called Mukumbi, land of cloud. Our schools in that great tract were widely separated, and children walked great distances every weekend, returning to their schools on Sundays, carrying little bundles of flour, beans, dried leaves, dried fish, nuts or whatever else their mothers could provide to last them the next five days. Between some of those schools there were distances of over 40 miles. I have a host of vivid memories of my visits to Chibesakunda, to the little school at Chibuta, near the White Fathers' Mulanga Mission, to Changalilo, Chishala and Mulilabantu. I began this story with my account of one such journey to Chishala where on my second visit, the teachers and their pupils had a little guest-house waiting for me with 'Come with Happy' inscribed on its front wall.

I usually travelled with one companion but sometimes went alone. Once, somewhere between Chibesakunda, royal village of another Bisa chief, and Changalilo, I suddenly came upon a lush green plain after cycling for a long time along twisting forest paths. I had seen no sign of habitation for miles but there was a passable track across the plain and I followed it on the assumption that it would take me somewhere! It was a beautiful day of blue sky and cirro-cumulus clouds and I was sweating lightly as I rode. Ahead I spotted what looked like a bridge made of tree poles and at once I caught the sound of flowing water over the din of my bike. What a perfect river that was!

It was unwise to bathe in some of those Zambian rivers where the water was sluggish and where there lurked tiny snails carrying the bilharzia flukes which could easily and insidiously enter one's body. But this was different. A stream about fifteen feet wide, sparkling in the sunshine as its clear waters rushed along. Who would not exult at such a sight! So, choosing a little bay below the six-foot high bank, I stripped, jumped in, soaped myself with a cake of Lifebuoy and, as I splashed, began to sing. Life provides us with few chances to sing with all our power. But I was alone and though the river birds stopped twittering, for shock, I could sing to my heart's content. I cannot clearly remember what I sang. It may well have been 'One Alone' from *Desert Song*. Anyway, as I stopped my song for a moment to splash my face with water, I thought I heard something. So I waited in silence, and, sure enough I heard it again, the unmistakable sound of suppressed feminine giggles. I had seen no one for miles. So I waited in silence again, but I knew now that the sniggers were proving uncontrollable. So I called out: "*Mwapoleni, Ba-mayo. Muli umutende* - Good day, mothers. How are you?" "*Endita, mukwai. Tuli umutende* - Yes, sir, we are well", bubbled out their answer through their giggles. As quickly as I could, I seized my towel, rubbed myself lightly and put on my shorts and shirt. Now I could greet the ladies.

Apparently they had come from some invisible village to wash clothes or draw water. Hearing the clattering of a bike, they had looked up from the river, seen a *musungu* charging towards them and ducked. It could have been a District Officer come to collect taxes. But I had not crossed the bridge. Crouching in their covert, not far from my bay, they waited for me to move on. They must have suffered suppressing those sniggers. We all could now laugh together and take farewell of each other merrily.

In that same great tract, when travelling with a young fellow called Chubi, we came upon a long stretch of *musebo* - the word for a road made by hoeing and so distinct from the *inshila* that are pathways trodden by feet. That *musebo* was about four feet wide. As we hammered along it, I suddenly saw that, some distance ahead, its surface changed from brown to white. "See that", I said. "The road changes colour". As we drew nearer, Chubi said, "Yes, it looks as if it's covered with chewed stalks of maize". And so it was, lots and lots of the stuff, well chewed and then apparently spat out to cover some ten yards or more. "Who would do this?" I asked, for we were passing through a virtually deserted region, the surface of the *musebo* telling us in no uncertain terms that it had not been hoed for some time. Chubi's answer amazed me: "Monkeys", he said. "Monkeys? But where would they get all the maize stalks to cover such a stretch of road with their spittings?" "*Katwishi*", he replied. "I don't know". Together we started looking all around us and then he spotted some tall stalks that must have been self-sown at the site of a long abandoned village. "Here's where they found the maize", he said, but it was a long distance from the *musebo*. "If that's where they found the stuff, why would the monkeys come to chew it and spit it out here on the road?" "*Musalula ku bantu*", he replied at once. "Insolence to human beings". Remembering my friend at Livingstonia five years earlier, and the vervets in his mango tree, I could believe that Chubi was right. Monkeys have a very different attitude to human beings than, say, deer or birds have. We seem to tickle their impish fancy.

I have mentioned how Nkamba the evangelist was called "grandfather of Kabuswe". In Mufulira I had come across this teknonymous mode of address, calling someone by the name of his child or grandchild. But it was in far commoner usage in this heartland of the Bemba. One day, cycling towards Lubwa from the Chipoma waterfall, I met Isaac Nsofu who had been a pupil when I visited the area in 1947. Now a teacher, he was still full of friendliness. As we parted, he said: "Please greet Ba NaMwila for us". "The mother of Mwila?" I asked. "Who is she?" "Ha", he replied, "can a man not know his own wife?" "How do you mean? Is my wife called NaMwila?" "Of course, since your coming here." "Then Catherine has been called Mwila?" "Sure". "And I am Shimwila?" "Of course. Have you not known this? You are always called this name when people speak of you."

Once it became known that Myra and I knew of our teknonymics, they began to be used all the time. You were a youngster till you married. When you married you were known as a man, *umuntu*. But not till you had begotten a child could you be considered fully grown. When at last your child in turn became a parent, then as *Shikulu* or *Nakulu*, grandfather or grandmother of So-and-so, your honour was complete.

Central Africa's Crisis begins to Concern the Christian Council

In the cool months after the last rain, the Christian Council of Northern Rhodesia met again. My friend Kenneth Mackenzie and I were chosen by the Mission Council to go to Kitwe in the Copperbelt for the four or five days of meeting. I cannot recall anything of that meeting except what happened when the Chairman rose one day and said: "Now, we've just about five minutes before lunch. So I suggest we give our blessing as requested, to the

Government's White Paper on the 'closer association of the two Rhodesias and Nyasaland', what they're referring to as 'the Federation'. If we deal with it now, then we can make a fresh start with our main agenda at two."

"Excuse me, Mr Chairman", said Kenneth at once, and rose to present his personal opposition to federation on the ground that it was being imposed on the voteless black majority by the wealthy, powerful white minority. Unfortunately, he expressed this in somewhat abstruse language 'above the heads' of some of those present. The Christian Council was still an all-white body, though a black 'observer' had been invited that year from a separated body, unacknowledged by the government, called the African Christian Conference.

Seeing that Kenneth was not being fully understood, I asked for the floor as soon as he finished. "If this plan is, as we are told, going to benefit all races economically and generate wealth, then let this Council call for a referendum of all the peoples of the three territories. If a majority of them say 'Yes' to the plan, let it come. If not, to impose it will be dangerous." It was the Anglican Bishop who answered me, first affirming his 'great regard' for me and then warning that what I had said, if it reached the ears of illiterate black people, might lead to subversion against lawful authority. I had no relish for a clash with him across the hall but had to counter his statement. "Chairman", I said, "what will bring what is called subversion will be the imposition of this federation in face of the widespread resentment and anger of the voiceless and voteless majority."

The chairman glanced at his watch. The time reserved for lunch was under threat. As he did so, the Revd Isaiah Mumpanshya, 'observer' from the ACC, jumped to his feet. "Mr Chairman, please may I speak. Some audible voices muttered, "No. He's only an observer." "Observers can't just speak like that", etc. The Chairman then asked for the approval of the Council to his allowing Mumpanshya to intervene which was reluctantly agreed. "All I have to say", said the observer, "is that my people do not want this federation with Southern Rhodesia and will never, never accept it". After this no one spoke, and the silence though brief was oppressive. "Let's adjourn for lunch' said the chairman at last and there the matter ended.

Automobile Trouble

In mid-1952, the new doctor at Mwenzo brought his wife to
Lubwa to have a baby. Tragically she developed poliomyelitis after
the birth and became paralysed, which necessitated their leaving
Zambia. But in the final waiting period before the birth, the doctor
was very restive and so I suggested that he should accompany me
on a journey to Kasama, capital of the northern province, which
was 140 miles by road eastwards across the Chambeshi. In return,
he suggested that we take his car, and that, to relieve his wife, one
of their children should go with us. It was a strenuous journey
because stretches of the road were very rough and the car was a
light Austin. On the return trip, after we had recrossed the river
by pontoon and had still about 70 miles to go before reaching
Lubwa, the car stuttered to a standstill. We knew we had plenty of
petrol and so had to trace some other cause. Neither of us had
much knowledge of motor mechanics but at last we found where
the trouble lay: a little detachable section of the petrol piping, near
to the carburettor, was blocked, presumably by some of the thick
dust that swirled around us all the way. We tried blowing it clear
but with no success. We had no thin wire with us and so, in
desperation, we decided that the only solution was to top up the
carburettor, drive a short distance till that ran out, top it again, on
and on over the 70 weary miles between us and our beds. We had
offered a lift to some heavily laden women in Kasama and they had
children with them. So sleeping in the vehicle was out of the
question. What we needed therefore was something to hold petrol
in, from which we could pour those dribbles into the carburettor.
The only available container was the little boy's potty which his
father had fortunately included in their luggage. So, syphoning
petrol from the tank, which involved first sucking up a mouthful,
through a length of rubber piping, we filled the potty as full as we
dared, knowing that the bumpy road would easily cause spilling.
The doctor sat beside me, holding our unlikely reservoir. As soon
as the car stopped, we both leapt out and gently topped up again. It
took us many hours to reach the edge of the mission, and suddenly,
there and then, the doctor declared that he could do no more. "Let's
walk the rest", he pled, and so we did, with his sleeping boy on my
back, having bade farewell to our passengers in the darkest hour of
the night.

Real Prayers

What names did people use for God, I often asked myself, before the coming of Christian missionaries? The question arose in my mind because the constant use of *Lesa mukulu*, literally 'great God' or *Lesa wa maka yonse* - 'God of all power', the Almighty, made prayers sound dull and repetitive. I had found 'mother of chickens' and 'God our father and mother' in the Mwenzo district. I therefore began asking senior folk to tell me what titles were properly used and soon we were popularising the use of such praise-names in our worship together: *Tengenene*, spreader of the heavens; *Chibuta*, the great bow of heaven; *Mwandanshi uwayanda ichalo chonse*, which conveyed the idea of the great architect setting out the whole creation in order; and others. It was especially from a great old saint, John Mpuku, that I heard prayers that bore no marks of translation from a foreign tongue or from foreign concepts. One petition of his in prayer struck me as so authentic and compassionate that I realised how sad it is that decorous taboos have often pushed our prayers in English into banal irrelevance. "O merciful one", old John prayed, "please enrich the flow of blood in the breasts of those who give suck"; for in a real way, nothing mattered more than that the babies of the villages should start the journey of life plentifully supplied with the best of all nourishment.

Chapter 11
RACIAL
BARRIERS

1952 had started sadly with that letter from the ANC. It proved a very full year in which somehow I had to keep my office work going while attempting to strengthen contact with the villages throughout the district. The revival of the Station Management Committee helped to cement relationships of mutual trust and, though that honest teacher continued his solo boycott of greetings with Basungu, friendliness trickled back like a shy tide. Yet, our invitation to a group of leading members of the community to come to our hillside house for a meal met not a single response. "I was busy" - "My wife was sick" - "Visitors came unexpectedly" - were some of the lame excuses offered when I expressed sorrow that no one had come to eat what NaMwila had prepared. Then at last, one man told me the truth, "I am sorry", he said, "but you see we cannot climb that hill for social reasons. For the building of those houses high up and away from us all symbolises *kapatulula*, the spirit of aloofness." We were going to have to wait for over a year before we could move down the hill.

Fuelling the Fear of Federation

There was meanwhile, no abatement of Welensky's campaign for Federation. The British Liberal Party's description of the scheme as 'conceived in fraud' was near the mark. When presenting the plan to the Queen, Welensky spoke of a 'multi-racial' society and the phrase 'Partnership of the races' was used by colonial officers in their concerted effort to sell the idea to their black subjects. But a leading Federationist let the cat out of the bag. "Don't be worried about partnership", he told an anxious white audience. "What we're talking about is the partnership of a man and his horse. They don't eat together, or sleep together, but there is a working understanding between them." Far away as we were from the line of rail and the hub of the plot, there was very little we could do. But I was more sure than ever that the whole scheme threatened the region with bitter conflict.

We were therefore not happy when it was announced that the Provincial Commissioner was coming on an official tour of inspection of the Chinsali district and wanted to visit Lubwa. Such visits meant lining up school children and going through a series of ceremonial gestures that became less and less desirable the more the colonial government proclaimed its support for Welensky's plan. The PC in the northern province was known to be one of the keenest advocates of Federation. But we had no alternative but to await him, show him round and bid him farewell.

We had been sent a precise timetable of his visit: leave Chinsali *boma* 1.35 pm; arrive Lubwa Mission 1.45; welcome by Missionaries and leading Africans; march past of uniformed organisations, inspect hospital, etc, etc, etc. But he arrived about 1½ hours late and the school children were now exhausted after a long wait, standing in the sun. "The young children have waited a long time", I told him, after formal greetings. "May we go straight to see them?" "No", he replied sharply, "I want you and your colleague here", pointing to the Principal, "to meet with me and the District Commissioner first before we do anything else"; whereupon he marched into our office, we followed, and he closed the door.

"Now", he said, "we want you to assist us by giving us as much information as possible about the local political situation". Neither of us two missionaries spoke. "Well?" said the PC, like a teacher addressing a couple of pupils caught red-handed in some school offence. The Principal and I exchanged glances, and then the Principal said simply, "Nothing to report". "Oh, really. I'm surprised", our guest retorted. "I'd have thought that you were in a better position than most to know what's going on in the minds of our African friends. How about you, Macpherson?" I found the form of address discourteous, but made no comment on that. Instead I asked: "What kind of information do you think you might get from us?" "Oh, come along", he chided. "You know what I mean, I'm sure. I'm talking about the political situation in view of the forthcoming Federation of the three territories and the Africans' reaction." "I'm willing to discuss any political situation", I answered. "But not here, not in secret session in our office, with our friends and neighbours outside, as though, because we are white we are part of your security network. And what do you expect us to report?

Secret stocks of weapons? Plots of revolt? Do you think that, if such were being planned, we'd be told?"

He was now showing irritation and changed his line of attack. Turning back to the Principal, he asked what was being done in the Training School to 'push Federation'. The Principal replied that, as he himself thought there might be some economic advantages from such a 'closer association' of the two Rhodesias and Nyasaland, he had mentioned that view now and then in his 'current affairs' period. "And you, Macpherson. You're Manager of the district schools. I hope you are also explaining these benefits to your teachers and instructing them to impart them to their pupils." "No", I replied. "Why not?" "Well, for two reasons: firstly, I do not support the federal plan and indeed understand our people's serious opposition to it. But there's a second reason: NRG has said that any teacher found speaking to pupils against Federation is to be disciplined, because this is a political matter and politics have no place in the classroom. So, for that reason, I would have to reprimand a teacher found advocating Federation to his pupils. You can't have it both ways."

The PC was angry now. He had a reputation of heating fast. Someone had told us that, years before, when he had been a DC, a prisoner had escaped one evening from the cell at the *boma*. Disturbed out of working hours by one of the *boma* Messengers, he had ordered the man's immediate recapture, 'dead or alive'. They brought the fellow back sure enough, but lifeless on a stretcher. The man had been incarcerated for some minor offence or other. Now, years later, I sensed that, despite promotion in the colonial service, the big man still had little control over his temper. As he reacted hotly to my statement, the DC looked extremely uncomfortable. He had taken no part whatever in the interview.

The PC rejected my remarks as ridiculous. He had, he said, rightly expected our cooperation in matters of security. "But we are not part of your security network", I replied. "No doubt you have agents in each district. And I object to being ordered into our office for such an interview as this. The people outside are our neighbours and friends. Clearly you have misunderstood our life and work here." "Government has to expect Europeans in the territory to support law and order. We will deal severely", he said, "with subversion and must indeed prevent it from happening". My colleague was still quiet, and so I had to express my own view in answer to this. "Personally I am sure", I said, "that if what you call subversion takes place it will be because of the imposition of Federation. Government's duty, I believe, is to take note of the feelings of the people rather than push Federation regardless."

"The feelings of the people", he retorted with irritation. "Our Africans, left alone, have no political views. Indeed, it seems to me that anti-Federation opinions came from certain Europeans, and we take a serious view of this. However, let's go and see these pupils of yours." We rose but I could not let that be the last word. "Governments have often tried to use the church as a tool, to hammer it into the shape they require. We're not here to be that kind of tool." Out we went. The day was now wearing towards late afternoon. Tired and hungry school children stood, limp and unsmiling, as the Commissioner's party 'reviewed' them. A cursory visit to the hospital followed, and then a cup of tea was served, the conversation consisting of those ineffable banalities that characterise such situations.

A good Welsh friend of mine, in government service, told me some time later that a file, with my name on it, had been opened on the PC's return to Kasama, and was locked away in the security safe. Some years later, while doing research on Zambian history, I came across a confidential memorandum of that provincial office in which the 'decline' of Lubwa was attributed to the activities of certain missionaries who had encouraged political agitators.

One of those 'subversive' missionaries was, clearly, my dear friend from college days, Kenneth Mackenzie. The son of a Strathpeffer shepherd, he was a man who moved from the narrower theology of the Free Kirk to an openness of heart and mind which gave his life a very special radiance. He was a stranger to even simple mechanics. In vain, we tried to teach him to ride a bicycle and later to drive a car. But his keen and compassionate critical faculties carried him straight to the point in debate. Few I have known have had his gift for speaking incisively and keeping his opponent's friendship. He loved what he liked to call 'the cut and thrust' of controversy. He was tall with a light spring in his walk. His black hair was closely waved and his eyes were blue. His use of English was rich, sometimes so erudite as to leave his listeners spellbound but uncomprehending. But his sense of humour was boyish and irrepressible. Above all he 'walked with God in truth'. Long after his return to Scotland in 1954 and while at full stretch in a busy

Edinburgh pastorate, he was, at the time of his sudden death in 1971, a leading protagonist of the anti-apartheid movement and as encyclopaedic as ever in his detailed knowledge of African affairs. He was always, as I wrote in an obituary note, a 'son of the morning'.

Two memories of him, in particular, must be included here. In 1951, he was invited, with very short notice to address the Christian Council on a subject expressly entitled 'A minor prophet and the modern economics of the world'. I too was asked to speak, my subject also being sent to me without option: 'The New Testament doctrine of grace'. We were both extremely busy in our districts when those letters reached us. The Council met at Chalimbana Training College, east of Lusaka at the chilliest time of the year. I remember finding it impossible to be warm in bed. Kenneth's address was early on the programme. He was six feet tall but for a rostrum he was given a coffee table. In a sparkling 100-minute talk, he presented the Council with the message of Amos, the herdman of Tekoa, and applied it to Northern Rhodesia, to the gross gap between white and black earnings on the Mines, to the totalitarian colour bar, to the conditions of rural poverty in a land where expatriates lived luxuriously and to the whole structure of colonial economics. Every now and then he had to bend, at the hips, to read from the papers on the little table. His rich voice gave point not only to the call of the Almighty for righteousness but to Amos's searing attack on the 'kine of Bashan', the wealthy leisure-loving women who despised and ill-used the poor folk in their service. "Oh, I know, I know, old Amos was right", said the Anglican chairman when Kenneth had finished, "but I can't go back to the Copperbelt and call my women cows!"

The other memory was of a long journey back to Chitambo from the line of rail through the hours of darkness. We were in the small pick-up which Kenneth used for his extensive travelling as Education Secretary. There were three of us, Kenneth, myself and Yonam Mpuku, the first black principal of Lubwa Training School. Mr Mpuku was suffering from a painful attack of mumps. The pick-up's cab could carry only two, and Mpuku was a big man. As Kenneth could not drive, I was at the wheel. So Kenneth had to ride outside with the inevitable large petrol drum for company. The road was badly corrugated and I had to move the vehicle fast in an attempt to reduce the shuddering. At last we reached Chitambo and were welcomed by Sister Agnes. "Kenneth, you're frozen", she exclaimed as the light of a pressure lamp showed up our weary faces. Kenneth was clad in short trousers with only a sleeveless pullover over his short-sleeved shirt. His teeth were chattering. "I am all right", he replied. "But what kind of a journey have you had?" she asked. "Quite good", said Kenneth. "The only trouble was that I was fighting a losing battle against a forty-four gallon drum". And so he had been. It had been impossible to prevent the heavy drum from dancing all the way and it could easily have crushed his feet if he had not held it at bay. But Kenneth never complained. Instead he was always quick to see the thousand and one jokes at the heart of the universe. Happiness came into any group of people with whom he was associated.

It was at that time, when spending a couple of days at Chitambo on my way back to Lubwa, that I was asked by the Sister to accompany her to a village far away where a woman was reported to be gravely ill after childbirth. The mission vanette had to serve as ambulance for part of the way, as far as the road bridge over the Lukulu. But from there, the approach to the village was by a narrow track along the riverside. Because of a very heavy storm, the path was so slippery that we had to move with great care. Huge pools of water had to be circumvented, and the tall grass overhanging the track was drenching. At last we reached the village where the woman lay limp and sobbing. It was a bad case of retained placenta. She was laid on a crude canvas stretcher, badly worn with age, and we started on the six miles back to the road bridge. The stretcher was then suspended from the canopy of the vanette and swung wildly as the driver pushed his vehicle through a sea of mud for most of the long journey to the hospital. Chitambo medical staff served an area stretching 225 miles south, 180 miles north and as far as the Luangwa River and the Zaire Pedicle to the east and west respectively. It was not uncommon for sick folk to be brought in to hospital by their relatives and neighbours, slung between two bicycles. In a very special way, the Church's medical work 'adorned the Gospel'.

One of our Foreign Mission secretaries had remarked to me, while on a visit to our field, that 'up-country' missionaries were often out of touch with what was happening not only in the wider world but also in the affairs of the Protectorate. Having been brought up as a 'political animal', I came to realise during our years in the northern province that it was very easy to lose touch with the world beyond ourselves. There were no daily newspapers and radios were often difficult to listen to because of bad reception and crackling interference. And if their cells died, it was sometimes difficult to obtain new cells unless you ordered them from somewhere on the line of rail. In the mounting crisis in central Africa, it was worrying to be so out of touch. Yet we sensed that people round about us were avid for news of the doings of Welensky and of Nkumbula and the ANC.

A Director of Information had recently introduced what was called 'the saucepan radio' into Northern Rhodesia at a price which peasant people might hope to meet by dint of hard saving. Between 1952 and 1954 I recorded an amazing increase in the number of those 'saucepans' as I visited village schools and congregations. Many times I would find people from neighbouring villages gathered together around someone's house, straining to catch the evening broadcast of news and commenting with feeling on what they heard. When the announcer quoted some action or some speech by Roy Welensky in particular, people would address their invisible arch-enemy vociferously. "Ah you, Welensky. Stupid. You think you can walk on we Africans. Wait and see. Go away to Rhodesia or somewhere. You are no good", and so forth. When I had occasion to spend a night at a village school, I would sometimes hear the voices of men with beer in them expressing their anger in stronger terms. As the rainy season carried us from 1952 to 1953, the determination of the Federationists deepened our foreboding and made us feel increasingly helpless. Moreover, though our relations with the Lubwa community had become freer and little remained of the early animosity, I was unaware of the activities of Kenneth Kaunda and his Congress colleagues, who seemed to exclude Lubwa from their programme of action.

Cycling 150 miles from Lubwa to Kasama and back

I was to meet Kenneth Kaunda soon, however, in an unexpected way. I had business to do in Kasama in April 1953 which included a visit to Noah Chulu, a probationer minister and former Lubwa teacher over whom the Presbytery had asked me to have supervision. Our itineration grant was very small and had to be debited at the rate of 1/3d for every mile we travelled by motor vehicle. I decided therefore to cycle to Kasama. This reduced the mileage from 140 miles via the Chambeshi pontoon to 76 miles via a canoe crossing at Mulema. I took with me a tall pupil from Mwenzo whose height and build suggested to me that we could make a good pace together; and certainly our first lap, to the river, went well. At Mwika, opposite Mulema, we had some difficulty in finding anyone prepared to ferry two men with bicycles by canoe. At last we persuaded one fellow to help us, but his canoe was small, the river was deep and flowing fast and he did not want to make two crossings. We therefore had to squeeze in as best we could and try to steady the bikes as the slim craft swayed to the swift stroke of a single oar, plunging first to one side, then to the other. When the oarsman had to swing the canoe against the current, water splashed briskly over the low sides, a small boy bailing it out as fast as he could with an old baked beans tin. "*E pela, mukwai, twafika*", said the boatman suddenly as we entered a thickening patch of reeds twenty yards or so from the land. "That's it. We've arrived". "Oh but please, we have to reach the bank", I replied. "We can't", he said. "The boat will be stuck in the reeds". So out we stepped to find the bed of the river cluttered with fallen tree branches. The swirling water reached to our waists. It was with the greatest difficulty that we managed to reach the bank, holding our bicycles above our heads as we stumbled forward, the matted reeds tripping us and all but making us fall. As we took farewell of the boatman and his boy, the lad said something quite audible about *ing'wena* - crocodiles!

There is a long plain on the west side of the Chambeshi beyond Mulema. I wanted to move fast over it, knowing that we would then have to push up through the hills towards Kasama and that our plan to do it in one day had to succeed. I had been whirling along for some miles when I heard a faint cry behind me over the rattle of my bike on the earth track. It could have been a bird, I thought, but I heard it again, louder than at first, and stopped to look back. It was then that I realised that my companion was not to be seen. I had no choice but to wait for him. At last Sichizya appeared and I saw that he was pushing his bike, stumbling and stricken-looking. "I've been calling for a long time", he said, not far from sobbing. "I'm dying of hunger". Then he admitted that he had not eaten before we started early in the day. We had now covered over forty miles. "I have some little things here", I said, for Myra had given me a box of scones to keep us going, since I planned to call in at Malole mission of the Franciscans where we would almost certainly be given a meal. My companion took the tin with both hands, and I sped off to find the nearest village. When I reached it, hidden in the long grass, there were only two women and some small children present. It was one of the most delapidated villages I had seen. I told the women about my hungry friend and asked if they could perhaps give him a meal of *ubwali* - boiled maize flour - and such *umunani* as they could spare to give it relish. "We have nothing". they said. "I will leave money for meal flour", I answered, but there was no light in their eyes. "If I call my friend, you will give him a little something, won't you?" I pled, and went back to call the lad. When we returned together, the women pushed a used and unwashed plate in front of him, containing a few boiled leaves cold from yesterday, and a blob of *ubwali* that the children had left, crusted and sour-looking. Sichizya swallowed with visible revulsion, nibbled a tiny portion and said he had had enough. Even on an empty stomach, their offering had nothing to attract him. We rose then, thanked them and left some money, and off we went. "Ba NaMwila's scones were good", said Sichizya as we rode side by side. He had eaten them all.

The fruitless visit to that dejected village had wasted a lot of time. We had not been cycling again for long when I myself became aware of hunger pangs, slow and dull at first but steadily increasing. We were now away from the level ground and climbing and, though I was still setting the pace, I knew that the tight straining of my thighs had to do with the hollow inside.

It was the time of the last rains, called in Bemba by two poetical names: *ikandang'ombe*, because the footprints of oxen remain and harden when there is no more rain to soften and obliterate them; and *inkuntansoke*, for it is the time when the water drains out of the tall grasses and they become limp and fall against each other in tangled clumps. The track was narrow with numerous rocky patches and with loose gravel elsewhere; and the drooping grasses on either side lashed us as we pushed our way upwards. I was determined to keep on pedalling and so, to maximise the thrust of my legs, I rose from the saddle. This shifted the centre of gravity forward and my back wheel bounced and clattered in consequence. I believe I was humming a tune to the slow rhythm of my legs when suddenly a louder noise broke in upon me and I realised that another cyclist was hammering down the hill towards us as the track bent to the right. Neither he nor I could see each other until we were face to face, and in order to avoid a head-on collision I had to throw my bike into the grasses on the verge.

He was even more surprised than I was, for he had been crashing along, never dreaming to find anyone else on that lonely stretch. It was none other than the ANC's provincial secretary as he now was, Kenneth Kaunda, with a guitar strung over his shoulders and a bulky load on his carrier, racing home at the end of an extensive tour of the northern and Luapula region where he had been recruiting hundreds of new members for the Congress. We had time for no more than a somewhat breathless greeting and exchange of information about the purpose of our journeys. For he had many miles to go and for us the long, hard, twisting hill track to Kasama lay ahead.

Myra's scones, it seemed, were sustaining Sichizya. For myself, as we pressed on through the hills, hunger was now more acute than I had ever known. My throat was parched, my eyes were stinging and I knew that if we were to stop, I would have the greatest difficulty in starting again. We had to keep moving. But my legs felt like limp sacks of dough, horribly heavy but scarcely able to maintain their thrust upon the pedals. Beyond reason, I could easily have sobbed aloud. Conversation was impossible; the track was too narrow and its surface made us swing from side to side to avoid the roughest patches. Then at last we reached the level, or at least a less steep stretch with a sandier surface. We could still reach Kasama before sundown if only we could keep moving. There had been no time to stop at Malole. A mile or so on the level gave me a little respite but ahead I saw that the path crossed a field of low mounds on which cassava was planted. Pushing my bike up and over those mounds was all but too much for me, grimmer than mountaineering, and my misery was aggravated by the watering of my eyes. To wipe them meant leaving one limp and aching arm to grip and turn the handlebars alone.

Somehow, we reached the provincial capital at last, with 76 miles between us and the beds from which we had gaily sprung in the early morning. Sichizya left me to seek the home of a relative and I then found the house of my host, that Welsh friend in the provincial administration who had told me in confidence about the secret file on me in the PC's safe. Glyn and his wife were out when I arrived. Their servant showed me my room and gave me a cup of tea. I cannot recall more than that. Two or three hours later, I was gently wakened from a very deep sleep and my body felt light and strong. Memories of that day's journey have remained ever since, vivid and pleasurable. Strangely, however, I find it difficult to recall anything of the journey back to Lubwa, except Catherine's question as she and Jamie rushed to welcome me: "Did you brought bacon?" - and I hadn't.

Lead up to the Imposition of Federation

In my biography of President Kaunda I described the events of mid-1953 in the context of 'the continental crisis'. June was the month of the coronation of Queen Elizabeth who had acceded to the throne on her father's death in February 1952. The celebration coincided with intensive bombing by the Royal Air Force against the Mau Mau in Kenya. The announcement of a knighthood for Roy Welensky strengthened the African conviction that Britain was supporting him in spite of massive black opposition. Yet I heard people around Lubwa say, *"Namfumu e Namfumu: te Welensky iyo"* - "The Queen is the Queen: she's not Welensky". This was a sensitive distinction, beyond what I dared to expect, for by that time even our best DCs were under heavy pressure to push Federation down the people's throats, so to speak. Our good man at Chinsali told me how sadly he was aware of a widening gulf between himself and the people of the district. "Kaunda often used to drop into the office for a chat or an argument", he told me. "He doesn't do so any more". The NRG (Northern Rhodesia Government) was meanwhile distributing little metal coronation badges to be worn by school children at celebrations to be held at all *boma*s as well as in all the towns on the line of rail. As Manager of Schools, I received about 5000 of those badges and the Schools Management Committee, which we had created in 1952 but which the Provincial Education Officer refused to recognise, agreed to send supplies of them to all our district schools. Pupils at Lubwa wore them for some days before the official ceremony and there was a lot of light-hearted laughter about them.

June 2nd was the big day and when we reached Chinsali *boma*, I saw that hundreds of the children from our remotest schools were already assembled. It was a day when, as often in June, a chill wind combined with glaring sunshine to give people headaches. As the hours went by and there was still no sign of Chief Nkula, the tedium became oppressive and so I was glad when some of the teachers started marching the children round and round, singing through the repertoire of songs which I heard constantly at those lively school concerts which I have described above. I noticed, and others remarked on this also, that the schools of the three Roman Catholic missions in the district were represented by very few children, though there was a strong turn-out of European priests in long white tunics, flanking their Dutch bishop. Their expatriate agents in the district far outnumbered the Lubwa missionary team.

Still we waited and the youngsters continued their leisurely circling of the area, singing as they went: *Umupila wa mapepala* - the Paper Football; *Kalulu alikwebele* - Rabbit told you; *Uyu mwana chinshi alelila?* - This child, why's he crying?; *Tulumbe bateecha besu* - Let us praise our teachers; and another that I had heard on several occasions - *Cha bulanda, cha bulanda! Basungu bapoke chalo chesu* - It's sad, it's sad! The white people have taken our country.

People were now weary and the clapping for the songs of the children was desultory. And so it went on until at last the Chief, bleary-eyed as he often was, came hobbling along with the DC. The ceremony was brief, the Commissioner reading a short statement: a tree was planted and 'God save the Queen' was sung by a few voices. The crowd dispersed quickly with little sound. Some of the children from schools managed by myself had a return journey of about 100 miles to make on foot.

Soon afterwards - though we did not hear this for some time - a member of Welensky's party raised a question in the Legislative Council about outrageous behaviour at Chinsali and, in the House of Lords in London, Lord Noel-Buxton said that school children had trampled on their coronation badges and "sung a near-seditious song as they marched past the DC". Around Lubwa, nothing significant happened, though at Chinsali the coronation tree was uprooted one night. Two months later the new Queen signed the order-in-council for the establishment of the Federation of Rhodesia and Nyasaland; and three weeks after that Kenneth Kaunda was elected Secretary General of the African National Congress by a very large majority.

Chapter 12
THE LENSHINA MOVEMENT

I have written elsewhere about Paul Mushindo who was in many ways a lonely figure in the local church. Though he never raised his voice, he was given to uttering heavy and sometimes unjustifiable rebukes to the local teachers, elders and evangelists. At the close of one session of an elders' Refresher Course, I came upon a group of men who were obviously rattled by something he had said. "*Ulya shikulu*", said one of them, "*chipasho cha Ba Ngungu*" - "That old fellow's just a replica of Ngungu" - Ngungu, meaning the aloof one, being the nickname of the old Scots missionary with whom Mushindo had worked for years on Bible translation. There had been a kind of love-hate relationship between Mushindo and the master who forbade him to imitate Europeans by wearing shoes. Yet Mushindo had, in no small measure, that solemnity which featured so strongly in the old missionary.

At an Elders' Session one day, with Mushindo in the chair, we came to the item of 'Any Other Business'. "Yes", said a usually silent and ineffective elder, "there is something. It would be good, I think, to instruct those who preach the word to do so with dignity". "Yes, dignity is good", Mushindo replied, "but tell us of what you are thinking". "That preachers should stand still in the pulpit as we were taught from the beginning: that they should place their hands upon the book-board; and that they should not make gestures." It was not, of course, a matter for voting, but the Moderator added his solemn support. I had been very tired that day and it was oppressively hot but that last item had caught my attention. As we left, Abel Nkamba called me and said: "What did you think of that just now?" I had not a ready comment, but he went on: "You know of whom they were speaking?" "No, who was it?" "Yourself", said Nkamba with a chuckle, and it flashed on me that he was right. "And certainly it was not Kangwa's own idea. He had been told to raise the matter". "By whom?" I asked. "By the minister, of course", he replied.

I could not help laughing. It was true that I used gestures as I spoke. I have done so all my life. You could gag me by tying my hands behind my back. But it is as much an African habit as it is French! Many speakers and preachers in Zambia and Malawi made wonderful use of their hands, often moving up and down in keeping with the words they were speaking. The old Scots pioneer, dour and solemn as he was, had frowned on that African gift and, with the monarchical episcopacy that so readily and perhaps understandably marked the missionary pioneers, he had forbidden those he trained to use gestures. Gestureless utterance had, like dark clothes and measured tread in Scotland, thus become a hallmark of ecclesiastical behaviour. It contrasted sharply with the glorious, spontaneous, infectious joy in worship that I had found in the Mwenzo district and on the Copperbelt. I could not help feeling that Alice Lenshina, and many other people, hungered for something that they could readily make their own, as they could not with that replica of nineteenth century Scottish patterns in which Ngungu had moulded Lubwa when he had superseded David Kaunda as exemplar and mentor in 1913.

As we longed for the first rains in October 1953, anger throughout the country was simmering at the imposition of Federation. It was as though the colonial government, with Britain's full knowledge, was closing the valve on the pressure cooker of popular anger, to stop its irritating hiss, and then announcing that all was peaceful. Locally the constant flow of people to Kasomo was inevitably affecting the rhythm of daily life for us at Lubwa. I visited Lenshina's village one Sunday and met a great gathering there: hundreds where a very few weeks earlier I might have found half a dozen. Then an unfortunate action by the local DC put the fat in the fire. He was a fine fellow and competent in the Bemba language. But any crowd of Africans were to be kept under strict surveillance in a situation in which NRG was clearly aware of 'security risks' while pretending that only a few self-seeking black agitators, and a small number of misguided missionaries, were opposed to the 'closer association' of the three territories. So, hearing of the milling crowds at Kasomo, the DC sent messengers to fetch Alice Lenshina to his office.

That *Boma* meeting, as described to me, was a most unfortunate one. A tall messenger in blue tunic with brief shorts over big muscular legs, wearing his broad-brimmed official hat and strong leather boots, led Alice Lenshina into the Commissioner's office and ordered her to squat on the mat before the huge green-topped desk. The DC would be seated as she entered and probably remained seated as she obeyed the *kapasu*'s command. His bi-focal lenses added, as they can do to any of us, to the severity of his expression. Though he could have spoken in Bemba he addressed her through the messenger as interpreter, something like this: "So you've seen Jesus Christ, eh?" "Yes, Bwana". "Well then, what was he like?... Was he tall?... Did he have a beard?" After a pause, Lenshina answered, so she told me later: "But the missionary at Lubwa didn't ask these questions". "I'm asking you", he retorted. "You're at the *Boma* now. Do you understand?" "Yes, Bwana". But she said no more. "All right then", said the DC. "Now, listen to me. I hear there have been many people at your village. I know your village. It has very few people. So I don't want to hear of big crowds there. Bwana Governor will not be pleased if you allow such crowds to gather again. There are trouble-makers in the country just now and they will be punished if they trouble this district. So no more crowds, and no trouble-makers, do you understand, eh?" And so she was ordered by the messenger to rise and leave the office. Her husband and other disaffected ex-employees of Lubwa mission heard her account of that interview with anger. But no one could stop the crowds seeking a glimpse of 'the prophetess' and many church members heard with pleasure that she was calling upon *baloshi* to bring in their instruments of sorcery so that they could be publicly burned. "She is helping to cleanse our country", said one keen young Christian teacher to me. "She is bringing happiness".

Illness and Ill-doings

The official start of the Federation was 1 August 1953, but the Federal Government was not formed until September and, in fact, it was not until October that the grim reality came home to the black people of the Territory that Welensky and Sir Godfrey Huggins were now their rulers. At the end of that month, our third child, Rosemary Anne, was born and at that very time I fell ill with a severe attack of infective hepatitis. Dr Wilson at once put me to bed and said that I must stay horizontal until all the yellowness had left my body. The jaundice made me weak, and though I had loads of office work to do, I had no strength for it. The supervision of our large and complex book-keeping was in the hands of the mission clerk but a colleague said he would 'keep an eye on things'. Most days brought a few visitors and one who came on a number of occasions was Mama Lenshina who called her own new baby Catherine after - so she said - our firstborn. Myra's hands were full these days with three little ones but I was unable to take my share of family duties. The weather was at its hottest and most stifling, and Myra was very weary at the end of the day. In addition to the tedium of inaction, I had to learn how to swallow a long glass of Epsom salts every day. But the hepatitis would not be hurried.

When Christmas came, I was still weak and lethargic. But bit by bit, I began to tackle some of the heaped up arrears of book-keeping and correspondence. Myra's mother came up from Lusaka to visit us and the mango trees were once again laden with their glorious golden fruit. Catherine and Jamie revelled in a feast of mangoes every day for breakfast and we had many more trees around us now that, at long last, we had been able to move to the house at ground level where the Principal had lived for years. He retired at the end of the year and we were all happy to leave the apartheid of the hill, even though our new house was much less well built. It had been built, so they told us, as a 'dare' by the old missionary from Chitambo with whom I made that 1800 mile journey in 1947. He had claimed that Dr Brown's figure was far too high and his challenge had been accepted. Our shoddy new home was the result. White ants found it a paradise. But it gave Catherine and Jamie the chance of playing with children from the teacher's houses nearby and Catherine developed a true Bemba accent. Rosemary was baptised by Kenneth Mackenzie.

I had been back at work little more than a few days when a plain-clothes black constable called to tell me that there was reason to believe that our clerk was engaged in some shady financial dealings with the store *kapitao* in a nearby village. The assistant manager of the store who, like the Scandinavian manager, lived in Kasama, was coming soon to check that village store's stocks and cash, so would I please arrange to check our cash at the same time? The assistant manager would be asked to call at my house as he passed on his way to his stocktaking. It was shocking news. Immediately I remembered that on a recent occasion when I had checked our cash, the clerk had said he had some entries to do first and asked for an hour or so to get the cash-book ready for me. As sharply I realised that word, passed to me apparently casually, by another employee that the new office-boy was the clerk's nephew was highly significant. But I had to contain those disturbing thoughts and await the man from Kasama. And once again, there was the seemingly inescapable offence in the situation that these two local men, clerk and *kapitao*, were about to be subjected to scrutiny by us two foreigners.

The baleful day came the next week. The young manager paid what would pass for a courtesy call at our house and then drove through Lubwa to the village store. As he did so, I walked to our office and, after the usual kind greetings, I asked for the key of the safe. "But, please, I have so many entries to put into the cash-book", said Chela. "That's all right. You can be writing them up while I'm counting. There should be quite a lot in the safe at this time of the month. So if you give me the key I'll start", and I held out my hand. "No", said Chela, but his expression was one of dread rather than of defiance. "Why not?" I asked. "No, please", he repeated, "I am too busy". "Give me the key now", I said and he could refuse no longer. Here, I knew, was one of those crises in which it would be foolish to act alone. If there was going to be a revelation of misuse of funds, it must not be him against me. He was what my father would have called 'a mousey wee man', but, in the short time I had had responsibility for the now integrated accounts, he had been cooperative. Indeed he had expressed pleasure when I relieved him of the burdensome tasks of the bank reconciliation, the journalising of transfers from one account to another, and the monthly trial balance. But of course we had had very little contact since I took ill and the replacement of the former office boy by this new lad had been done by him without consultation.

With the key in my hand, I left the office and went to ask Yonam Mpuku, the Training School's new Principal, to help me with the checking of the safe. He came at once and we did the whole job together. It did not take long for there was very little in the safe. Then I went to see Chela's progress on the cash-book but he had done nothing. I found him staring blankly ahead, looking crushed. All I could do was to take the pile of loose chits and the cash book and ask him to help me to complete the entries. This meant that he saw me extract the total of what should have been in the safe. There was a shortfall of over £500. The Principal and I then showed him the cash total and I asked him for his comment. But he simply shook his head. "The manager from Kasama is at the store", I told him but clearly he knew already. "I mention this", I went on, "because the police say that you and Mulundika have been doing something together with cash. Is that true?" "I can say nothing", was all he said.

There followed a horrid period. The police worked quickly and within a few days a young English officer appeared in a landrover. Before he called on me however, he moved stealthily about the community and spoke most insultingly to Principal Mpuku and other senior colleagues. "Where's the money?" he demanded. "I know you. You're all in this. You Africans are all liars." When I heard this, I prepared to tackle him severely. His response was of that kind that reveals the gross misunderstanding in many people's minds about the church. "You're a minister", he said with the hint of a sneer. "You think everyone's good. I'm a policeman and I know better". "I wouldn't be a minister", I answered him, "if everyone was good. But if you condemn people in the way in which you have spoken to my colleagues, then you should quit the police. For it's your job to treat people as innocent unless their guilt is proved". It was not thereafter an easy thing to have to accompany him to a number of remote village schools for whose teachers' salaries the signatures of receipt had been forged. This discovery showed that poor Chela must have been desperate in those last weeks before that terrible day of reckoning.

Our baby girl had a slight chill at that time. Mrs Cross was due to return to Lusaka and I was to drive her there and do some business for the mission on the line of rail. On the morning of our departure, I said to Myra that the chill seemed to be clearing. Catherine and Jamie were entertaining Rosemary by 'monkeying' as we took our farewells. The next day, in my mother-in-law's office in Lusaka, I was handed a telegram. As I was expecting word about some item of the business I had to transact, I opened the envelope without a thought. But instead it told me that our baby had died. In the next few hours, with the generous loan of a car from a Scots garage proprietor, and a driver to share the wheel with me, I set off to drive non-stop to Lubwa, arriving some time in the early hours of the Saturday. The little burial service had had to take place on the Friday, with a tiny grave in the little cemetery, not far from the church building, where they had buried David Kaunda in 1932.

The result of a post mortem examination done by the Medical Officer in Kasama revealed that Rosemary had died of viral pneumonia. On the Friday, Myra said, there had been a knock at the door and a voice calling softly, "*Odi*". It was that teacher who had made his personal protest against the threat of further repression under the Federation by refusing to exchange greetings with any *musungu*. "I have heard that your baby has died", he said. "I am very sad for you". Then, after a few more shy words, he said: "May we pray?" and knelt down in our sitting room. His prayer was brief, simply asking that we be given strength in our sudden sorrow. From that day, he resumed human relations with us and the other missionaries.

Very soon after my dash back to Lubwa came the trial of our clerk. The court building consisted of six or eight brick pillars supporting a roof, with a small platform for the magistrate's table. It was full to capacity and scores of spectators sat on the ground outside. The original 19 charges against Chela had been reduced to six. There was no way in which I could dodge the distasteful role of chief witness for the prosecution. Right away, I realised that our clerk was pretending to be unable to answer in English, which was unfortunately necessary because the District Officer who sat as magistrate knew little or no Bemba. I realised too that the interpreter was mistranslating certain key parts of the evidence in the interests of the accused. At one point, I had to ask the magistrate to call for an accurate re-rendering of a badly distorted statement. With the dreaded Federation now in its eighth month, an open court conducted by a white magistrate with another *musungu* as chief prosecution witness could have provoked a hostile reaction from the crowd. Yet I had a definite sense of support when I challenged the interpreter's distortions and even when, at last, the sentence of six years imprisonment was pronounced.

Chela's defalcations totalled around £800 in cash plus about £400 worth of food stocks, filched from the mission granary. Yet six years for conviction on five of the six charges was not a light sentence, especially in view of a recent outrage which had earned its perpetrators a mere eighteen months. Two young white men who had been involved in some kind of fiddle on the Copperbelt, had decided to take flight before it was discovered. Having probably lived carelessly and spent wildly, they had little cash as they drove across the Zaire pedicle into the northern province. By the time they reached the Chambeshi pontoon crossing at Mbesuma, their funds were presumably very low. So, well after darkness had fallen, they knocked at the door of the brick store belonging to the African Lakes Corporation.

Little stores of that kind were in the charge of a *kapitao* who was given a room or two in the building as his quarters. Most of those *kapitao*s were married and so their families slept on the premises with them. That night, Nsofu the store-keeper heard the knock after he had gone to bed. His little shop was of course, not electrified; a candle had to be lit before he could shuffle to the door. "Hello", said a voice from outside and Nsofu would know it was not an African voice. "Open the door. We want to see you". What could this be? A District Officer, perhaps, or even Bwana Kapaso, the European police officer. But why so late? "Bwana, please, the shop is shut and I am asleep with my family." "We want to speak to you now, Open up", said the voice and so, fumbling with the key of the padlock that kept the shop shut from inside by hasp and staple, Nsofu opened the door enough to see the two white men outside. It was all over in a moment, as they thrust their way in, demanded all the cash from the till, shot Nsofu when he refused and removed the metal cash box as he lay writhing on the floor. I believe they stole £59.

Our Dr Todd, skilled surgeon as he was, was unable to remove the shot embedded in the *kapitao*'s spine. Nsofu lived but suffered permanently from that gunshot. The young men were apprehended soon after they had attempted another such raid this time by daylight, at Nkonde's 'First and Last African Hotel' at Isoka Boma at the moment when I happened to be leaving the hotel. Their guilt was easily proved in court. They were then deprived of their freedom for a year and a half. British justice seemed scarcely colour blind when Chela's sentence was laid alongside theirs, and this did not go unnoticed in the norther province. The colonial tradition of legal inequity thus died hard. In the heyday of Rhodes's Company's rule, a white man, Davis, and a black man, Mwaluka, were both convicted in the town of Livingstone, for common assault and each fined £2. But Davis's earnings were probably over 40 times as much as Mwaluka's.

Chela's case involved me in a brief encounter with the Scandanavian general manager of that chain of stores, of which the little shop beyond Lubwa was one. I told him that many people believed that his *kapitao* was as guilty as Chela and that indeed he had 'softened' Chela with beer in order to persuade him to 'lend'

cash from the Lubwa safe to put his own till in order when
stocktaking was imminent, on the assurance that it would be paid
back very soon. No doubt that kind of transaction had taken place
on a number of occasions in the period when there was no check
on the Lubwa cash-book and safe. The general manager dismissed
my remarks truculently. "All that matters to me is that my boy's
cash tallies with his records of sales", he said. When, however, the
little store went up in flames as word came across the Chambeshi
that another stocktaking was planned, it was clear that Mulundika
was desperate, knowing that the man he had manipulated no longer
held the key to our safe.

1954 was overshadowed for us by our baby's death. Phineas
Mbao, our building *kapitao* at Lubwa, carved her name and the
dates of her birth and death on a flat piece of the rock from the hill
and it is there to this day, surrounded by Christ-thorn. Myra's
physical strength was slow to return. I myself suffered a strange
experience when the removal of a badly rotted tooth left a small
chip of the root in my jaw. That chip created a septic situation and
raised a large swelling on my cheek, in size and colour like a turnip.
One day, in the office, I was aware of a strange itching not on but
under the skin of my face which became sharp and painful until
suddenly the chip of root punctured my cheek from inside and
squeezed itself out. But the turnip remained and so I had to go
south to have it lanced.

Bitter Fruits of White Superiority

During that first year of the Federation, there was an uneasy
and sullen atmosphere in rural areas like Chinsali. The towns were
scenes of overt protests against that colour bar which black people
believed was to be further entrenched by the promoters of
Federation despite their talk of multiracialism. Under Kenneth
Kaunda's more dynamic approach to the ANC's programme,
boycotts were organised against certain butchers' shops which were
notorious for their humiliating treatment of black customers. Then
Dr Hastings Banda was forbidden to enter Northern Rhodesia
where he had planned to open a non-racial medical practice in
Lusaka. The government of Southern Rhodesia declared Kaunda
and the ANC President, Harry Nkumbula 'prohibited immigrants';
their PI orders describing them as 'alien natives', an amazing
contradiction in terms. Meanwhile Kaunda's editorship of the

Congress Circular helped to show the people that their struggle was part of the universal conflict between exploitation and justice and that it was vital now to change the situation in the Protectorate by 'non-violent positive action'.

I often trembled for the future of Christianity in Africa, knowing that it was becoming increasingly common for 'white supremacists' to proclaim themselves champions of Christian civilisation against 'world communism' and to brand all their opponents as puppets of the Kremlin. The foreboding was not lessened by news from China that was passed to me quietly one day, in my office, by the gentle lady who had recently taken charge of Galilee, our girls' boarding school. She had been with the Church in Manchuria for years until the great revolution in China forced the withdrawal of all foreign missionaries. That day, she had come to see me about the discovery of weevils in many of the bags of beans in the boarding foodstore. Something would have to be done quickly to find fresh food-stuffs to replace these bags. As she was about to go, she said, "Oh, perhaps I should tell you. I've had a letter from China, a very sad one. I can't get it out of my head". "Tell me about it", I replied.

The letter had been smuggled out via Hong Kong. It was from one of her Chinese colleagues. It told, without comment, how at a meeting of the local presbytery attended by about 30 elders and 30 ministers, the proceedings had been roughly interrupted by the arrival of soldiers. As the captain brought in his armed men, he ordered the ministers to line up against the wall. As the so-called secular world often does, he apparently ignored what are called 'ordinary members' and treated the ministers as though they alone were the church. "I have come to tell you that Christianity and all worship of foreign gods is now abolished in this province. To be a Christian is now a criminal offence. I am therefore giving you ten minutes in which to declare that you reject and curse Christ and to undertake to return immediately to your places and to disband the churches there. When you have cursed Christ, I will give you free bus or railway passes to enable you to return home quickly so that the churches in your areas can be disbanded at once". As he finished, he checked the time on his watch. Silence fell, disturbed only by the fidgetting of some of the soldiers. "Five minutes to go - four - three minutes left". Then two ministers stepped forward and bowed to the captain. "You curse Christ?" "Yes". "Then stand over there".

Who could know what had been going on in the hearts of those two: "My boy's just finishing high school"; "How could my wife manage alone with five children and my sick old parents to care for?"; "It'll only be with my lips I'll say the curse, never in my heart, never where Christ is". Who could know? "Thirty seconds - fifteen - five. Ready - fire", and the twenty-eight other ministers slumped dead on the floor, some crying in pain, some calling on Jesus, like Stephen the first of the martyrs whose stoning was watched with approval by the man who was to become the greatest of all missionaries.

"The behaviour of some white people in China had caused deep and widespread resentment over a long period", said my gentle colleague. "The soldiers couldn't have done that without the belief that many people would approve of action against those ministers who seemed to be friendly with members of the race of white exploiters". There was surely a dangerous parallel there with the situation of Christianity especially in southern Africa where race relations were indeed worse. My lady colleague had told me earlier that the 'white seats' in the Lubwa church had shocked her. "We'd never have had anything like that in China", she said. "There were no race barriers at all in our Christian fellowship." So my heart had to echo the old spiritual that had come from those great grand-children of Africa whose fathers had been dragged in fetid cargo ships to the plantations of America: "Sometimes it causes me to tremble, tremble, tremble - Were you there when they crucified my Lord?"

Incident with a Snake

There was a young man from a village near Lubwa, Edwin Palama, who had gone to Senga Hill for training as an agricultural teacher. Senga offered special courses for primary school teachers to enable them to develop the cultivation of maize and other crops at their schools both to provide food for their pupils and to let the children learn the vital work of agriculture along with their other lessons. I had been north-west again and called in at Senga for a night's rest. The head of the Training School told me that Edwin had been repeatedly sick during the term and badly needed a rest at home. Would I take him with me? I was glad of the young man's company as I had been travelling alone. But I was shocked to see how 'peely-wally' he looked, to use an old Scots phrase. However, we set off in the early part of the day, hoping to reach Lubwa in the evening.

When we were still over 50 miles north of Kasama, I noticed something on the road that looked at first like a bamboo cane. As we approached it, however, Palama and I realised that it was a snake, a very long dusty green one. The traffic was very light and the reptile may have been enjoying a stretch in the sun on the sandy road, away from the prickly grasses in the wooded country on either side. I had very little time for a decision and so I drove over it. But my rear mirror showed me that it was writhing and lashing about. I certainly had not killed it. "We can't leave it like that", said Edwin. "It might attack someone else since it is now angry". So I stopped the vanette, jumped out and went to look for something with which to put it out of pain. There were fallen logs in plenty, but none the size we wanted; and I had forgotten to carry an axe. "Let us use stones", my sick companion suggested. He, however, had no strength himself. Marksmanship has never been an accomplishment of mine. But I had to do something. So, selecting a large sharp stone, I went as near as seemed safe and hurled it at my wretched victim. Palama was some yards behind me at that moment, but, as the stone struck the creature's neck, he cried out. I swung round and saw, with horror, that he was pressing his hand to his right eye, obviously in sharp pain. "Something came from the snake", he said. "It hit my eye. I can't see",

Leaving the snake still writhing, I rushed to the vanette to get our thermos flask, which was full of hot tea. We had nothing else to use for bathing Edwin's eye, but I had little hope of the efficacy of a tea bath. "Let's go quickly to Kasama", I said and we leapt in and drove off. "How's your eye now?" I asked as we hammered along. "I can't see. It's like blackness". Could it be the snake's poison, I wondered; and there were still enough miles between us and Kasama to let my dread mature; the thought that my foolish action had blinded the young man's right eye for life; that I whose marksmanship was useless could have burst the scaly reptile's sac of venom with such force that a jet of poison should have traversed that gap of yards with such deadly effect. We were about three miles from Kasama hospital when Palama said: "I think I am seeing again, only a little bit". At the hospital, we found a helpful Sister who, since there was no doctor there, had to tackle all emergencies over a great stretch of the northern province. She bathed his eye

and told him to hold a pad over it for a while. "I can now see well",
he said at last. "It must have been a drop of the snake's blood", the
Sister said as we thanked her. I had a singing heart of gratitude for
miles afterwards.

People were meanwhile still flocking to Kasomo. Alice
Lenshina seemed fully recovered in health and was putting on
weight. She was also displaying unmistakable authority over her
hearers and her entourage, which now included a number of
employees of Lubwa Mission. I went one Sunday to meet with
them and was warmly welcomed. After a festival of singing and
prayer, I stayed to chat with the people, Lenshina acting as chairman.
At one point, a rough fellow stood up and, pointing a finger at me,
across the heads of other listeners, he said that it was very bad that
the Mission had not provided transport to carry Mama Lenshina
and her choir when they had recently travelled about twenty miles
to visit Chief Nkula. With a vanette costing 1/3d a mile, we were
in no position to offer such assistance. But before I had started my
response, the lady herself rounded on the man and ordered him to
sit down and not to speak so foolishly again. "People bring pennies
when they come here and we have enough to hire a lorry if we
want. We do not expect our friends to carry us". But, of course,
here was a hint of potential conflict between the local Churches
and what was irresistibly becoming a mass movement. For, if the
services at Kasomo were, as we would have wanted, under the
auspices of the CCAR, then offerings received at them should have
been handed to the treasurer of the District Church Council.
Throughout 1954, however, relations were seemingly cordial.

Chapter 13
SECOND
FURLOUGH

Our next overseas leave was to have started in January 1955, and so I was attempting, in the latter months of 1954, to cover as much work in the district and at Lubwa as possible, with the demands of the Bible translation task still upon me. But it was now clear that Myra's recovery was too slow and so, after a consultation between Dr Wilson and Dr Todd, it was agreed to ask our Edinburgh committee to authorise an earlier furlough and travel by air rather than by sea.

John Ngwele, whose first marriage had been childless, had been very upset when his wife's family called her back to her home on the banks of the Zambezi. He had however decided to begin again and his marriage to a Bemba woman from near Lubwa was going well, with the promise of a child. Since his first in-laws had blamed him for his wife's barrenness, he was now glowing with delight. Canadian missionaries who had come to Lubwa for language study were very glad when he agreed to work for them when we left. Our departure was hurriedly arranged, its first leg being a journey by lorry to Kasama, via the Chambeshi pontoon. Caleb Simpamba escorted us and waved us off as a small plane carried us south to Ndola where we would join a larger plane for a three-day flight to London.

The first day's flight took us only as far as Nairobi where the airline had reserved overnight accommodation for us in the Norfolk Hotel. The Mau Mau 'emergency' was still on. Official British statements described Mau Mau as a savage uprising. I was anxious to hear how our Scots fellow missionaries in Kenya saw the tragic conflict. Fortunately, I was able to contact one of them who lived in the capital city. The official news of the response of the 'security forces' to the outbreak of Mau Mau and especially of the bombing raids of the RAF on forest 'hide-outs' had for long been very disturbing. But what the missionary in Nairobi had to tell was far worse. For some time, he said, word had been reaching him through

missionaries of various denominations about atrocities committed
upon village folk by soldiers. At first he had dismissed these as the
exaggerations that one might look for in a situation of confused
turmoil. But the weight of attested evidence became too great to be
ignored. Indeed, he came to the conclusion that, by virtue of his
residence in the capital, it was his duty to collate such evidence and
make it available to the government. As he tackled this unwanted
task, he found that testified statements alone made up a bulky
memorandum and moreover that the story they told of cold-blooded
killing, rape, the burning of villages and the terrorising of small
and wholly defenceless communities called for more than a
memorandum sent by letter to the colonial authorities. He resolved
therefore to submit his written document to the Chief Secretary
and on the same weekend to make reference to the scale of such
barbarities in a sermon to an English-speaking congregation. His
action was followed swiftly by a visit from a high-ranking official
from the Secretariat with a clear warning that the memorandum
might result in his deportation from Kenya as an undesirable person.
His response was that such an action would evoke an immediate
reaction from the Church of Scotland which had contacts with
both Westminster and Whitehall.

He was not in fact deported. But there were to be further grave
revelations of 'official' atrocities, some of which would be replicated
five years later in central Africa. The fact that such conduct by
forces, equipped with the latest weapons, had characterised the
reaction of European imperialism to outbrusts of pent up anger
from its 'native subjects' in the Americas, in Asia, in Australia and
all over Africa could in no way diminish the horror of it. For this
was not the romantic valour with which Kipling and Newbolt had
clothed the building of Britain's empire. This was the reality of
smash and grab, have and hold. It was ruthless bullying with no
regard for the weak, merciless to women and children and bound
to accelerate conflict on racial lines in many parts of the world.

From Nairobi we flew to Wadi Halfa in the Sudan for another
night on the ground; thence to Malta and, on the fourth day to
London at last. At the Wadi, we bought ivory candlesticks which,
as was his custom I'm sure, the vendor gave us 'at a very low price
- only for Madam'.

As we thought back over the three Lubwa years, we wondered,
as we'd often wondered before, about the purpose of that period.

It had been in some ways a time of shadows: the baleful shadow of Federation; the pervasive gloom of racial tensions even in the mission community; the blighting of Chela's life; the sudden ending of Rosemary's sweet sojourn of only three months' duration. Perhaps it can only be in retrospect that we can hope to see the sense of some of life's experiences. If so, no wonder that the 23rd Psalm is so readily appropriated by people of all nations, whether we sing it as 'The Lord's my shepherd' or '*Lesa e Kakumba wandi*'. For thus we affirm that, for all our unbelief and the shortsightedness of our souls, Someone is our pathfinder even through the valley of the shadows. And, more than that, by the reality of the ineffable sympathies of love among us, we are given, even in mourning, the oil of joy and the garment of praise.

We were in Scotland from December 1954 to October 1955. Much of our time was spent at North Berwick, the beautiful East Lothian seaside town facing the Bass Rock, where I had spent many happy holidays in childhood. My brother taught in the High School there and had a house behind the town. Catherine started her schooling in very pleasant surroundings and wee Jamie often accompanied us to the school to meet her as she came running out at the end of the day, full of chatter.

As in 1950, I was sent to a host of places to meet church folk and speak to them about 'foreign missions'. On one occasion, I was introduced as a missionary minister from Lubwa (with the 'u' pronounced as in 'tub', and not as it should be, as in 'put'), with a 'parish' stretching from Blantyre on one side to the Copperbelt on the other. Elsewhere, a minister with a resonant voice and generous gestures described me as having "served the Master in the great Northern Rhodesian Copperbelt, stretching from shore to shore" - with a sweep of his hand from left to right - "of the mighty African continent". I could almost hear an angel chorus singing 'Bravo' as I rose to speak and then hissing 'Tut-tut' as I endeavoured, without discourtesy to my host, to reduce my sphere of service to size. For, in a real sense missionaries, chatting together, could have much more accurately spoken of 'you in your small corner and I in mine'.

One incident in the course of that spell of deputation work I can never forget. The manse in which I was to spend the night was, typically, very big; but it housed just the minister and his wife. I must have been sent there to speak at a Friday evening meeting of the Woman's Guild, and arrived some time in the afternoon. The minister was relaxed, reclining in a deep armchair, with his legs stretched at full length. His wife went to the kitchen as soon as we had shaken hands. As she left the sittingroom a small dog of the Cairn terrier variety entered like a football kicked straight at me. Without ado, it went in to the attack. My host, with like alacrity had got in a step ahead, with a rambling description of his parish, combining without strain a salty cynicism and an unmistakeable love of his job. My role was that of fascinated listener, punctuating his eloquence with "Yes, I see", and "Hmm" and "Ah, that's interesting" and so forth. But Cornelius or whatever else the Cairn was called, was at me now in earnest and so, as I listened and responded, I had to hold the beast at bay by kicking at him. His master was wholly unconcerned: maybe this was his way of ensuring an alert audience! As what was being prepared in the kitchen was clearly more than bread and scones, I had a lengthy ordeal at the little monster's teeth.

At last the lady came to call us, noticed that I was losing the duel and called the dog off. "Come through in a minute", she told us. "I'll put him in the kitchen". As we went in to the dining room, my host put a question to me at last about my own work, and picked up his question again as soon as grace was said. The main dish, if I remember aright, was a tasty cheese pie and the table talk was brisk. In retrospect I was to realise that, yes, at one point, the lady had gone to top up the teapot or something like that. But we were back in the big armchairs before I suddenly perceived how Cornelius had avenged himself. For, as I sat down I saw that a round chunk, about 2 inches in diameter, had been excised from the front of my right trouser leg. For a beast of dynamic exuberance, he had perpetrated an act of astonishing stealth. I must have sat at table with my feet tucked under my chair so that my trouser legs hung forward. That had given the little wretch his inspiration when he had slipped in from the kitchen with the topped up teapot. I had realised from the start that he had a set of lethal teeth. But his skill at cloth clipping was his chief distinction. Once I had verified by touch what I at first rejected on the report of my eyes, I had to interrupt my affable host and show him what had happened. "Oh dear", he said, "that's bad".

What were we to do, was the urgent question. In a little over half an hour I was to address the Woman's Guild. "Slip into George's dressing gown", said my hostess, "and I'll patch them for you. It'll only take a minute". So I returned to my chair in the gown, she went off to her workroom. What she brought back was, at best a darned-on patch which naturally failed to restore the crease and, being of a slightly different shade of grey, the patch was almost as eye-catching as the hole itself would have been. With five minutes left, however, I could not but say thanks.

The Guild met in a hall with a low platform, the ladies seated round card tables draped in white cloths, with a vase of daffodils per table. Their eye-beams were on the exact level of my patch as I stood to speak. I could not fail to see a short sharp shock on one face and then another and so to the rest, and as quickly a look of contrived unconcern as if they had seen nothing. But, inevitably, one or two could not refrain from another furtive, furrowed glance, and the unease was almost tangible.

I began, therefore, by speaking of my boyhood fascination with the 'romance of missionary heroism'; with the marks of the lion's bite on David Livingstone's arm that was to confirm that the body which Susi and Chuma had carried from Zambia to Zanzibar was indeed that of the legendary explorer; and with many other tales of intrepidity in the face of wild beasts. "I, too, in a smaller way of course have", I went on, "been attacked by a fierce animal and suffered material injury, though not of course to my body. Indeed, it happened very recently, today in fact, when a huge and ferocious Cairn assailed me". A sound of tentative emotion greeted these words, a blend of incredulity, amazement and relief. "I mention this", I said, "to release us all from the embarrassment that enveloped the hall when some of you became aware of the state of my trousers". At once the tension slackened and I tried then to transport them to the Copperbelt and to our huge rural parishes of Mwenzo and Lubwa. My suit had to be discarded however, as soon as I got back to North Berwick. It was beyond repair.

1955 was the year of the All-Scotland Crusade when Billy Graham came as the star speaker. The Africa Secretary of the Church of Scotland's Foreign Mission Committee asked me to give some time to this event as a Supervisor of Counsellors. This may have been because he knew that I had taken part, in my student days, in some of the missions organised by the late D.P. Thomson, one-time Evangelist of the Church's Home Board. As a Supervisor, it was my job, in collaboration with another Supervisor, to interview persons who were volunteering to serve as Counsellors. We spent some time on those interviews, realising that some of the volunteers we met were 'the salt of the earth'. But we also had reason for concern. I asked one limp and dreamy-looking woman what she would do if, after one of Graham's meetings, she was paired with a girl in her teens who had come forward in response to the evangelist's call. "I would just say to her, 'Dear, you must be washed in the blood of the Lamb'", she replied in a barely audible whisper. When I then asked her how she would explain that formula, she came up with nothing. Others would disagree; but I could not see how that advice would help a modern urban lass whose only acquaintance with lamb's blood would be with what lies in the runnel below the sloping tiled display shelves on which butchers place mutton and other meats to catch the attention of the passer-by. Nor were we any less disquieted, my fellow Supervisor and I, by the response of a hefty ex-boxer-like fellow to our question about his previous experience of counselling. "Me?" said he. "Oh, this is no new thing to me! Stockbridge, 1943, in just one night, all my own work" - and at this he punched a fat fist into the palm of his left hand with a resounding crack - "48 souls for the Lord". When we then asked about 'follow-up' he dismissed the question brusquely: "That's the Lord's job, not mine". We both found ourselves reluctant to let loose among innocent and tender enquirers so seasoned and truculent a 'head-hunter', lest all that would come of it would be more trophies for his private collection.

The Foreign Mission office had, as usual, filed an application for sea passages for our return to Africa, soon after we reached Scotland. I enquired about that application in May and was assured that the matter was in hand. We were therefore jolted sharply when, some weeks later, they told us that the application had been lost by the shipping agents and that we would have to return by air. Myra and I had agreed that we simply must replenish our stock of sheets and other household necessities which cost a lot less in Edinburgh than in Ndola. We had therefore been buying such items whenever we spotted a good sale. I mentioned this to the office, realising that we had already collected more than our air baggage allowance. We were told to pack what was necessary and not to worry about the cost. But when I reported the weight, there was clearly some concern about it. The FMC had to be assiduous in the task of keeping costs as low as possible, as we fully realised.

As October drew near, we assembled our *impedimenta*, ready for flight; and it was a motley collection of well-worn containers, including a valise, stuffed to bursting point. We were going to spend a night with Myra's younger brother in Sheffield and another night at the home of her aunts in Essex. I weighed our stuff before leaving North Berwick and found it heavier even than I had expected. I repeated the process in Sheffield and decided that we simply must leave some things behind. So, while awaiting the London train there, Hugh and I whipped various articles out and he took them home in an old suitcase. We were going to have to pay excess baggage charge at the Airport out of our small 'out of pocket' travelling allowance. So, when we reached London, I resolved to weigh it all once more on the scales in Fenchurch Street station. Railway scales must often disagree, but the discrepancy between the Sheffield scales and those in London was alarming. Once again, therefore, and with the reluctant permission of a surly official in Fenchurch Street, I sifted through our remaining 'absolute necessities' to find anything that could be deemed expendable. The aunts, like Hugh, were then left with our little pile of jetsam and we flew out at last.

The handling of air baggage was probably less violent than that of rail or sea baggage. But we winced when the old valise was tossed on to the tarmac at Ndola with towels and sheets sticking out. Our anguish increased when a Northern Rhodesia official demanded a full list of everything new that we had with us and proceeded to charge us customs duty on the Dinky cars that Jamie had been given for his fourth birthday just before we left, and which, of course, had been well used from the moment he received them. We were glad, however, that no one had inspected our hand luggage which contained a heavy paraffin iron, a teapot, some china and cutlery, and Jamie's blue and red Triang van, which were in no sense overnight necessities.

Chapter 14
BACK TO THE
FAR NORTH

It was to Mwenzo we were bound, once again. The Scots minister was due for leave after his first tour of four years and so the Mission Council decided to send us there in the first instance rather than back to the Copperbelt. As the Mwenzo vanette was stranded somewhere north of Lubwa, on the side of the road, we had to make the 650 mile journey by Thatcher Hobson's bus. It was a big dusty vehicle with a kink in its chassis that made it move with its back wheels not directly behind its front, rather as a dog walks. But at least it was an omnibus and not one of those lorries that had carted African travellers in former years, with neither seats nor cover from the rain.

The news that we were not to return at once to the Copperbelt had been a disappointment. I thought of it as my first love. But Mwenzo had enchanted us during our brief five months there in 1951, and I had greatly enjoyed the chance to work with another, and distinctively different, Zambian language. For China-Mwanga was more akin to the languages of southern Tanzania and northern Malawi than to Chi-Bemba. The differences in sound can be well illustrated by one example: 'He gave me permission' is *alinsuminishe* in Bemba but *wanzumilizizya* in Mwanga, a much stronger sound. And again, astoundingly divergent meanings belong to words in these two languages, that sound alike. For instance *amakasa* in Bemba are 'feet', but 'arms' in Mwanga; *ubukata* in Bemba is 'glory' while *uwukata* is 'laziness' in Mwanga. Lastly, for this short list, the jackal '*ichimbwi*' of the Bemba is the lion of the Mwanga. A missionary of the Brethren told me that he sincerely believed that we were near the original site of Babel in that area! But Mwanga and Bemba, in common with all other Bantu languages, are rich in proverbial folk wisdom. I especially liked the Mwanga maxim: '*Nd'usi nu nyokolume uwayinyokoluma* - If you have no maternal uncle, maternal-uncle yourself', or, in other words, meet the challenges of life with initiative.

A new Pastor clarifies Christian priorities

The welcome back to Mwenzo was very kind. The minister there was now Yaphet Mugara, who, you remember, had acted as chairman of that 'people's court' which had cleansed the place from the dark threats of yon hospital employee who had pinned evil letters on trees by night in the early weeks of 1951. Mugara's was an emphatic character and he took his role as pastor and leader very seriously. Yet he also inspired people with a sense of what Paul meant when he called the church 'the body of Christ'. This was illustrated soon after our arrival, at a meeting of the District Church Council, which was in effect an assembly of evangelists, elders and deacons from all the congregations of the district, from Ntatumbila in the west to Muyombe in the east-south-east and Muyileka and Katyetye in the south. Mugara spent many weeks visiting these congregations on foot. Like Kenneth Mackenzie, he had not learned how to cycle. But from time to time, the leaders of those congregations were summoned to the DCC for reporting and for planning.

One of the evangelists - let's call him Meshek Siyame - was becoming tired. His 'flock' felt that he was giving too much attention to his fields and too little to the life of the *ecclesia*. His face sticks very clearly in my memory. He looked as though someone had dealt him so heavy a blow on the left cheek that his nose and mouth had been knocked off centre. When it was his turn to speak about his area, he said that there was really nothing to report, "Only just an adultery"; a young man from the Mines had spoiled the daughter of Bright Situnga, and the girl's parents were very angry. "So I am asking, please, that the girl be suspended from the Lord's table". Some of the other members present tutted in censorious agreement. But Mugara rose and his indignation electrified the atmosphere. "Keep this unclean wound in your own place and heal it there", he said sharply. "Do not come here again to speak of such things as though this was the harvest of your field. What about the widows? Have you had their houses repaired? Has a field of *cassava* been prepared for blind Tatakulu Siwenu and his wife; has the congregation helped the young widow Nawulanda to clothe her children for school? These are the fruits we await from you, Siyame. If there are no crops, perhaps there has been no planting and weeding. How can we answer the Lord of the Harvest if we are lazy?"

It was a heavy rebuke. As I listened, I wondered how it would be received in a Scottish elders' meeting. But Mugara then called us all to stand, read a very apt passage from Paul's letter to Timothy and prayed a prayer that blended truth and tenderness as Siyame's tillage was commended to Christ. As the DCC adjourned, many of the elders and deacons quietly shook Siyame's hand. But it was no partisan gesture to signify solidarity with him against his minister. Rather it was a wishing of good cheer for one who had had to undergo surgery but would be well now.

Loosening the Bond between Church and Schools

Negotiations had been going on for some time between NRG's Department of Education and the voluntary agencies for the transference of primary schools to Local Education Authorities. 1955 was the year in which the schools managed by Mwenzo were to be taken over by the new LEA for Isoka District; and so I found myself involved in this process soon after our return from leave. Many of our teachers and most of the church members had misgivings about this move. Anything initiated by the government was more suspect than ever since NRG had 'betrayed' the people to Welensky. There were, of course, a few teachers who chafed under the discipline of mission management, especially in respect of beer drinking. But though the seemingly laxer morals of white education officers encouraged their hope of a looser rein, the official statements on the matter stressed the need for good character in teachers of the young. What I feared was that NRG would be in a stronger position to force teachers to toe the line and to penalise opposition of the Federation.

I was sure that the situation required me to visit the schools and assure the communities round about them that the church was as interested as ever in the vital work of primary education. I therefore began a vigorous programme of district touring as the rains drew to a close in March. Just before my first trip, I was visited by the Education Officer who was to have oversight of Isoka district. He walked into Mwenzo dressed in spotless white shirt and shorts as though he was about to play tennis. I was amazed, therefore, to learn that his vehicle was stranded about seven miles away and that he had walked in to ask for help. It augured well, I thought, but he made it clear, as we talked, that he had no relish for village touring and would certainly not use a bicycle. The next day, after his vehicle had been fixed, we went together to Nachipeta where there was a lower primary school. As we approached the classrooms, the headmaster came to meet us, but when I introduced him to the man who was to be his manager later in the year, that gentleman merely inclined his head slightly. The teacher's extended hand dropped limply, while our visitor puffed daintily on a Matinee and blew whimsical smoke rings. It was not that he wanted to be rude. It was simply that he was quite unready to communicate in the manner of the local people. As I described the school, he stood still, obviously feeling no need to look closer at its buildings, let alone to meet its pupils. The Matinee was now shortened to about half an inch, whereupon he flicked the stub away, landing it some feet ahead on the dry ground. As we moved to return to the vehicle, I saw a swarm of little boys scrambling for it in a whirl of dust.

More Translation work

At that same time, we began a new translation project. The Bible Society in Edinburgh, which had published the original New Testatment and then the Psalms, was willing to take on a book of Old Testament Selections, since it was not practicable to undertake the translation of the whole Old Testament in Mwanga. Caleb Simpamba was available to help with this project and we set to in earnest, basing our selections on William Manson's 'Bible from Day to Day' which provided a helpful heading for each passage. Other Mwanga people acted as readers and consultants as the work progressed but it was Caleb's gift for dynamic translation that mattered most. We were encouraged by the comment of one acknowledged authority, a retired evangelist called Sinyinza: "*A muvwango witu* - it is how we speak". When I meet people who have rejected new English translations on the ground that they depart from 'the fine old language' of the Authorised Version, I often mention that, in Africa, no one would think of using any other form of the language than that which people can readily understand.

At the same time, too, we had to accept the necessity to demolish a striking looking classroom block at Mwenzo because faulty roof structure had damaged the walls. That building was special for two reasons. It had been adorned by the use of white and red bricks together to produce what we called a 'Fairisle' pattern. But its special significance, known to only a few, lay in the fact of a bitter tragedy in the life of the mission builder, Joel Silumba.

Some years earlier, that man and his family had been engaged, along with the rest of the community in burning off the long dry grass around their houses as a safety measure. For, after a few weeks of the dry season, when the sun had drawn all the moisture from the grasses, they were so brittle that a tiny spark could ignite them. People were therefore careful to do this burning off as soon as conditions were right. Because it was a routine operation, however, it was done without anxiety.

As the builder had been burning, his youngest children, too small to help the adults, had been playing in a small thatched hut not far from their house. Their father's attention was momentarily distracted when, in an instant, the gentle breeze eddied into a strong gust of wind and carried the flames leaping backwards. No one had realised where the little ones were and, as the hut was due for demolition, no one worried as it caught fire. Then suddenly the yells of the toddlers were heard over the roar of the flames. One of them was rescued but died soon after. The other child could not be reached. A terrible silent anguish settled upon their father and, for many months, he spent his days sitting staring ahead, nibbling at some food put before him but speaking not a word.

When the Mission Council had authorised the building of the four-classroom block, the missionary in charge was at a loss to find someone capable of building it. Then one day he said, "Look, friend, the children of the villages around us need this school. Only you can take charge of the work. If your little ones had not died, they would have come to learn in it. Will you not build it for their friends?" The builder rose and a gentle smile crept over his mouth and eyes, a smile I was to know well. "*Kandizenge*", he said. "Let me build it. I shall start tomorrow." It was therefore sad for him as well as for the community when, in 1955, his 'Fairisle' structure had to be reduced to the size of one classroom and an office, because of warping of the main roof timbers and consequent damage to the walls.

The Los Angeles Ladies

I was laying plans for a tour of the eastern reaches of the district as far as Uyombe, in Malawi, when, one evening after dark, we heard a vehicle approching and a search light beamed from it upon our front door. As we blinked our way towards it, we heard American voices declaring themselves to be a three-woman team from Los Angeles. "We've come to do some recording of local music with your natives", they told us and then wanted to stay with us for a few days to do so.

They were a host in themselves, those exuberant extroverts. They never left us is any doubt about their likes and dislikes in the matter of food. When Myra asked one of them if she'd have a certain dish at dinner, the answer was, "Yah, so long as it's sterile". They seemed to see it as their vocation to create Matthew 25 situations: "We are strangers, so take us in". They obliged us to let our lives be organised to suit their programme, and wanted to involve a number of local church people in recording sessions. They talked loudly and listened little, seemingly quite insensitive to our problems in responding on the instant to their random requirements. I could never forget the visit we paid to Chieftainess Wayitwika and how they took command of that royal audience.

The ladies were traversing large tracts of east and central Africa in pursuit of indigenous hymns of which they would then have discs cut for distribution, at low cost, to people like ourselves. The vehicle they used was a Willis Overland station wagon, furnished with all modern conveniences which included a neat little cupboard designed to hold three toothbrushes in little clips, far enough apart to ensure that their bristles would not touch. But, said their leader, "What we are trying to teach the natives everywhere we go is that they must lead spiritual lives and eschew all the insidious temptations of materialism by which Satan in threatening Africa". Yet Satan, I could not help thinking, would have been delighted to borrow their Willis, even for a week, to speed up his nefarious activities, and to show his victims the glories of that four-wheeled specimen of triumphant materialism.

The coming of the ladies was, however, yet another testimony to the Zambian proverb: "Where God cooks your food, there's no smoke". For when they heard of my plan to tour the eastern end of the parish - which I mentioned more than once with a note of urgency so that they might get the message that my time was limited - they said they would carry me with them. "We've been awaiting a word from the Lord as to where we should go from here, and this is his answer". So, as swiftly as they had come, they prepared to depart. It was a long journey to Muyombe and they gave me little time to arrange how I would return, but their offer was too good to be declined.

The Willis had a small built-in refrigerator and so our ladies had a better stock of perishables than we had at Mwenzo. After three hours of travel, the leader suddenly stopped. "Now we eat", she announced and in a flash, they had opened the back of the vehicle to provide a table. Deck chairs appeared from some other repository: a table cloth was spread and I watched as they uncovered cutlery and crockery, condiments, sauces and all the requirements for a restaurant meal. Grace was spoken by the leader with great emphasis as though the One addressed was hard of hearing. I was worried, however, by the appearance of the sky and I said so. "Perhaps we should go on a little further", I suggested. "There could be a heavy storm any moment". But the ruling hand was raised to silence me, "Listen", she said, "We've committed this safari to the Lord and he'll fix the canopy" - which he did!

As my perfidious storm clouds melted away, one of the team said: "Now how about a Bible quiz?" with alacrity they cleared the table, put everything in place and fired off with a question to me about someone like Shealtiel. In my first years as a theological student I had to sit exams that required the reading of the whole Bible. But as the quiz progressed, I was exposed as an unlettered pagan, and I began to feel desperate - especially because they seemed to interpret it as a contest between `the saved' and the 'unsaved'. "We've still a long way to go", I said. "Perhaps we should start off again". The ruse worked, though my score at half-time was scandalous. "We'll pick it up again when we stop for tea", said the leader, and off we went.

When we were not far from Muyombe, we found signs of recent heavy rain. I was driving at the time and realised that a long stretch of the road ahead was under water. "I'll take the wheel here", said the leading lady, and we changed places. "But first we pray", she announced and in the now familiar tone that demanded a hearing, she asked that we be led safely through the flood. I could not but admire her control of the Willis as she then steered it like a speed boat, sending great sheets of water out on either side.

Mulekatembo and Nachisitu

I had carried a bicycle so that, when we reached Muyombe, I could visit the neighbouring schools at Masangani, Mpemba and Chifungwe and then go backwards to Mulekatembo. There was a lower middle school there and the local evangelist, Jonas Sichone, was arranging a gathering of elders and deacons for a short study conference which I was to lead. A local trader met me on my way to the school, and carried me to the road where his wife gave us tea and scones. She seemed very young. "She is number three", her husband explained and they both laughed. "And where are the others?" I asked. "Here", he replied, "but it's her turn to do the housework this week so they are in the field over there". The state of polygamy was called *impali* and I asked the lady how she liked it. "It is very good", she said. "The senior wife is like a mother to us. And we like to have different duties each week. Life is not dull this way." She certainly had a happy disposition. Between them, those three women had provided their husband with a very large family.

The refresher course or study conference at Mulekatembo was a lively affair. The periods of prayer and of discussion were interspersed with spontaneous bursts of song and dance, enlivened as so often in central Africa by the ululation of women trilling above the praising voices. One of the subjects for discussion specially requested by some women elders and deacons was 'Christ and evil spirits'. I was glad, as I have been on many occasions in Scotland as well as in Africa, that the Gospels show clearly that Jesus did not pooh-pooh people's fears about the power of these spirits of confusion that possessed and prostrated many lives. For who today, without blinkers, can dismiss the reality of a power of evil greater than the sum of individual sins in our society? The confident young minister who undertook to sort out the old lady who, they told him, believed in the Devil, was aptly cut to size by her response: "I'm glad to ken that Satan's dead, but I'd just like to know who's carryin' on the business".

At Mulekatembo they would have claimed that life provided plenty of evidence of 'powers of darkness' in their midst. But there were audible titters when one woman asserted that she knew where the *iviwanda* lurked, to pounce out on the unwary. "Look", she said, pointing to the local cemetery away in the trees, "when you see holes, as wide as my big finger at the edges of graves, *cenjeranji* - be careful, for that's the kind of exit they use from the dens of darkness". When however you have lived on the fringe of communities which see life as a whole and all human experiences as spiritual, it is hard to return to the European separation between the spiritual and the material which so effectively - though reverently - puts religion away in an ornate casket in the display cabinet, to be looked at now and then but not to be touched.

From Mulekatembo, without a vehicle, the best way to Nachisitu was across the Mafinga mountains. For that 35 mile walk, my companion, alas, was a lad whom I had known in Mufulira, and who now wanted to train for the ministry, but who was not quite right in the head. As the track was single file almost all the way, he followed close on my heels, wearing sandals cleverly made from slices of Michelin car tyres. His feet slapped the earth with an insistent rhythm that would have been trying enough on a 5-mile walk. Talking ceaselessly, he recounted incident after incident in which nasty people had despised him or told lies against him. The pulse of his voice and his sandals gave me a sense of being pursued and thus spurred me on to keep a brisk pace and shorten the ordeal of his company.

The track crossed the top of the hill at a point where the downward slope began almost at once. One minute we were hauling ourselves up by clutching tufts of grass, the next we were having to tread carefully lest we should start to slide. But soon the hillside began to level out again and we walked comfortably with a wide vista ahead of the valley in which Nachisitu lay. The village itself probably had a population of no more than sixty but, as we drew near at last in the late afternoon, we found hundreds milling around as if in a great open-air market. I had come for a weekend of worship culminating in the sacrament of communion. The great congregation was drawn from all the neighbouring villages and the air was filled with singing and good cheer as we at last reached the house of the head teacher, where I was to stay. It had been a day of relentless walking and I gladly accepted a mug of sweet black coffee from my host as he showed me my room. I drank it, lying on my bed in that cool dark place. The next thing I knew was that someone was shaking my shoulder. "We are all waiting for you", said the senior church elder. "Sorry", I replied, rubbing my eyes. "Have you been waiting long?" "Yes", he said, "for about one and a half hours. But the teacher said you were sleeping". Darkness had fallen as we went out together to the classroom where the elders waited by candle light.

What took place on the Sunday was a festival rather than what is often called 'a service'. Young folk with guitars sang and danced as the congregation flocked into and around the place of worship. It was just after harvest time and the offerings in grain, vegetables and eggs were generous. Smiling faces and kind greetings were everywhere. As I found so often in my visits to distant areas, the people of Christ had indeed 'Come with Happy'. When my sandalled companion and I set off at last to walk north-westwards to join the road back to Mwenzo, a great crowd escorted us, singing all the way. This was not an encounter of the people with the alien wares of an imported foreign religion. It was a great company feasting together on the Bread of Life.

More Racism

By previous arrangement, I was to meet a Native Authority lorry at the road end as it made its way, with a load of chiefs and their councillors, to a meeting at Isoka *boma*. Mr Sandals left me as the lorry arrived, to make his way back by lifts to Mulekatembo. I appreciated his willingness to accompany me to a place I had not visited before, but I was worried about his future, especially since he claimed two honoured church leaders as sponsors of his application for ministerial training.

The recent rains had made a terrible mess of the approaches to the many palm log bridges of that tortuous road between the Malawi border and Mwenzo. As the lorry slithered towards one of them, the driver stopped and jumped out, he had drawn into the side as far as he dared, knowing that the verges were quagmires in many places. "We'll have to lay branches over this mud", he said, and at once the men on the lorry spread out to axe at the trees and trim off sharp twigs to make a rough platform over the muddy approaches. Nyela School being not far up on the other side of the bridge, I said I would go and give the teachers their salaries, to save time, and they all agreed. It had to be a brief visit, though the over-due salaries were warmly welcomed as was a small stock of New Testaments and of the Psalms for sale in the surrounding villages.

As I was walking out from Nyela, I heard a vehicle passing in the direction in which we wanted to go, up the plateau. It sounded too light for our lorry but I gave it little thought. The shadows of evening were lengthening as I reached my friends at the bridge, still bedding down branches to ensure a safe crossing. "I heard a car", I said to someone. "How did it get across?" What they told me was shocking. A car, driven by a white man - a Mumbunu from South Africa from his accent, they guessed - and with a woman and small child in the back, had appeared from the east. Its driver had bawled at the men to let him pass. The lorry driver had gone to explain what they were doing and to ask him to wait till they finished. "But he refused. He called us bloody baboons and told us to go to hell and get out of his way. So we had to let him pass. His car somehow got over but the branches were thrown all over the place, because we had not tied them yet". "Where was he going in such a hurry?" I asked. "There he is", said one of the chiefs, a tall man with the beaded band of chieftainship on his brow. I looked and sure enough I could see the rear brake lights flickering somewhere on the long hill up towards the plateau. "He must have stuck in the mud", the chief added wryly.

We had a consultation then about what we should do. The lorry could now cross the ramp of branches. "Let him sleep in the mud", said one young fellow, but the decision was that he should be offered help. "He has his wife and baby with him", said the driver. Mwenzo district was far from the racist vulgarities of the Copper-belt, and I was grieved and angry that this shameful thing had happened. "Let me speak to him", I said and this was at once accepted. So I walked ahead of the lorry and there in the swift-falling darkness I found the man gazing at his back wheel which he must have embedded further in the muddy verge by revving fiercely when he realised the car was stuck. "Good evening", I said. "I see you're in trouble". His response was curt. He was obviously a short-tempered fellow, as shown by the way he answered something that his wife said. The baby, I noticed, was in a carrycot on the back seat beside its mother.

"My friends on the lorry down there are willing to help you", I told him, "but I believe you insulted them when you met them at the bridge". His reply was an oath muttered behind closed teeth. "Do you wish help?" I then asked, and he nodded in the affirmative. "Then I shall call them". They came, and in a couple of minutes, the car was on the crown of the road again. At once, the man jumped in and drove off without a word. We were all shocked, but even more so when, on reaching the top of the hill, he stopped, got out and called, in cutting sarcasm, "Thank you... Bwana". "We should have left him in the mud", someone said angrily. "No", answered an older voice, clearly carrying authority. "He had his child and it might have suffered from mosquitoes in the night. It was right to help them". In our Mufulira days, Myra had said once after witnessing a horrid exhibition of racism, "How long will the people go on suffering such treatment?"; and that night, in the far north, under the high stars, I repeated inwardly the Psalmist's cry: "O Lord, how long?" and "When will they ever learn?"

Chapter 15
MORE STORIES
FROM MWENZO

Mwenzo mission had its bank account at Barclays in Kabwe, just under 600 miles to the south. However, we had a good way of getting cash for most of our needs. We crossed into what was then called Tanganyika, and at the Asian-owned stores at Tunduma, only six miles from us, we were able to obtain coin and notes in Northern Rhodesian currency in exchange for a cheque. This was mutually helpful: the traders did not have to carry bags of coin to their banks in Mbeya, 70 miles further into Tanganyika; and we had ready cash for teachers' salaries, labourers' wages, purcases of food supplies for the boarding school and the hospital, etc, etc.

Every now and then, however, the system broke down because the traders' cash supply was short of our needs. In such cases, we had to order notes and coin from Kabwe. I think I had to do so three or four times during our two periods at Mwenzo. On receipt of our cheque, sometimes for around £6000, the bank packed a so-called gold box for us, screwed down its lid and put a blob of sealing wax over each screw head. Then at an insurance rate of less than 50 pence (ten shillings) per £1000, the box was taken to the despatch office of Central African Road Services for delivery to us. CAR's buses and trucks, which had superseded Thatcher Hobson at the start of the Federation, ran an incalculable service. We could never guess when their vehicle would reach us. Thus I had no idea when to expect the arrival of the 'gold box'. It could come on any day of any week and at any time of day or night. I recall vividly however the manner of such arrivals. I would perhaps be in the office chatting with one of our workers when he would say: "O, by the way, your money is at the road end. CARS came in during the night". But neither of us registered any sense of urgency. At leisure, I would go out to that nexus of little roads that our London-born headmistress of the Girls' School called Picadilly Circus. And there, beside some bags of grain, some travel-battered suitcases, a crate of live hens, a sewing machine, a bundle of personal belongings packed into a large aluminium basin all wrapped into a length of cotton, I would find the scratched and much-used box, measuring around 12" x 8" x 5" in which £6000 nestled together in tranquility. For no one ever touched that box, even though it sometimes lay in the little thatched and wall-less shelter at the Circus for hours on end. Sadly, that could not happen nowadays.

Our quaint elderly Irish lady doctor

The doctor at Mwenzo had gone on leave soon after our arrival. Once again, therefore, we were indebted to a unique little old lady, Dr Hope Trant, for her willingness to serve as doctor for the best part of a year. I had met her briefly on that extended round trip which I had made in 1947 with the old missionary from Chitambo. She was then running a resthouse at Tunduma. She loved animals and took me round to see her various pets. Black servants had charge of the donkeys, the ducks, the goats, the cats and the monkeys. "This is Marko, my donkey boy... Luka my duck boy... Yohane my monkey boy" - all men with a positive role to fulfil - "and this is Mateyo my mosquito boy", the only member of the team committed to destruction. Dr Trant, who hailed from Eire, was one in a million. They told me she had been a VAD in the first world war. I don't know what had brought her to southern Tanganyika but she had lived there I believe for many years. At one time she controlled a network of resthouses for white travellers. You could say that she thus served the policies of apartheid; but her walk and conversation were full of kindly humanity.

Now in 1955, she decided to move into the doctor's house at Mwenzo on condition that she could bring Audrey, her colobus monkey with her. Audrey was vehemently anti-feminist, we found, as we observed her from a distance. But she apparently excluded the lady doctor from this antipathy; possibly because Dr Trant dressed in trousers. I've no idea how old the colobus was. But she was big and strong and keen to wreak mischief when the doctor was at the hospital.

One day, Audrey managed somehow to gain access to the pantry. Jacob Sinkala, the doctor's factotum, found her there and tried to eject her, whereupon she chased him towards the kitchen. As he slammed the door, the beast hammered on it and then, seeing a hole in it, she pushed her hairy arm through to try and grab her enemy. She wearied of that game, however, and ambled off. Sinkala watched

his chance and, with a handful of broken bricks, started to keep her at
bay so that he could go into the house and prepare the doctor's lunch.

Old and new Understandings of Life and Death

During our short stay at Mwenzo in 1952, I had gone one day
to the village of the grandfather of Revd Yaphet Mugara, an ancient
man called Mugulwa Sichizya, who held the rank of sub-chief under
the Chieftainess Wayitwika. Mugara had gone with me for our
special task was to baptise the old man and his wife. They were
both over ninety but active and alert. As Mugara had not then
been ordained, the sacrament was administered by myself. But the
grandson gave the message and at one point, for emphasis, he gripped
his old grand-father's long white beard. Infant baptism casually
given is surely a poor thing compared with the baptism of someone
of whatever age, whose soul is saying 'yes' to Christ.

Four years later, when Yaphet Mugara and I were talking one
day, near the hospital, about his forthcoming tour of the Ntatumbila
area, about 50 miles west of Mwenzo, a lad came running up, knelt
before Mugara and said simply: "*E Mugulwa wafwa* - Mugulwa is
dead". He must have been 96 but we could not but sorrow for his
passing. For some moments my colleague was silent, then suddenly
he spoke. "You will bury my grandfather", he said. "I must go to
Ntatumbila for they're awaiting me there." And so it was done.

It is difficult to see how, in our western societies, we could
have avoided the formalisation and the professionalisation of the
work of burial. And I know that a compassionate undertaker can
be of real help to bereaved people. But we have lost something by
denying friends and neighbours the chance of enacting their
sympathy by preparing the body for burial and digging the grave.
At Mugulwa's funeral, I found myself drawn into just such a corporate
expression of neighbourly regard. The tall slim old body was laid out
on a wooden stretcher, covered by a white cloth. Together we then
dug the pit for its commital, sweating heavily in the heat of the sun.
Thereafter, having put our shirts on again, we bore the old man to
the grave, to the exultant singing of songs of resurrection.

As we were gathered round the deep hole and I was speaking
the words of Christian assurance, a man slipped quickly and
respectfully between me and the local elder. He had a young white
cock in his hands, its feet tied by bark rope, as he began to lower
himself into the pit to lay it on the old man's chest, as sustenance

for his long journey ahead. "No, no", someone said to him but not unkindly. "He does not need this. He is a Christian" "Oh, sorry", said the man and climbed out again, clutching his offering. I was now speaking the formula of commital, when the cock crowed triumphantly as though to affirm the reality, for the ancient saint, of the resurrection morning.

When Yaphet Mugara returned from the west, he was eager for my report of his grandfather's burial. Then he told me of what he had found at Ntatumbila. When he and his team were still some miles from the big village, he said, word had been brought to them that the wife of the headman had died giving birth to twins. Dread had at once seized the whole community and everyone had fled the village except Ntatumbila himself and his wife's sister. "I was sure, you see", said Mugara, "that I had to keep my promise to those people even when I heard of my grandfather's death. But at that time I was thinking about the report I'd received of bad behaviour by some youths in the Ntatumbila area, about a sudden increase in drinking and coarse dancing and about the weakness of the church there. The word about the death of the headman's wife was a new thing altogether. But it made me sure that God was sending me there for important work."

As they reached the deserted village, he went on, he had found the headman and his sister-in-law alone with the corpse. One twin was still alive but very weak. The other had died after a breath or two. "Even as we were speaking with them, the baby died in the woman's arms. It was very sad", he said. But Mugara was a man of quick thought and action. So, at once, he began to prepare the three bodies for burial, while his companions went, on his order, to dig a grave at the village cemetery. Then when all was prepared, he led the small party from the house, singing songs of eternal life. The villagers could be seen huddled together at the edge of the forest and Mugara called to them, with his strong voice, to come to the graveside. None came, however, and so he carried through the burial service, encouraging the mourning company as best he could in the praises of the risen Christ. "But my heart was angry", he told me, "and so, as soon as the grave was filled in, I went towards the crowd at the forest's edge". I wished I could have heard what he said to them but I knew him well enough to be able to imagine the power of the breath of his rebuke upon the dying embers of their faith.

The end of the story was that what had been originally planned as a routine visit for a sacramental weekend became a confrontation, for Mugara, between darkness and light, fatality and faith, the hostile power of evil spirits and the healing power of Christ. As the weeks went by after his return to Mwenzo, we received constant reports of what it was right to call a great revival of the church around Ntatumbila and of those same guitars playing no longer for midnight dances but for the praise of God. Maybe revival can come only when faith is seen to be, not a mere affirmation of the notion of cosmic benevolence, but a healing of our deep disease and an outpouring of love in action. Jesus's brother was right, I am sure: "Faith that does not express itself in conduct is dead". (James 2.26)

Unexpected Hospitality

The garage in Kabwe, after a long delay, had sent the wrong part for Mwenzo's stranded vanette. As we were expecting another baby in August, I had to undertake a tour of the south-eastern part of the district entirely by bicycle. The road to Isoka was very heavily corrugated and the 70-mile cycle ride there from Mwenzo was a jading experience. For when you tried to move off the ribs of the corrugation on to the verge, it was often so pitted and scarred by runnels made by the last rains that there was no choice but to return to the juddering corrugations. At last, however, I sighted Isoka just before nightfall and as I was making for Nkonde's 'First and Last African Hotel', I met Mpanji Kapitila who taught at Chiwanda lower Primary School. He was alone in his house, he told me, and gave me a warm welcome to spend the night there. He did not mention that he had no food in the house. Instead he excused himself after spreading a bed for me, leaving me in a comfortable chair dozing by the light of yet another of those little smoky lamps made by poking string through the lid of a vaseline jar full of paraffin. He must have been away for nearly an hour when his return startled me from sleep. As he came in, I noticed blood on his head. At my insistence, he told me his tale of woe.

"I wanted to go and waken my store *kapitao* friend", he said, "so that I could get this small tin of meat. But, you see, I had no light on my bike and I was going very fast. Suddenly I crashed into a *Boma* messenger coming the other way. It was a severe crash and we were both thrown on the ground. For a moment, as we shouted and blamed each other we could not see each other or even our bikes, till some person came with a torch."

He cooked a tasty dish of rice with the Fray Bentos corned beef. Then as I ate, he told me of his 'very big confrontation' with his wife and of his order to her to return to her mother. There was a ring of imperious implacability in his tone, interrupted now and then by little sobs. I heard him out and then began to urge him to try to see his wife's point of view. I pled with him to throw a bridge across the gulf that now separated them, especially since he had declared that he still loved her. But his silence radiated resistance. Then suddenly he cut into my pleading with a dramatic cry: "Sir, do you expect me to lie down for ever under petticoat government?" He had not budged from his intransigence when we went to bed. Next morning he set me off on the way to Muyileka after a tasty breakfast of fried eggs and coffee.

Kitten versus Snake

To reach Muyileka, I was advised to take the track over a hill called Mpando. It was relatively easy running for some miles and took me through Malale where there had been a thriving sub-school, unaided by NRG until the Education Department had abolished all sub-schools in 1951. The ex-teachers were respected church leaders. As I approached the village no one was in sight, nor did anyone appear, as was usually the case, to greet my visit. In village communities strangers were always welcomed. I dismounted and pushed my bike to the nearest house, only then noticing that a good crowd of people was assembled in a circle in the middle of the village, intently watching something that I could not see. As I approached them, they burst into cheering and clapping and as suddenly fell silent again.

It was a grim duel they were watching: a long green snake, bloated with anger, being baited by a scruffy kitten. So intent were the spectators that no one noted my arrival. So, standing at the back of the circle, I watched and their fascination caught me up. The snake raised its head and made three movements as though the fourth would strike its assailant down. But at the third, the kitten soared over its head, struck it from behind with open claws and then danced insolently round to face it once more. The blow of the cat's claws had hurt the snake badly but once again, infuriated by the little beast's provocative dancing and contemptuous spitting, it raised its head to strike and once again on its third swing forward, the kitten leapt behind it for another swipe at its neck. The action was repeated a third time but the kitten now had mastery and proceeded to rip the snake's skin open behind the head, till at last, with a swift collapse, it went limp. At that the people rose and cheered tumultuously but the little hero resisted their curtain call and hopped coyly away to the shade of its favourite tree. "You see", said an old man to a group of delighted youngsters, "If you are determined, though you are still small, you can overcome anything".

Tough Terrain

The ascent of Mpando was deceptively easy, and I managed to stay on the saddle without strain until the path levelled out on what was a high plateau. Spinning along an open track, I was amazed to find wild irises blooming in profusion. My companion on that tour was a hefty young man from Mwenzo, the youngest son of Benjamin Sikombe whom Alexander Dewar had taken to Scotland in 1901. But Yaled was new to hill cycling and had already dropped behind. It was always Indian file on those forest paths and hill tracks. I knew that many miles had to be traversed before Muyileka; I knew the village and school were in low country going towards the Luangwa River; and I also knew that my hefty friend cycled as many others did, in the wrong way: a low saddle; the arch of the foot, not the ball of the toe, pressed on the bar of the pedal; and the knee bending outwards. Moreover, the level track on the plateau urged on my pace.

Then, all of a sudden, the level ended and below me lay the basin of the great river. The drop ahead must have been at least 1500 feet, and it was sheer. But the mountainside was covered in trees growing at almost 90 degrees to their roots. So, shouldering my Raleigh, pannier bags and all, with my light camp bed tied to the handlebars, I began the descent. Climbing down such a gradient would have been bad enough with free hands. But the 'antlers' of my bike kept catching in the branches while my left hand clutched the trees and a strange shaking seized my legs, forcing me to stop every twenty yards or so to recover their steadiness. What made things worse was that I could not find a ledge on which to sit and rest, nor any place to lay my bike. The sight of what I was sure were the thatched roofs of the Muyileka classrooms helped, however, to keep me going. I can't recall how long the descent took me, but at last I reached the plain for the last lap. Teachers and pupils welcomed me kindly and my bed was spread in the school office. Yaled Sikombe arrived after dark and fell asleep at once.

Here as in most of the schools, I had cause to admire the teachers' constancy in running their schools and caring for their young charges in situations of great loneliness. To get, for example, salt or paraffin, they had to go the way by which I had come, to Isoka.

Musyani's Absalom

Katyetye was our next school and church centre after Muyeleka. The village was a *chinanawene*, the residence of a lesser chief of the people called Awiwa. When I first heard that name, I was startled, for the word means thieves. My hesitant questions about its meaning received the same answer everywhere: "Yes, that's its meaning". For the ancestors of the Awiwa had been so called because of an event that had made them flee from the land of the people of Mwanga. The Mwanga chief, Musyani, so they say, had an ambitious son, like David's Absalom, who could not wait to take over the throne. He therefore conceived of a plan to have the royal drums stolen. The people regarded those drums as the prime insignia of kingship. If Muchinga could seize them, he could be assured of popular favour. And so it was done. But the old king's servants discovered the theft almost at once and soldiers were despatched to chase the thieves, perhaps not knowing who they were.

The prince and his young admirers were fleet of foot and had reached the river Kalungu before their pursuers sighted them. To escape they had to plunge into the river and swim across. The king who had been carried by the pursuing soldiers witnessed their crossing and knew that there was no catching them now. "*Chiwange. A wiwa watupu!*" he cried. "So be it. They're no better than thieves". And thus Muchinga became the founder of a breakaway state, known to this day by a name that they themselves cherish: the Thieves.

I never traced the origin of Chief Katyetye's name, however. *Katyetye* is the wagtail; and many a time, as I've pedalled along forest paths, a *katyetye* has run for a stretch in front of me. Some event long ago probably caused that name to be given to a sub-chief of the Awiwa, but I never learned what.

After a school inspection and then preparations for the celebration of communion, I had to tackle the long ascent to Isoka from the valley. It was a tough journey, they told me, and I would have to cross the Kampumbu river. I would not be meeting again that amazing elephant highway that stretched for part of the way between Muyeleka and Katyetye, a track as wide as a two-way motor road, so trodden that no grass grew on it and pitted with great holes left in the drying mud, at the end of the rains, by the elephants' huge feet. Indeed, with a shimmering sun directly overhead, obliterating shadows, I had crashed twice into such holes before I learned why they were there and how the great jumbo highway, so they told me, stretched for hundreds of miles along the banks of the Luangwa. When I spoke of the highway as a *musebo*, my companions laughed; for a *musebo* is a hoed road, and no hoes had been used on that great track. But I was now leaving elephant country for other unknown hazards.

One River too deep

Wild pigs known as *ngulube* seem to love to dig for roots on forest path-ways. Their snouts sink hollows of a couple of inches' depth and under a foot in diameter, holes deep enough to jolt a bike badly or to throw a cyclist to the ground. There were many such pig pits on the tortuous track from Katyetye to Isoka. But the biggest hazard was the swirling river Kampumbu. The local villagers knew how to cope with it and so I had not realised, till I reached it, how turbulent it would be. As the rains had ended some while ago, I wondered how the river would look at the height of the wet season. I am a poor swimmer. But the alternative to crossing it somehow was to make a huge detour that could add perhaps even two days. I had never met the local people till then but, as always, I found readiness to help, a gift not to be taken for granted.

"Don't worry", they said. "You will be carried. Here is Situnga, he often carries people over. And you, Jeriko, come here, You take the bicycle." Jeriko was a lanky youth who at once whipped off his shirt, rolled up the legs of his shorts and waded in, holding my bike, with its pannier bags, above his head. The waters hammered at him as if he were an unwelcome invader, spinning him round as they lapped under his armpits. Situnga was now ready, having gone to replace long trousers by shorts. He too had discarded his shirt. He was probably in his forties, shorter than Jeriko but powerfully built. As he came down to the waters' edge, he took a last long draw on a home-made cigarette which he then handed to a woman nearby who proceeded to finish it for him.

I had not ridden on anyone's shoulders since those bygone days when Mwangonde Faulds, on leave in Scotland, used to pick us up and let us have a look at the dusty tops of my father's tall bookcases. This was, however, no time for hesitation and I had to clutch at the assurance that Situnga would not put himself and me at risk nor would his neighbours allow a foolhardy act. But I had no reason for confidence in myself as a shoulder rider. Situnga was now squatting low to make it easy for me to mount. I weighed around ten and a half stone but he seemed to have little difficulty in standing upright under such a load. As soon as he moved into the water, I realised he was picking his way among rocks and submerged branches. But in he went and in a few seconds the water was up to his neck and my shorts were soaking. I was now gripping his head fiercely, unable to relax my tenseness. Just then, we reached the main channel and Situnga spun round and back again, jolting as he negotiated the hazards underneath. I thanked him as warmly as I could but his reply was "*Awe, kusi na chimwi* - Not at all, its nothing". As I took the westward track, I saw my friend and young Jeriko enter the Kampumbu again apparently unconcerned. I had heard once from Dr Currie at Mwenzo of how his father, a missionary in southern Malawi, had been borne in like manner through a river at dusk, only to find as they reached the other side that it was a woman who had carried him.

Family Affairs

In August 1956, not long after the death of my father in Edinburgh, Myra gave birth to Myra Isabel. We had all gone to Lubwa for that event which took place without hitch. It was Catherine and Jamie who insisted that the baby should be called after her mother. Little Myra was baptised a few weeks later at Mwenzo by Yaphet Mugara and some of the women elders called her Namposya, which was a royal title of the Mwanga. Jamie, meanwhile, at the age of four, announced two discoveries. First, he told the nursing sister that his daddy loved him even when he was bad. Then, more dramatically, Myra and our house servant James

Sinkala happened to converge one at a time at the door of our large pantry where they spotted the wee lad, standing on a chair, helping himself to a tray of fudge. He had not heard their approach and neither of them spoke. For a moment or so he munched on happily. Then, as often happens, the back of his head felt the touch of their eye-beams and he turned round. "Oh", he said. "Now I really am a fieth". It was Paul the apostle who once remarked that without law, there would be no sin.

Lumpa in spate

Bad rumours were coming up to us in those days from Chinsali. The Lumpa movement, as it was being called, had broken with the local churches in 1955. We were in Scotland at the time and I had been disturbed by reports of a campaign, organised ostensibly for evangelistic renewal, which had resulted in what some village folk resented as a form of inquisition. "Have you ever been to Kasomo, the village of Alice Lenshina?" people were asked quite often by campaign agents who had been recruited from as far away as the Copperbelt. The answer "Yes" was to align oneself with a movement which was considered fit for excommunication because Lenshina had allegedly given baptism to those who publicly renounced 'the ways of darkness'. The antipathy had been aggravated by the movement's ready welcome to a number of prominent people, ex-teachers and others, whom the churches had disciplined for some lapse or other.

There was no easy prescription for this type of phenomenon irrupting as the movement had done suddenly and with great magnetic power. It would have been easy to reproach the churches, Protestant and Roman Catholic alike, with jealousy as the forest paths broadened to highways by the feet of thousands of pilgrims from as far away as Tanzania and Zimbabwe, Malawi, Zaire, Angola and Mozambique as well as from all over Zambia. A juster judgment seemed to be that the two big churches of the region were encumbered by regulations based on written rules as well as on use and wont which made their response to Lenshina's appearance both rigid and lacking in confidence. Thus the gulf was fixed and the movement effectively outlawed. But its numbers and its fame increased as hundreds of church members, suspended from the sacrament of communion because of an admitted visit to Kasomo, openly joined the ranks of Lumpa.

On our trip to Lubwa for the birth of little Myra, I decided
that I should visit Lenshina. The relationship between her and
ourselves had been cordial from the time of her 'resurrection' in
1953. While it could not but be difficult to embrace such a vibrant
new thing within the staid framework of Lubwa's presbyterianism,
I had been sure, as I mentioned earlier, that the church had to meet
the movement with flexibility and expectation. Instead a pharasaical
reaction had set in and Lumpa had been condemned for illegalities.
"The letter kills", Paul, the ex-Pharisee, had written long ago. "The
Spirit gives life." How often and how grievously down the ages the
institutional church has opted for the spurious security of legalism
for fear of the unpredictable caprice of a spirit that "blows where it
lists". On the one hand, I did not want to embarrass the church
further by seeming to side with 'separatists', but on the other, I
believed it was right once again to greet the charismatic lady, whose
first visit to Lubwa had been made in obedience to what she surely
believed was Jesus's command to her to greet me and to ask for help.

To approach Kasomo by vanette would have been wrong. The
noise of the engine would draw the attention of whatever crowds I
might find there and could cause a tumult. So I went by bicycle
and was almost in the village before anyone was aware of my
coming. Someone went to call Lenshina and I was shown into a
large and finely-built thatched *insaka* or palaver house to await
her. She appeared, dressed in a brightly coloured length of cotton.
But I had to believe my eyes, for she was over twice the size she
had been in 1953. Her once slim face now displayed an ample double
chin and she walked heavily. I told her that I would like a brief
chat without observers and she at once assented, sharply ordering
her hangers-on to move away.

I had not seen her for two years and she had passed through
many troubles. But she asked at once, kindly, for news of our family
and especially Catherine whose name she had given to her own
baby in 1953. I began by asking her about a rumour I had just
heard that "some were saying that Macpherson had taken the Book
of Life" when we had first met in 1953. "That is not true", she said.
"I showed you the mark of the Book. But I did not have it myself.
It belongs to Jesus". Where then, I asked, would such a rumour
come from? "Ask Mushindo", she said with acidity and I realised
that the 'movement' was in sharp conflict with the 'establishment'
at Lubwa. I then said that I was sad to learn that she and her people

had left the church. "But we have not left", she retorted. "We are Christians but we have been put out". "Why?" I asked but all she would again answer was: "Ask Mushindo", pointing to Lubwa where the Revd Paul lived. I refrained from further probing as I realised that the matter agitated her visibly.

A bunch of children had meanwhile drawn near to the *insaka* and were now peeping in. Suddenly Lenshina rounded on them and, with a shout of frenzied anger, sent them scurrying off like chickens. She was obviously under severe nervous strain and by no means at ease in her role as prophetess of a new revelation. As the frenzy subsided she as suddenly became limp and weary. It was time, I knew, to say farewell. I was not to see her again until 1965 when, with the General Secretary of the United Church of Zambia and Paul Mushindo, I was sent to visit her in the detention camp at Mumbwa, west of Lusaka, to which she had been sent after the horrific outbreak of the 'Lumpa War' in 1964.

An unexpected Transfer

The Central African Regional Committee met in Blantyre in 1956 and I was once again elected to represent our Northern Rhodesian work. The Committee's agenda included the urgent matter of filling the post of Principal of the Overtoun Institution at Livingstonia which had been vacant since 1951. The Institution had carried on with an Administration Committee but insistence had grown that a Principal was needed. But for me this was a Nyasaland problem and as I did not know the qualities of our mission staff there, I sat back and listened quietly as the matter was introduced and the discussion began. When, therefore, on the next day and during the lunch break, the Regional Secretary came to see me alone, I was surprised. Would I accept nomination to the Principalship, he asked? Various conversations outside the formal meeting had shown him that others agreed. And so, in a twinkling, it was said and done, and I went back to Mwenzo with most unexpected news for Myra and for our colleagues and friends.

We could not move at once, however, for a missionary from Nyasaland was to come over to the Lubwa district and we would then go east by the lorry that brought him westwards. Moreover the man who was on leave from Mwenzo was not due to return until December. I was anxious to push on with the Old Testament selections in Mwanga in the time left to us, and also to visit the rest of the district. But we were glad of a week's holiday at Chimala in Tanganyika, made possible by the use of Dr Trant's van as far as Mbeya. Baby Myra travelled well and we all enjoyed the bus journey from there to our holiday rest house. The Tanganyika Government appeared to place no restrictions on the building of villages near the roads and so we passed scenes of bustling activity and numerous roadside markets. NRG's policy of pushing villages away from main roads meant that the long distance traveller saw little of local life. Around Mbeya we were amused by an amazingly thin layer of tar rolled on to a stretch of road to be used on the forthcoming visit of Princess Margaret.

Mwangonde Fauld's last journey

The big event of those last months however was an unexpected journey to Karonga following receipt of a telegram from Mrs Faulds. She was coming, she informed us, to inter Mwangonde's ashes at Karonga, and would I drive her there? After quick consultation it was agreed that I should take the chance of a preview of Livingstonia and so I prepared the vanette for a round trip. Matthew Faulds had died in 1955 while we were in Scotland and I had conducted his cremation service. Bangubosa was now living up to her reputation for sudden decisions involving other people's cooperation. But I was in no way reluctant to visit Karonga. Uncle Matthew had drawn vivid word pictures for us, as children, of the lakeshore community in which the mission was set, the mission house that had been engulfed, inch by inch, by the rising of the lake, the warm breezes off the water and swarms of *khungu* fly in their millions lying like clouds on the face of the deep.

For Auntie Doris, the journey through the Karonga hills from Chendo to the lake was packed with memories. It was eighteen years since they had left Nyasaland and her delight in the prospect of reunion with Miriam Nyachirwa and her old friends was irrepressible. Conversation was difficult, however, as we wound through the hills, for the track was stony and the empty vanette clattered ferociously. Then suddenly I had a bright idea: if I took on board a load of large stones they would greatly reduce the noise and moreover we could use them to surround the grave at the lakeshore. I did not then know that there are no stones at all by the lake, and so it proved an even better plan than I imagined. Mwangonde had trekked on foot through those hills many times.

It was therefore most fitting to have hill stones around the lakeshore grave.

When we reached Karonga at last and were warmly welcomed by the Revd Andrew Kayira and a crowd of senior church members, we learned that they had not expected us. The message Mrs Faulds had sent to Livingstonia had not been passed on to them. But they sent out messengers at once, north and south, along the shore and away into the hills of Wenya and Misuku, calling people to come for a special ceremony three days later.

They came streaming in at once from far and wide and when the chosen time arrived there must have been nearly four thousand there. As elsewhere in Malawi the singing had to be heard to be believed. "*Yamara nkono ya nyifwa*", they sang, "The war of death is finished", dancing and clapping to the strong rhythm of a Ngoni war song turned into a paeon of resurrection triumph. Innumerable tributes were paid to Mwangonde and then the District Commissioner spoke briefly. "I, of course, did not know Mr Faulds", he said. "I was a boy at school when he left Karonga. But I've heard his name all over the district and I can affirm that his influence is still strong among the people everywhere." Hundredweights of rice, scores and scores of eggs, vegetables and coins were heaped upon Bangubosa and many wept openly as they embraced her. For myself, the experience brought a keen awareness that I knew dear old Uncle Matthew better now than ever.

Karonga's farewell to Bangubosa was so overflowing in affection that it was very late when at last we started the 70-mile journey to Livingstonia. It involved the fording of the river Lukuru, 'the big one', but fortunately, after months of dry weather, the water ran low. Much of the lake-shore road was rough and as we clattered along, I feared what we were to find only too true at journey's end: that scores of the eggs showered upon Mrs Faulds and packed in the only way possible, in the hundred weights of rice, were cracking and silently scrambling themselves into a sticky mess.

My lady passenger had been accustomed to make that journey by machila in the 1920s and '30s. Her memories of the climb of over 3000 feet from the shore village of Chitimba, by way of 22 hair-pin bends, began to fill her with foreboding. Perhaps we would have to do it on foot, she suggested. When, therefore, we began the ascent well after nightfall, she became very agitated and insisted that I drive at little more than walking pace. Her trepidation was genuine but it was embarrassing for me; for driving uphill in first gear meant that the radiator boiled again and again. We had to stop frequently to let it cool a little and we had no can of water to replenish it. It was late at night when at last we reached Overtoun Institution.

The next day I was introduced to the staff by the chairman of the interim Administration Committee that had held the fort since sudden illness had prevented Dr Robert Walker from assuming the principalship in 1951. Till now, I had always regarded myself as a youngster among the Northern Rhodesian missionaries. But at Livingstonia, the junior members of staff bowed respectfully as we shook hands and, as principal-designate I suddenly felt the weight of my ten years' service. There was, however, little time to stand on ceremony as we had to start off as soon as possible for the 270 mile journey, via Rumphi and Njakwa, back to Mwenzo. I did however renew my acquaintance with a man who was to become a specially valued colleague, Revd Stephen Kauta Msiska, and also with the owner of Chihoro Castle, as he playfully called his house, William Chiswakhata Mkandawire, the Institution's accountant.

Mwenzo's gift of sweet Memories

The last few weeks at Mwenzo raced by. The first rains came in November and the flying ants poured forth in their millions from holes in the earth. Children chased them with wild delight and, as the ants dropped their wings, they roasted them over their picnic fires. Meanwhile gorgeous dragon-flies winged around the marshes and dung-beetles feverishly dug out the softening earth to bury the cattle-droppings in which they had hidden their eggs. Lizards that had haunted the eves of houses in the dry months dropped to the ground to forage in the fresh green grass for the scores of different types of tiny insects that were being born prodigally into that festival of life. And the air was heavy with the pungent fragrance of cypress and eucalyptus.

The missionary couple whose place we had filled for their year of overseas furlough returned shortly before the Livingstonia lorry was due to carry us away. As there were no removal contractors, we had to do it all ourselves, with no way of checking the weight of our crated belongings. Nor could we guess whether our crates would exceed the capacity of the lorry. We believed it would be a five-tonner but it would have to carry 44-gallon drums of petrol for so long a journey. Thus we were greatly relieved when Gibson Mavumbanya arrived, with his 'lorry-boy' and took charge of the loading operation. He was a wise and experienced man, as we were to appreciate often in the next few years. We were especially grateful to find a cushioned bench for the family. But there was just enough space and no more for our crates and bundles, the two spare wheels, the tool-box and the petrol drums.

It was sad to leave Mwenzo. In some ineffable way, we had found there in 1955-56 what we had found in our brief stay in 1951: a joyous fellowship that showed no signs of being spoiled by the racial strains that we had found at Lubwa. There was a delight in friendship which was spontaneous and wholly free from affectation. I remember meeting a man one day whom I had not known well and had not seen for some time. "*Ye Musyani watulota!*" he exclaimed as we met and wrung each other's hands. "Musyani has dreamed of us!" The great Musyani was, of course, the founding ancestor of the Mwanga kingdom, dead perhaps well over 300 years. But who would not respond 'with happy' to such a greeting? So too with "*Kuku, kuku, wana witu*" - that greeting that was accompanied by a gentle embrace, right cheek to right cheek, then left to left, and holding hands; a greeting hard to translate but having in it the root idea of the word for kindness or grace '*icikuku*'. Perhaps 'Welcome, welcome, folks' is as near a rendering as any for the essence of the greeting. We had been addressed with those words on countless occasions; and so we left Mwenzo aware that we were debtors in love to many, many people, and so more conscious than ever of the joy of Christian fellowship.

Chapter 16
LIVINGSTONIA
- THE LAST LAP

The last lap, that is, out of the thirteen years during which I was paid by the Foreign Mission Committee of the Church of Scotland. They were to be followed by four years, under the Home Board, in a teeming Church extension parish in Greenock, after which we returned to Zambia for twelve years' work in education and academic research.

We were aware that it was not long before we would have to do something about schooling for Catherine and Jamie. Teaching at home was far from ideal. When we had expected a return to the Copperbelt to follow our year at Mwenzo we knew there were schools there; but education was totally segregated on racial lines and schools like the one for whites in Mufulira were seed-beds of racism. The unexpected move to Nyasaland meant that we would have to return to Scotland in two or three years' time. For, just as we were resolved not to send our children, as some missionaries had done, to boarding schools in Rhodesia or South Africa, it was no less clear that we could not put them into the local school at Livingstonia. There was a great lack of school places there for a host of bright black children, and if I, as Principal, had arranged for our two to be admitted to the elementary school there, it would, we were sure, have been an abuse of my position.

Nonetheless, there were good reasons for looking forward to our new sphere. For instance, the colour bar was less visible in Nyasaland than in Northern Rhodesia because the settler population was much smaller and there were no mining enterprises such as those on the Copperbelt. In consequence, relations of black and white had a greater openness. This, in turn, was making 'the integration of church and mission' move faster on the eastern side of the Luangwa; an acceleration aided by the historical fact that the Gospel had been proclaimed in Nyasaland a generation earlier than in the west. These factors, along with Mwangonde Faulds' inspiration and vivid memories of my 1947 odyssey, whetted my appetite as the five-tonner hurtled along on a glorious December day.

Ninety-seven years earlier, a little steam boat had chugged into Lake Malawi from its southern end, with David Livingstone on board. A missionary colleague told me what he had heard from some of the old folk in a village near Cape Maclear. I have never found this story in print but was assured that it was held as a strong communal memory among those lake-shore people. They said that when the chug-chug of the boat was heard far away, the local headman called his people together and spoke to them in this wise: "I have heard that they are saying in the south that there is a smoking canoe on the water with *Azungu* in it. If this be true, and if that canoe comes to our place, I say that we must not allow the *Azungu* to come here with their smoking spears and their cruelty." The people affirmed agreement, for they had heard many terrible reports of *Portugueza* and other *Azungu* who beat people and raped their women and sometimes killed, *Azungu* who stole ivory from the chiefs of the people with no shame. "No, we will never allow a *Mzungu* to put his toe on our shore", they declared. So then the *Mwenemuzi* selected those of his young men who had the finest skill of spear and arrow; the women boiled poison for the tips of their weapons; and they waited and waited as the chug-chug came slowly nearer.

As the steamer rounded the headland south of the bay, Livingstone would be on the deck scanning the sandy shoreline. There were canoes beached and he could see the roofs of houses but there was no sign of life. The steamer would have to drop anchor some distance from the beach and so he would have to be rowed ashore in a small boat. Standing in it, he would be scanning the view closely. Lakeshore villages must have a lot of life about them. Then, suddenly he spotted a head peeping above some tall reeds. The young headman's curiosity had got the better of him. This *Mzungu* carried no weapon, no *futi* to kill people from afar. In the instant their eyes met and Livingstone removed his cap in greeting, bowing slightly as he did so. "Spears down", hissed the headman to his warriors, and stepped forward as the stranger reached the shore. Livingstone was smiling kindly. He had clearly come in peace. This was very surprising, very different from what people expected from the *Azungu*. "How beautiful upon the mountains", the lakeshore or the plains, "are the feet of them that bring good tidings of peace".

School readers in northern Malawi told the story of Livingstone under the title 'Chiswamsango', the pathfinder, the one who cut through the undergrowth to 'prepare the way of the Lord'. As in Zambia and in all the regions he traversed, that is how he is remembered in Malawi. Without him, there might well have been no missionary enterprise in central Africa and certainly no Livingstonia.

Peace through the Gospel
Dr Robert Laws, Edward Young and their six companions arrived at Cape Maclear in October 1875, only two and a half years after Livingstone's death in the land of the Lala in Zambia. Malaria struck heavily at those pioneers and so they moved north to Bandawe in 1881. Then, in 1894, Laws began the construction of the Overtoun Institution on the high Khondowe plateau in Phoka country (called Poka, with an aspirated 'p'). One of the many scenic wonders of Khondowe is the fall of the Manchewe river to the Lake with a sheer drop of many hundreds of feet. In caves behind the curtain of the waterfall, Phoka people took refuge from raids of their Ngoni neighbours in the 1890s.

The lakeshore area was in a state of turbulence when Laws's party arrived. The high region of central Malawi had been occupied by the Ngoni around 1855 at the end of their long wanderings which had taken them as far north as Tanzania. There, their great leader Zwangendaba had died. He had led them in flight from the grim upheaval that befell the Zulu empire of Tshaka in 1818. Like the Israelites, like the Anglo-Saxons, the Vikings and many more of history's intruders, the Ngoni had ended as conquerors a great trek that they had begun as fugitives. Nicknamed Mazitu and Mapundi in various parts of Zambia, Malawi and Mozambique, the Ngoni had been dreaded over a wide area for a generation by the time the missionaries appeared among the Tonga and other loose-knit lakeshore communities who were bearing the brunt of Ngoni raiding.

Somehow in the midst of countless hazards and alarms and the utter unpredictability of each new day, the missionaries managed to translate a few selected passages from the Bible. One chosen from the Old Testament was that vision, in Isaiah 11, of an end of all hurting and destruction, when even wolves and sheep would live happily together and when the leopard would lie down with the kid. One day a probably halting rendering of these words was read to a congregation of Tonga crofters and fisherfolk. They would listen with respect but, away from the missionaries, they would deride the ludicrous idea mercilessly. "Leopard lie beside kids - not on your life. These Azungu are crazy - *balikufuntiratu!*" But time went on. Then came William Koyi, a Xhosa student from Lovedale in Cape Province who had volunteered to help the missionaries to gain access to the Ngoni court. His language being akin to Chingoni, he might be acceptable to King Mwambera as a Tonga emissary could not be. With great courage, and unarmed, Koyi at last found himself in the royal presence. Progress, however, was slow and it took a long time for Mwambera to agree to allow even one black teacher to enter his territory. But Koyi's ministry of reconciliation succeeded at last and it was the Ngoni who, before his early death in 1886, nicknamed him Mtusane, the go-between, the bridger of the gulf.

So it came to pass that, one fine day, a great congregation gathered for the festival of Communion. On one side of the minister sat an elder of the Tonga people, so recently ruthlessly raided; and on the other an elder from among the wild Ngoni as a missionary had called those arrogant intruders. As the service proceeded, one man in the congregation was twitching with excitement. As soon as the benediction was spoken and the people rose to go, he rushed among his friends crying, "Today I have seen it. With these two very eyes of mine. Yes, I have now seen it. He was right". "What have you seen, brother?" they demanded. "I have seen the leopard lie down with the kid". For, in Christ, as Paul said, there is a new creature, a new humanity altogether; he breaks down the middle wall of partition and makes foes into friends.

Khondowe

The plateau that Robert Laws chose, high above the mosquitoes and far from everywhere else, as the site of what he dreamed to make the university of Central Africa, is a place of splendid vistas. When we arrived, the rains were beginning and the air was piquant with the strong perfume of the eucalyptus trees that edged the road to the principal's house. The dust-laden haze of the dry months had been laid; the visibility was sharp and the colours bright. As the edge of the table-land was just a short step from the houses built for senior missionaries, the massed tops of the trees in the valleys roundabout presented a Persian pattern of rich reds and many shades of green on the millions of new leaves, spreading below us like a mighty carpet. Here and there, that carpet was holed, as it were, by the clearings of the scattered villages from which many of the estate labourers climbed every morning to the Institution. If you did not live on the plateau, you had to face a daily climb up the rain-scarred tracks from the *malambo* beneath. And from 3000 feet below great milk cans were carried, before dawn, on the shoulders of a team of lakeshore men who handed them over, half way up the mountain side, to a team of porters from the plateau.

On its landward side, Khondowe is ringed with mountains, the most striking being Nyamkhowa, 4000 feet above the Institution. On these mountains live small communities of Phoka hill people in villages with names like Hanja, and Mbura and Chakaka. From time to time, on shopping expedition to the stores of Mandala and Kandodo (the London and Blantyre Company at Khondowe), they would visit our houses with gourds of strong dark honey. They seemed shy, those slim men of the mountains, plaided in lengths of black cotton, belted with strips of goat skin.

The British annexation of Malawi, under Sir Harry Johnston, Consul of Her Brittanic Majesty, had been quickly followed, in 1891, by the imposition of universal taxation of the black population. The colonial subjugators were determined, like Rhodes's agents in the two Rhodesias, to extract the maximum amount in taxation and to apply it, profitably, to the costs of what they called 'administration'. But for all those decades till Malawi became an independent nation in 1964, the people of the mountains above Khondowe systematically eluded the collectors. There were no motor roads and so the colonial bwanas had to climb the steep tracks on foot. Invariably, they would find the scattered villages deserted and would turn back in frustration and anger, without attempting to reach the more remote settlements. As the afternoon sped towards evening and the officers were picking their way down the steep slopes with the great mass of the mountains obtruding a dark shadow between them and the westering sun, something would make them turn back and there they would see the hill folk, silhouetted along the sky line, waving them farewell.

Robert Laws's understanding of the Gospel was based on an incarnational theology, comprehending the whole of life. Proof of the breadth of his vision was provided by the deliberate inclusion of every type of artisan skill in his pioneer team, and by his determination to relate sound agriculture and farsighted forestry to the evangelistic, educational and medical programme of the Institution. The Homestead, at the north end of the estate, had been ambitiously planned. By our time, alas, it had dwindled to little more than a vegetable patch. The poor quality of soil combined with the difficulties of missionary recruitment combined to defeat Laws' dream of a community self-sufficient in food. We now had to depend therefore, on the purchase of maize and other grains from buying centres in the Henga valley to the south which our lorry had to collect in all weathers. Similarly, the forestry plantation at Vungu Vungu had never fulfilled the original grand design and tree-planting had not been maintained systematically. Yet what remained of the tall cypress and juniper trees made Vungu Vungu a delightful spot for a picnic.

The founder had been a man of unique qualities of leadership, thinking ahead not only of most of his colleagues on the field but also of the home church. Yet, like us all, he was a child of his own time. So he ordained that, while the houses of staff members with university training would have a lake view for inspiration, artisans' houses were to look inwards to the Institution; and the bigger and better houses were allocated to the graduates. I heard too from Malawian friends who remembered Laws personally that, if sent with a note to his house, one had to stand some distance away and signal to call attention. Only when summoned, could the emissary approach the big house with his missive. The Doctor could also be interviewed in his office in the General Administration block but his office there was upstairs and a clerk would have to be asked to request the favour of an audience.

Truly "we have this treasure in clay water-pots" as Paul said. But, in the case of Laws, as of Chisholm of Mwenzo, there were few cracks in the pot; it was not for nothing that he took as his own watchword another word from Paul: "The love of Christ constrains us" (2 Cor 5.14). Laws would have agreed, at least in retrospect, I am sure, that a fellowship in commitment exerts on us, in innumerable ways, the constraints of the spirit of truth and love: and that this is so even when at first such constraints evoke frustration, irritation and even pique in our souls.

Take, for example, the dream-house designed for the Institution's Principal, and so, in the first instance, for himself. It was to look as like as possible to a house in his native Aberdeen. Khondowe had no granite, and so he had to accept a grey rock called soapstone instead. The house was to be double-storeyed, with basement quarters below for servants. Its rooms were to be generous in size and to include a private study, while the council room in which the Senatus was to meet would have a more official study attached. The building was nearing the height of the ground floor rooms when Laws went on furlough. In his absence and at the instigation, I was told, of Dr Elmslie, the plan was then radically altered. A single-storeyed house, the staff agreed, was big enough and so a roof was erected, using corrugated iron which was painted red. The result was something that, from a distance, could have passed for a tobacco barn. Its great lounge remained a lounge, but the dining room and the private study had to serve as bedrooms. A smaller room at the front provided a third bedroom. But the most drastic modification was that the stair-hall had to be used as the dining room and also as a passage from the house to the council chamber. Thus the lounge and dining room were as far separated as possible. I do not know how the Laws family reacted to such a *fait accompli*. But it seemed that the original plan to house the servants in the basement immediately below the ground floor was abandoned and separate servants' quarters had to be erected away from the house. *Sic transit gloria mundi*.

Opposition to Federation

The story of the growth of the African voice in the politics of Nyasaland and the two Rhodesias has been recorded by scholars in recent years. It is enough to say that the earliest organisations of the proto-nationalists of Malawi, were led to a notable degree by men who had received formal education at Livingstonia and Blantyre. It was the rise of Roy Welensky and his alliance with Godfrey Huggins of Southern Rhodesia which alerted black people to the real menace of the plan of those vociferous spokesmen of the 'settlers' to consolidate 'white supremacy' north of the Zambezi with the support of the South African government.

Welensky's universal unpopularity among the indigenous peoples of Zambia has already been mentioned. But I found in Malawi a less pessimistic mood and a more articulate resolve not to acquiesce under the already three-year old Federation. Indeed Malawi had already witnessed several clashes between the colonial government and followers of the Nyasaland African Congress. There had been riots at Cholo and then at Chikwawa and

Chiradzulu in the south in the first months of the Federation. Cholo was the scene of a second wave of unrest in which police rifles killed two Malawians. That had been followed by the burning of some estates owned by white planters and as 'the forces of law and order' intensified their efforts to suppress black anger against the Federation, district officers were faced with large-scale tax evasion and defaulters who were caught filled the jails to overflowing.

The political tension, however, detracted in no way from the welcome we received. The stone house was full again and this seemed to please the community. The Institution was now 62 years old but I was only the fifth principal. The head of the Engineering Department who had served as chairman of the Administration Committee, handed over to me very helpfully and I began at once to visit the departments of the Institution and to call on the homes of the staff.

In 1956 there were nine departments: the primary and secondary schools; the Teacher Training Department; the Theological Department; the Medical Aid Training School attached to the David Gordon Memorial Hospital; the Commercial Training Department centred on the General Office; and the three related departments offering five-year apprenticeships in Electrical, Motor and Water Engineering, in Building and in Carpentry. In order to get to know the pupils, students and apprentices of the Institution I undertook to visit each department at least once a week and spend an hour or so in general discussion and in Bible Study with them.

I believe it was on my first visit to the senior Primary School that a slim lad, with Arabic features, leapt up at the end of my brief greeting with a question: "What is civilisation?" he called out. His tense expression and piercing gaze told me that he was in deadly earnest. "What do you think it is?" I replied, after the manner of Socrates, sensing that his question sprang from a burning rejection of 'the white man's' vaunted claim to a civilisation that justified his superiority over Africa's peoples. "Is it civilised", he fired back, "to fly in aeroplanes over where people are sleeping, also little children, and burn them with bombs to death?" "No", I answered from life-long conviction, "it is barbaric. I can find nothing but cowardly evil in bombing, nothing civilised and no courage". At once the passion left his eyes. "Thank you, sir", he said and sat down. I was sure that, had I replied with a description of civilisation as the property of Europe and contrasted with it the ways of 'backward peoples', he would have hated me cordially. For him, I guessed, Welensky's Federation was the supreme exponent of white arrogance and the RAF's 'wiping out' operations in the Mau Mau emergency in Kenya demonstrated a like assumption that 'might is right'. His young soul was aflame with indignation against the 'oppressors' and he spoke for multitudes like himself.

In the Footsteps of Mwangonde Faulds

We had been in residence for only a few weeks when I was asked to add to my duties the managership of the thirty or so primary schools in the Karonga district. It was an unexpected chance to tread in the footprints of Mwangonde Faulds. There were two Assistant School Managers in the district, Revds Andrew Kayira and Yoram Msopole, supervising primary schools on the lake-shore and in the hills respectively. I had, of course, met Kayira when Mrs Faulds and I had gone from Mwenzo to Karonga to inter her husband's ashes there. On my first visit to those schools, I realised that those two men were experienced administrators and that they had excellent relationships with the local communities and with the teachers. Why, I wondered, were they only Assistants to the Manager? It was to take some time to have them recognised as Managers by the Government Education Department. During that time, I was to have the chance to visit all the Karonga district schools and to find how tough was the terrain that Mwangonde Faulds had traversed by bike and on foot. For he had had no motor vehicle at his disposal. Of course his touring had taken more time and given him less time for office administration but his journeys, whether by bicycle or on foot, had enabled him to form strong friendships and so to leave a sweet memory of a kindly caring pastor.

On my first visit to Lubwa in 1947 - well over 400 miles from Lake Malawi - I had met a student there from Karonga. "Did you know Matthew Faulds?" I asked him, but immediately knew it was a foolish question, for Mwangonde had left Africa in 1938 and the student was no more than 18 years old. "Yes, I knew him well", he replied. "He used to come to my village". His home was in the Misuku hills, a long way from the Faulds' home on the lake-shore. "You must have been very young", I said. "I was just a little boy", replied the young man. "But when Bwana Faulds came, he was used to play with us children and to know our names. He spoke my language very well". So now, 19 years after Mwangonde's farewell, I was to visit his beloved haunts.

The minister in charge of the congregation on the Kondowe plateau and the smaller congregations on the hillsides below was Stephen Kauta Msiska. We had formed a reciprocal affection on the instant of our first and very brief meeting in 1947. He included me now on his 'preaching plan' and so I took my turn in visiting the church folk beyond the bounds of the plateau. Stephen promised to arrange a visit, as soon as possible, to an almost legendary place on the lake-shore called Mlowe. The village was famous simply because of the existence there of the Mlowe Health Centre and of the wonderful work being done by the man who had dreamed it into being, Ernest Michael Mtawali.

Mtawali had worked for some years at the hospital on the plateau. As a Medical Assistant, he was trained in general diagnosis and could prescribe treatment for the general range of illness. He was greatly respected by all the hospital staff and had the full trust of the missionary doctor and sisters. His use of English was excellent and he had a quick wit. The story was told of a hospital committee, attended by the District Commissioner from Rumphi, which was reviewing the examination results, written and oral, of the trainee Medical Orderlies. "This chap", said the DC of one of them, "clearly thinks he is the whole cheese". After a thoughtful silence, a local headman touched Mtawali's arm and whispered, "Why does he say that this young man he is whole cheese?" "He means", replied Mtawali behind his hand, "that he thinks he's the cat's whiskers", thus further confounding the headman's confusion.

For some years Mtawali had worked at the David Gordon Memorial Hospital on the plateau. Then, one day, he mentioned quietly that he was planning to resign and go down to Mlowe. The Scots sister was shocked and tried to plead with him to drop the idea at once. "We need you here", she said. But he had made up his mind. "I want to move from curative to preventive medicine", he explained and he believed Mlowe was the ideal place for such a project. For some time he had been propagating his idea in the lake-shore community. Malaria, as they all knew, took a relentless and grievous toll and both infant mortality and the deaths of women in childbirth gave a sense of mourning and deprivation to the area. A new approach to sanitation was vital and the menace of polluted water must be checked, he declared. Stagnant water, in which the anopheles mosquito bred, must be done away with completely. The local sub-chief organised a collection of money to start off the plan for the erection of a 'health centre' and £35 - a great sum at that time and place - was handed over to Mtawali.

Stephen Kauta took me to visit Mlowe at the end of the rains in 1957 and we spent a happy night in the great man's home. By then the project had already scored signal success. The ante-natal death rate was almost nil and as a result of the deep, stone-lined circular latrines, mosquitoes had quit the area in their millions in company with those noisome bluebottles that had done a brisk commerce in intestinal diseases, especially in children, by ferrying myriads of germs from the shallow, putrid latrines to little human bodies. Fatalism was now in flight before the forces of faith and hope, that Mtawali, in the love of Christ, had mustered.

Chapter 17
WINDS OF
CHANGE

In March 1957, Ghana won its independence from Britain under the leadership of Kwame Nkrumah. The celebrations were attended by Harry Nkumbula, President of Northern Rhodesia's African National Congress, and T.D.T. Banda, secretary-general of the Nyasaland Congress. They met Dr Hastings Banda there in Accra and no doubt the doctor was urged to return to the land of his birth. Letters from people like Henry Masauko Chipembere had been pleading with him for some time to fulfil his people's need for 'a kind of hero'. Around the middle of the year, I received a letter from Hastings Banda in Ghana asking me to tell him my opinion of the various leaders of the Nyasaland Congress. They were little more than names to him, he said. He would therefore appreciate my frank comment, to help him to distinguish between those who could be trusted and those who were self seekers. I appreciated his problem, especially now that he seemed to believe that he could not for long resist those insistent pleas. But I replied to say that I did not wish to meet his request, for I would be taking too great a responsibility. Indeed, I did not know the Congress leaders well. I could have reported local comment about some of them, but decided it was better to decline. I did not hear from him again for quite a while.

A Hazardous Trip to Karonga

As the rains ended in April 1957 I planned a tour of the Karonga schools on the lake shore, which Andrew Kayira supervised. The narrow belt of flat land between the mountains and the lake was naturally very wet and the grey-black earth of the road was quickly turned into squelching mud by the rains. I heard it called 'cotton soil', I never knew why; but it was certainly very different in texture from the heavy brown clay-laden earth of the roads around the Khondowe plateau and in the hinterland.

On that journey in April I was accompanied by Kayira and Stephen Kauta. We had had meetings at the plateau and were able to save expense by travelling north together. I cannot recall the purpose of Kauta's trip but the three of us enjoyed each other's company to the full. However, as we moved towards the Lukuru river, I sensed Kayira's apprehension. There had been a severe rainstorm in the last few days and all the streams and rivers were in spate. Lukuru, 'the great one', had figured in Mwangonde Faulds's vivid tales of his Karonga years. The day was moving to twilight when we first heard the rush of the waters. "We'll ask the villagers about the crossing", said Kayira. "They'll know if any vehicle has crossed today."

The local news was worrying. The customary fording line had been altered by the shifting of a broad sand bank during the recent torrential rain. "But if you are careful", said one of the villagers, "you should manage if you follow that line"; and he pointed to a new landing place on the other side which only heightened my apprehension. For I was driving an Austin 10 van with a much lower clearance than the Landrovers that the government officers used. But, as we were now nearer Karonga than Livingstonia, we decided to try. About 12 yards across however we stuck; and I could feel the sandbank dissolving under the wheels. The van then tipped slightly under the rush of the water and that was that. With shoes and stockings in my hand, I waded back to the bank where my companions were standing.

Heavy clouds lay above the mountains. "You'd better stay in the van", said Kauta. "We'll stay here watching the river and if we hear the water speeding we'll warn you. If you feel the van moving, you tell us". So the night was passed, my friends with hankies tied around their heads, slapping at the assailing hordes of mosquitoes, and myself straining to hear any change in the thud-thud of the river against the van and fighting exhaustion as best I could. The clouds, however, held back their torrents; the movements of the van were slight; and at last we saw the first beams of dawn flashing over the black mass of the Livingstone Mountains on the Tanzanian side of the lake.

We were hungry, but first we had to find help. Lupembe village was not far off, on the north bank of Lukuru, so I went there to report our plight. The response was immediate. All the able-bodied men came to the river, once they had collected their powerful little axes, followed by the children. Our crisis was at once lightened by laughter. But our helpers wasted no time. Two tall slim young trees were selected for felling and, as soon as they had fallen, the little axes swarmed into the kill like lion cubs, sharing their parents' quarry. In minutes, the trunks had been stripped of every single branch and twig. Twig or branch stumps could damage the undercarriage of a vehicle and so the little axes smoothed the trunk flush. There was a hint of competition between the teams that stripped the two trees and a shout of triumph burst from the winners who clapped for themselves and jeered their rivals playfully.

Then came the great moment. Stripping to loin-cloths, a group of men began to probe gingerly with the narrow tips of the trees, under the car, until at last the tips came through to the other end, evoking another lusty cheer. It had been a delicate operation and some of the men had plunged their faces under the water as they slid the trees in behind the wheels. Now, with two teams of four at either end and with a great cry of "*Pezulani* - Up with it" they lifted our vehicle right out of the water and bore it to the far bank. '*Pezuleni*' belongs to the slang of the South African and Zambian mines, where no doubt some of our rescuers had once sojourned.

We had no way of expressing thanks except by words. "*Iyai, kulije kantu*" said the men of Lupembe, "It's nothing. We are happy because you are safe". As I switched on the ignition and to my great relief the engine fired, another cheer arose from the crowd, the children cavorting and turning cart-wheels as we started on our way to Karonga. But we did not get far, for there was water in the sump. We drained it but had no spare oil with us. However, as often happened, we found a willing teenager who raced off on a rattly bicycle to purchase a gallon of oil for us from an Asian trader at the *boma*. As we awaited his return, one of my companions said: "I didn't tell you this sooner, but you know, not far from where we were stranded, a woman was taken by a crocodile just a few days ago, while she was drawing water from the river. But God has been good to us." Spontaneously we affirmed our gratitude in a verse of one of the Tumbuka hymns:

> *Wati wabe na lusungu*   He will be merciful
> *Ku abo vyalema lero*   To those who are weary today.

There could be no self-congratulation, in such a song, that, while that poor woman had died in the crocodile's jaws, we were safe. Rather it was, as surely it must be, inconceivable not to acknowledge our real sense of blessing for the cutting of our fetters of fear. Thanksgiving cannot be stifled because blessing is not experienced everywhere at the same time.

Kayira's home was very close to the shore of the lake at Karonga. We were welcomed by the whole family and fed sumptuously on *nsima* and fresh succulent fish, followed by scones with jam and tea. Family prayers took place by the light of a storm lantern before the younger people went to bed. We three men, being very weary, were more than ready for rest ourselves, but the insistent song of the night-breeze off the lake, as it set the tall reeds chattering, kept me awake for quite a while.

Next morning we began our tour of the lake-shore schools. Because government equipment grants in Nyasaland were then even more parsimonious than in Northern Rhodesia, headmasters had to ingather fees from their pupils and so carried a heavier responsibility, involving the added strain of having sometimes to turn a child away, not just because there was no place for him but because he had no money. Andrew Kayira, and his colleague in the hills, Yoram Msopole, were thus involved in a monthly book-keeping task.

Despite these burdens, the two Assistant School Managers had established relationships of caring and trust with the teachers under their supervision, yet maintaining and expecting high standards. The more I saw of their work, the more I admired these two men and the more I was convinced that, even though they were fully stretched by their combined roles as school administrators and ministers of huge 'parishes', they should be nominated to full and not just to assistant managership of those schools. Fortunately I was able to persuade the Joint Council, then integrating the work of the local church and the Scottish mission, to press for government recognition of such a change.

A splendid District Commissioner

At Karonga, I had an experience which came as a very pleasant surprise. When Kayira and I returned from our tour, a letter was waiting for him from the District Commissioner, Joe Maynard, inviting him and me to dinner. The Maynards and the Kayiras had the kind of relationship that should exist between a local government officer and parish minister. Yet never before - nor indeed after - did I find such a relationship. Elsewhere, white was white and black was black and, one could add not inaccurately, never the twain would meet around the same dining table.

The DC, I gathered, had eaten at the Kayira's House. He and his wife were exceptional people. It was not surprising therefore when less than two years later in the bitter days of the so-called 'Nyasaland Emergency', Maynard was transferred to 'special duties' at provincial head-quarters. He was so much the friend of the people of his district that he would have perhaps been an impediment to the military in their concerted exercise of ruthless 'pacification'. But more of that later!

Kenneth Kaunda's Cousin

The farthest north of the lakeshore schools was at Kaporo. Its name means 'slave' and there may well have been associations there with the Arab slave traffic, masterminded by a man called Mlozi, in the early 1890s. At Kaporo, a young man called Robert Gwebe Nyirenda came to greet us. I did not realise then that he was a nephew of the mother of Kenneth Kaunda, Helen Nyamu-Nyirenda. Robert was then, I guess, in his thirties. He and I had a long chat together, during which he spoke passionately about his people's deep opposition to Welensky's Federation. I was glad of the opportunity to hear a black man speak in detail and with such a combination of intellectual conviction and deep emotion. I was glad, too, that he could speak to so openly to a white stranger like myself. I could not fail to understand his tears as he spoke of the real threat of the northward extension of the hated system of racial oppression that flourished in the south. "Please somehow help us", he pled. "We still look to Livingstonia."

A few days later, near Karonga boma, I was nearly knocked over by a bicycle that came hurtling down a shady lane and onto a track of sun-dried pitted clay. The rider was tall and white-haired, and a crack on one lens of his spectacles had been covered by a strip of sticking plaster. I learned later from Andrew Kayira that he was none other than Robert Gwebe Nyirenda senior, father of the young man at Kaporo and ancient uncle of the future President of Zambia. He was then in his upper eighties.

A Night on the Lakeshore

I have another memory of the Kaporo area. Kayira and I had decided to sleep on the shore, I cannot clearly remember why. It was very warm near the water's edge and little groups of sleepers were dotted along the beach. Like them, we slung a mosquito net over our sleeping bags. I was still not accustomed to the nocturnal music of the lake and the breeze in the rushes, and so, though I slept deeply for a few hours, I woke very early, feeling restless. I was aware of a great urge to refresh my jaded frame with a bath in the lake. So I rose softly, not to disturb Kayira, took my cake of Lifebuoy soap, and tiptoed towards the dark water. The faintest fingertips of dawn were poking from behind the black mass of the Tanzanian mountains beyond but a heavy mist enveloped the water, suppressing that first light to the merest glimmer. I had a glorious bath, soaping myself again and again, and longing to burst into song yet not able to do so for fear of awaking the sleepers. As I laved, I was aware of a quickening rush of dawn light and turned round to face the lake. What I found startled me sharply. Of course it was no more than an optical illusion. I had seen its like two years earlier at dawn on the banks of Loch Tay, in a spell of blistering warmth, while we were on leave in Scotland. But the force of the illusion was in no way reduced now. It seemed as though the peaks of the Livingstone range were right overhead, wreathed in swirling mist. Some freak refraction must cause such illusions which go as quickly as they come, especially in a land where dawn is very swift. So, for me, there on the upper reaches of the great lake the illusion fled as the sunrise swelled to the glory of morning. But my heart was beating faster than usual.

Our first Colleague from Ireland

I told you, some time ago, about the quiet Scots missionary lady who joined our staff at Lubwa in the early fifties because, along with scores of other missionaries, she had had to leave China after the so-called 'communist revolution' there. Another missionary enterprise affected by events in the Far East was that of the Presbyterian Church in Ireland; and so it came about that their first contribution to the work of the Church of Central Africa Presbyterian in Malawi was the appointment of the Revd Bill Jackson, who arrived in 1957 with his wife and baby boy. He was to prove a splendid colleague, assiduous and effective in the study

of Kya-Ngonde, the main language of the Karonga District. For
the Joint Council resolved that he should work in that area, though
in the first instance he would have to live at Khondowe. During
his initial months of study, I continued my special relationship
with Karonga. In the next two years we were to learn more of
Jackson's worth and of his courage. Since then we have heard that
he has served in some of the most dangerous areas of Northern
Ireland and has associated actively with endeavours to replace
recrimination and savage conflict by reconciliation. In 1957 he came
to join us with that quality of enlightened understanding and
positive grace that were so much required in that time of accelerating
but long overdue transition.

Increasing Consultation with local Colleagues

Overtoun Institution was, as I mentioned earlier, what would
probably now be called a polytechnic. Departments which planned
their own courses and selected their own students shared the use of
accommodation and grounds mainly in two impressive buildings:
the college on the higher ground and the long double-storeyed
structure that housed the technical departments, at the junction of
our main roads. I became aware, on arrival, that, as can so easily
happen, there was a lack of consultation especially between the
departments of primary education, secondary education and teacher
training which shared the college building and its grounds. Because
there was no need for curricular coordination between them in
view of the fact that they each were obliged to follow teaching
programmes in accordance with Nyasaland Government policy, it
was in the delicate areas of space-sharing and the use of common
facilities that consultation was needed. So, with the approval of the
Senatus, a committee was set up, consisting of the head and deputy
of each of the three departments, with myself as convener.

It proved at once that it met a distinct but bottled-up need and
so there was no problem in finding agenda for it. It began to serve
as solvent for a number of potential stresses and personal tensions.
In our urgent task of integrating the work of the Scottish 'Foreign
Mission' into the life of the Malawian church and community, it
played a timely role.

For instance, there was the matter of the repair and maintenance
of staff houses. From the start of Livingstonia in 1875, the church
in Scotland had providently and indeed inevitably budgeted, in two

separate accounts, for 'FM Houses' and 'WFM Houses', ie houses of male missionaries and their families for which the Foreign Mission Committee in Edinburgh took direct responsibility, and the houses of women missionaries whose support and welfare increasingly became the concern of the 'WFM' working as a splendid handmaid of the whole enterprise by taking special care of women agents in foreign fields. In the earlier decades, the housing of 'nationals' employed by missions - and initially called 'native staff' - had been left in the hands of the missionaries on the field who could rely on unpaid help from local populations for the building, in local materials, of thatched houses in keeping with local styles. Bit by bit, however, the Scottish church had made special grants for the building of some African staff houses in burnt brick and with corrugated iron roofs, which, though notably smaller, would harmonise with the standards of other buildings on mission stations. Thus mission stations became visibly different from and, in every way, grander than the villages round about them.

In this way, also, the seeds of a problem were sown for us who came later. We had, at Khondowe, the *madoda*, houses built on either side of the main road to the Institution which housed a few of the mission's married staff of 'nationals'. We also had a few houses for such people as the local minister and the senior hospital assistant. But we did not have funds for their repair and maintenance. Now, in 1957, we had a growing number of well-trained Malawian staff, some of whom had attended special courses abroad and one of whom, the deputy head of the secondary school department, was a university graduate. And those colleagues, fruits as they so clearly were of the vision and labours of the pioneers, were not separated from missionaries by that wide educational gap that had seemed to make social integration less urgent when very few local employees had completed primary education. The mission, in terms of the formal educational patterns it had imported, was thus producing social strata which were bound to cause tensions, sooner or later.

"Principal", said the deputy headmaster in his quiet voice at one of the early meetings of the Consultative Committee, "may I ask: is it possible to have some improvements in our housing, for instance, whitewashing of interior walls? Houses like mine haven't been..." But he was cut off sharply by a missionary who, forgetting to address the chair, snapped in hot anger: "What'll you be wanting next? Do you like your egg turned? Get some whitewash like everyone else and do it yourself."

It was my turn to chip in, albeit too late. The teacher had raised an important matter, I said, and it was right to raise it here. But I could hear the missionary still growling, and so I had to spell out my comment carefully. Now was clearly the time, I said, to do two things: (a) to recall and explain the purposes for which the old FM and WFM Repairs Accounts had been set up; and (b) to search openly together, in a time of financial stringency, for a new system that reckoned with the realities of our situation today.

"But why can't he decorate his house like everyone else?" asked the missionary, still obsessed with one idea, the laudable principle of self-reliance. "You and I don't decorate our houses", I replied. "Perhaps we should. It would save expense. But instead we follow the practice of the Foreign Mission Committee over the last 80 years". The Committee then resolved to ask the Senatus to take such action as I had suggested. As we closed the meeting, my missionary colleague was obviously still unhappy. "Don't let people like Ngana get everything they ask", she said earnestly. "Where can we get the money for African staff house repairs?" "That's our new problem", I said, "but look! you worry me. You are like a farmer who works tirelessly to clear the ground, turn the soil, sow the seed, weed the field while the corn comes to fulness - and then curses the harvest". She looked at me, straightly and smiled a quick smile: and I blessed her for her readiness to discard outmoded attitudes in face of current realities. "We have this treasure in earthen vessels", said Paul as we noted earlier, "so that the glory may be God's not ours".

Another Wound for healing

The Consultative Committee, not long after, faced another crisis. As matters for its agenda were reaching me, the senior teacher in the primary department sent along a note: 'Agenda: Use of first Names'. Mr Chirembo was a well-built upright man, more thin-skinned than thick, a leader of church praise and member of a respected family. His note was cryptic. So I went to see him and asked what lay behind it. "I'll explain at the meeting", he replied politely. "It's difficult", I said, "to chair a meeting when there's something on the agenda of which you have no idea. I'll be glad if you'd tell me what you have in mind in this mysterious item!" He laughed pleasantly at that. "Well, it's a simple matter really. It's about whether teachers and others in authority should be called by first names before their pupils". "And has this happened recently?" I asked. It had, he told me. A woman missionary involved in a branch of primary school work had entered his office when he was surrounded by pupils and said, "Webster, I've got to see you today about that equipment business". "I'll come as soon as I'm finished here, Jenny", he had replied. Her reaction was quick. He had insulted her by using her first name and so she had reported the matter to the Mission's Education Secretary who, in turn, had warned Chirembo of disciplinary action if he showed such familiarity again. "But she used my first name first", he said to me. "Is it all right for her to do so just because I'm an African?" I thanked him for 'putting me in the picture', as we say, and decided that it was right to place the matter in its cryptic form on the agenda.

"Now we come to item 4, the use of first names", I said as the Committee completed the amiable and positive discussion of the first three items. I knew that this was one of the situations in which a homily could not be avoided, a clear, exhortatory statement presented incontrovertibly. And so I began: "This item is about how we address each other in the presence of our pupils or students. As I see it, it is really simple. We live and work together and so it should be easy for us to use first names, whether we are local people or whether we have come here from abroad. And of course if I call Mr So-and-So by his first name in friendship, I want him to call me Fergus. I hope we all agree."

Five of the silent faces round the table indicated agreement. The woman missionary who had quarreled with Chirembo looked at me intently and I detected the darkness of displeasure in her eyes. But that other colleague, the one who had blazed up about the whitewashing of Mr Ngana's house, expressed approval audibly, shaking her head vigorously up and down.

"That seems to be agreed", I went on, "and of course it should be. We're here, all of us, because of the Gospel and we should expect to find deep friendship in what the New Testament calls 'the body of Christ'. But I think we'll also agree that, when we speak to each other in the presence of our pupils or students, we should use a more respectful form of address, Miss So-and-So, Mr So-and-So. I hope this is also agreed by us all..." Again, the silent faces registered assent. "Good", I said. "Now let's move to item 5".

As the meeting closed, I felt grateful to both the parties in what could have become a horrible clash: to Chirembo for making it clear by the look on his face that he accepted my 'magisterial' approach to the issue, in general rather than particular terms, and for accepting annonymity in an issue that had made his ego burn; and to the lady for refraining from anger, even though at the cost of biting her lip. It is no wonder that the apostle Paul, in his letters about the Gospel, had to reiterate so often the need for reciprocal compassion among those who bear the name of Jesus.

Local Symptoms of the Central African disease

As postscript to that memory of Webster Chirembo's cryptic *agendum*, I recall him as a man of strong political emotion, bitterly resentful of the perfidious imposition of Federation and full of anger at how it was developing. Thus much more than personal pique lay behind what could have been regarded as a petty, parochial crisis. For Welensky was very busy: a Franchise Bill, accepted by the white-dominated Federal Assembly, was raising the property qualifications for the vote which would reduce the number of eligible black voters. Moreover, his Electoral Extension Bill - sounding so progressive and liberal - was in fact further curtailing African participation in political life by a cunning reshaping of electoral areas. And, as we shall mention later, the political situation was going to move swiftly towards racial confrontation under Welensky's leadership.

It had worried me, in Northern Rhodesia, in the years before Federation and just after its inception, that the churches, mostly white-led, were so woolly in their witness about an issue that was so obviously embittering the whole life of Central Africa. It was good to find a much clearer attitude on the part of the Church of Central Africa Presbyterian in Nyasaland, with both the Synod of Blantyre and the Synod of Livingstonia pronouncing on such matters as the Franchise Bill and the Federal Extension Bill and speaking on behalf of the country's voiceless indigenous population.

A Dog in the Sanctuary

For us, as a family, 1958 began with the birth of Alison Mary, who was delivered by the doctor and sister at Ekwendeni Hospital on January 10th. She was the heaviest of our babies at birth, 9lbs 7ozs. Some weeks later, she was baptised by Stephen Kauta, one of about twenty babies mustering forty parents. The great church at Livingstonia was packed and we parents were squeezed closely together on the front pews.

Now it so happened that, not long before, we had taken over a dachshund, called Pip, from a family who were going on leave. I have never found the frenetic little, squiggly, bow-legged yelpers attractive, and Pip had no notable points of charm to redeem the situation. It took him some time to accept a new family and new surroundings. Yet he would follow us, unbidden, wherever we might go. We were therefore especially careful to see that he was always securely penned into the kitchen when we went to Sunday morning worship.

For some time Myra had not been attending that service because of Alison's arrival. On the Sunday of Baptism, however, we were all at church. Pip, we believed, was duly imprisoned. But suddenly, I heard the pattering of his Teutonic claws on the brick floor and the quick breathless panting that accompanied his movements. "That's Pip", I whispered to Myra. There was nothing we could do, however, packed as we were in the middle of a long line of parents with babies and young children. At that instant, I was acutely aware of a malevolent eye-beam drilling the back of my head, as a concentrated eye-beam can certainly do. In the ensuing agitation, I glanced round, as much for momentary relief from the beam as to identify its emitter. There she was, about eight rows behind, a respected Scots colleague who loved cats but had a pathological loathing for 'man's best friend'. "Hilda's seen Pip", I said to Myra, "and she's furious".

Pip, however, had no social inhibitions. He was having a jolly time and had now reached the chancel. I was very afraid that he would mistake some item of chancel furniture for a wayside tree and commit the ultimate offence upon it. He disappeared briefly into the dark tent of Kauta's cassock. If the good lady had been near she would literally have kicked him out, but the minister showed no discomfiture and continued, in his sweet and kindly voice, to lead the people's worship. It was when he came to the New Testament lesson that I suffered my worst agony. For it was from Paul's letter to the Philippians that he read, from the first verse of chapter 3. Verse 2 in the Tumbuka language said, "*Chenjerani na zinchebe*". In English, Paul was telling us all to "beware of dogs". My physical jaw-clamping struggle to stifle a paroxysm of laughter was acutely sore and it was some while before I knew that I had won. Fortunately composure had returned when we stood to make our promise to bring up our new baby in the nurture of Christian faith and life.

Two-wheeled Evangelism

On many Sundays I was not on the plateau. The preaching plan for the district sent me hither and thither to services in the surrounding valleys and *dambo*s. Every such journey involved a steep descent and then, after the day's work, a hard ascent again to home. Some of the little 'preaching places' were accessible on foot, but others were too far for what people in central Africa often call 'footing'.

Junju was one such place, and I recall one particularly tough journey there. It was during the rainy season but I had decided not to take a motor vehicle. Motor conveyance was not available to church elders and others on such missions and 1958 was no time for manifestly discriminatory actions. I enjoyed cycling, but when that Sunday dawned, it was clearly going to be a very wet trip. Cycling always brought on heavy sweating and so it seemed to me better to dress as lightly as possible, to let the rain soak me if it came, hoping to dry out in intervening sunny spells, and then to change into respectable clothing for the service. This meant carrying a water-proof bag for my suit and clerical attire, and wearing shorts and a light shirt for cycling. Unwittingly, I had taken a nylon shirt, hoping for ventilation through its 'aertex' pattern of tiny holes. Instead it clung to my wet skin clammily all the way. But worst of all was the indescribable clay mud of that main arterial road to the south, during the rainy season. Travelling by vanette or lorry could be hazardous, with passengers having to leap out to push the vehicle away from dangerous skids in the cocoa-brown mire. On that visit to Junju I learned that the clay could simply force a bike to a halt by wrapping the wheels in a coating so thick and slimy that the space between wheel and mud-guard was packed tight and clay stacked up behind the brake blocks. I had to hunt for a piece of a tree branch suitably shaped and strong enough for the work of scraping away the clay knowing that, in a short while, the drama would have to be replayed. And if the descent to Junju had been grim, how much grimmer was the homeward ascent going to be! But "how shall they believe in him of whom they have not heard? And how shall they hear without a preacher?" (Romans 10.14).

The roads in northern Malawi were tougher than most of the roads of Zambia. I have mentioned the 14 hairpin bends on the road up to Khondowe from the south, the road in fact on which lay the village of Junju; and, much more perilous the steep descent of 3200 feet, by way of 22 hairpins, from the plateau to the lakeshore at Chitimba. The latter road was named Golodi, after a Mr Gauld who was in charge of its construction in the pioneering period of the Livingstonia Mission. Because of those unavoidable hazards, drivers of mission vehicles were required to pass an additional and exacting driving test. Negotiating a five-ton lorry down Golodi was a challenge calling for cool nerves and wise judgment. We were very fortunate in having as our senior driver at the Institution our friend Gibson Mavumbanya Msiska.

Not all users of those roads were careful, however. Thus it happened that a gruesome accident occurred in 1958 which shocked us all. A young man, employed by an Asian trader, had been sent to the northern province to collect a load of maize. He was very small, but in charge of a very big lorry. As he drove north he must, it seemed, have decided to go beyond his employer's orders and pay a quick visit to his parents at Sangilo on the lake-shore, between Chitimba and Karonga. That meant taking the huge lorry first up the convoluted track through the Henga valley, via the 14 bends, and then down Golodi and up again, in the minimum time. He would then pick up his load of grain as he went south from Rumphi Boma.

One assistant, or 'lolly-boy', accompanied him on his clandestine jaunt. They made the ascent of the Henga valley and the descent to Sangilo successfully. But on the return journey, Bend 6 defied his skill. His assistant had jumped out to set a large stone behind a back wheel while the wee man strove to make the multi-point manoevre that the sharpness and steepness of that worst of all bends demanded. What probably happened then was that he failed to change down and engage first gear for another upward movement. So, as the gear lever stumbled in neutral, the lorry rolled back, missed or bounded over the 'lolly-boy's' stone and somersaulted over the precipice. His assistant could do nothing but watch as the huge vehicle plunged through the tree tops. By the time we arrived, in response to a distress call, we found the little man's body already affected by the great heat as it lay, lifeless under the roof of the driving cab. It looked as though he had been thrown out as the lorry plunged and then, by a macabre trick, pinned, where he lay, by the upturned mass of metal. As I approached the scene of his needless death, I saw to my horror that on his chest lay the 'Driver's Manual'. Afer a post-mortem examination at the David Gordon Memorial hospital on the plateau we had to carry his body to his stricken family at Sangilo. To our amazement - for such was not expected in that area in those days - a night raid was made on the lorry a few days later, by looters who removed all its valuable mechanical parts. The odometer showed that it had done very little travelling since purchase. We heard nothing at all from its Asian owner.

A 'clever little rabbit' called Austin

For that sad journey down to Sangilo, I had used, as hearse, the little old green Austin 10-horse-power van for which I had given 10. We had first met the van at Lubwa in 1952. Its owner, a cousin of Dr David Wilson, was employed in the Water Affairs department of NRG. Brian paid an unexpected and delightful visit to us in Livingstonia in 1957. He was then driving a Landrover. "I suppose the little green van went off the road some time ago", I said, remembering how we had had to haul it out of a swamp six years earlier. "Not at all", he replied. "It's still in good shape. I use it locally around Fort Jameson every now and then." As we talked on he told me that he was keeping it until he could give it to a friend. I told him then that I would like to buy it from him. He declined a purchase but in the end he agreed that I would make a donation, not to exceed £10, to the new inter-racial library in Fort Jameson which Brian was trying to promote, against the opposition of some of the white community there. Fort Jameson (now called Chipata) lay not very far across the border from our Loudon Mission. It had been named, of course, after Dr Leander Starr Jameson, Rhodes's swashbuckling agent whose infamous 'raid' into the Transvaal in 1895 made the South African War inevitable.

The Austin's body had suffered from much battering on rough tracks, but it was in fine shape mechanically. If missionaries wanted to use mission vehicles for personal purposes, a lake-shore picnic or a trip into the Nyika Plateau, they naturally had to pay a mileage charge. To be able to have picnics with our young family, using the Austin, was therefore a great boon. Moreover, I used it sometimes for work when no mission vehicle was available; and it could be handled on Golodi's 22 hairpins much more easily than a 30-cwt truck. Indeed it won high praise for the way it skipped in the wet season through the treacherous cotton-soil of the 55-mile stretch from Chitimba to Karonga.

On one occasion in very heavy mud, I slithered past the dark-blue Postal Landrover whose driver, 'Danger' Mkandawire, had a reputation for getting through in the worst conditions. On that day, he was stuck and fuming as he struggled to heave his heavy vehicle on to slightly firmer ground, with the help of a bunch of local lads. If I had stopped to help, I would certainly have stuck too. 'Danger' knew this and shouted, "Don't stop. Keep moving. On you go. *Kalulu Kachenjele.*" The title caused a shout of mirth from his helpers meaning as it did 'clever little rabbit'.

When we left Livingstonia in 1959, the little green Kalulu went into creative dispersion: the engine to power an electrical generator at Mlowe Health Centre; its chassis to serve as a trailer, to draw petrol drums up from the shore at Chitimba where they were off-loaded by the lake steamer; and its body into immediate action as a shelter in Mavumbanya Msiska's farm, in which he and his family could hide, shaded from the sun, and pot monkeys which came in marauding bands to plunder the maize just before harvest time.

A welcome Visitor

1958 was marked by a number of memorable visitors. Dr George MacLeod, founder and Leader of the Iona Community, was Moderator of the General Assembly of the Church of Scotland and was on an African tour which included South Africa as well as the three territories of the Federation. That form of miscalled 'evangelical' Christianity which turns faith into an introverted and emotional declaration of 'surrender' to Christ while turning a blind eye to one's share in corporate sin and social injustice, has long flourished, not surprisingly, in white South Africa as in America's southern states. Early on his tour, Dr MacLeod was greeted by a wealthy white man of that persuasion who said something to the effect that he hoped the visiting Moderator was going to proclaim the red-hot gospel and nothing else. Indeed, he was, replied the great man, and he would be challenging South Africa, in Christ's name, to end the scandal of racial discrimination and the oppressive injustices done to her black majority. "Oh them", said the 'believer', "if I had my way, they'd all be driven into the sea".

In Blantyre, in southern Malawi, Dr MacLeod met a gentle white lady who told him that she just wished that the Africans were less agitated and extreme in their political expression. At that time there were, at long last, five black members of the Nyasaland Legislative Council who supported the African Congress, among them Henry Chipembere and Kanyama Chiume. A new militancy was characterising their utterances and they were demanding an end of the colour bar, especially in the civil service, and a new constitution founded on universal suffrage. The status quo of settler life was shuddering and the gentle lady told the Moderator that she believed it was un-Christian to say things that might lead to violence. "What's your attitude to the H-bomb?" he replied, to her distress. But there was integrity and consistency in the convictions of the man who campaigned against the abomination of the nuclear arms race with the same incision with which he exposed the inhumanity that flourished in consequence of the southern African doctrine of 'white supremacy'.

Wherever he went, George MacLeod brought a challenge that sprang from the Gospel of Christ as "the power of God unto salvation". With this he blended wit and good humour and it would be impossible to forget the impact of an address he delivered to the students of the Overtoun Institution on 'the history of Christianity'. The liveliness of the questions that followed showed how pungently he had expounded his massive theme. "What is the true Church?" asked one young secondary school pupil, obviously troubled, as so many have been in those areas of the world to which European 'foreign missions' have exported the contentious divisions of institutional Christianity. The pupil knew well of the rivalry of Roman Catholic and Protestant missions, not to mention the numerous splinters within the churches of the Reformation. "Surely", replied the Moderator, "the true church is in the eye of God, and indeed only He can know who is of it. But its members, in terms of the Gospel, are all those who love the Lord with heart and soul and mind and strength and their neighbours as themselves."

Dr MacLeod, in his moments of highest inspiration, displayed exceptional fluency with a rich vocabulary. "There will have to be interpreters", it was agreed before his arrival. But even our one black Bachelor of Divinity could not keep pace with the great man's flow and I had to stand, wincing, helplessly on one occasion when MacLeod's declarations for an incarnational understanding of Christ as offering, in the Cross, the cure to all the world's distress, were translated as opposing the application of Christianity to issues of social, economic and political justice. When, therefore, as he was striding over with me to give his great address to the Institution, he suddenly asked, "Must I have an 'interrupter'?", I decided to take a risk and dispense with interpretation, in the belief, happily vindicated, that he would find and exploit his own transcultural wave length.

His visit was memorable also for his jokes. One in particular brought tears of mirth to his hearers' eyes. It was the tale of a captain of a great ship in the Pacific whose spy-glass one day picked up a tiny island. As the ship moved on, the captain was sure he could see someone on the shore, and so, when within a short distance of the isle, he dropped into a small boat and made a landing on the beach. Sure enough there was a man there, gaunt, wiry and bearded, yet neatly clad in a skirt of banana leaves. They at once shook hands and the captain was amazed to hear how, many years ago, this English seaman had been the sole survivor of a shipwreck. "And how have you lived?" "Well, it's been lonely sometimes but I get plenty of fish and there are tasty fruits on some of the trees." The old sailor's appearance testified to a sound diet. "Will you let me take you home?" the captain then asked, and, after some thought, the man agreed. "Well, now that that's settled, why don't you give me a quick look at your island home, a sort of farewell tour for yourself?" "Sure", said the sailor, "let's go". Just as they were starting, however, the captain noticed two sticks, about five feet high, supporting two short sticks in the shape of a house gable. "Hello. What's that?" the captain asked and immediately the man's expression altered and a solemn reverence came over his demeanour. "That's my church", he said with a Sunday morning voice. "Jolly good", replied the captain. "So you keep yourself spiritually as well as physically in trim. Bravo!"

Off they went and the captain, as he puffed and panted along, envied the splendid health of his host. It was a pleasant isle and its lonely inhabitant was delighted to point out its fruit trees, its spring of fresh water, and its most fertile patches as they made their way around the coastline. Suddenly, however, the captain stopped in his tracks, for there, in front of him, stood another erection of five-foot sticks in the shape of a gable. His trained seaman's sense told him that they were due opposite to the beach on which they had met. "Excuse me", he said, interrupting his friend's inventory of natural foods, "What's this?" At once the man's eyes darkened and his lips curled with suppressed antipathy. "That", said the old salt icily, "is the church I don't attend".

One of the much publicised projects of the Central African Federation was the establishment of what was described as the multi-racial University College of Rhodesia and Nyasaland. The facts that the school systems denied black pupils an equal chance to obtain the entrance qualifications of the College and that residential life was segregated were not publicised. In due course, its official opening by Queen Elizabeth the Queen Mother was announced and a tour of the territories of the Federation was arranged for her.

Myra and I were among a group of guests invited to meet the Queen Mother on her arrival in Nyasaland. In advance of the visit we had heard that there would be separate functions at which she would meet people according to skin colour. But when we reached Limbe in the south, we were told that all that had been changed and that the three races, African, Asian and European would be mingled together at all the special occasions. There was word that, for example, Mr Marshall had had to offer his dinner suit to Mr Gondwe at the eleventh hour, so that the latter could be suitably dressed for an evening banquet.

There was, of course, no proof available to us of what was nonetheless a strong rumour, namely, that the radical recasting of the programme had been made on Her Majesty's express order when, just as she was leaving her previous port of call, she had been shown the schedule of segregated functions planned in the Protectorate. And indeed, when we met her personally, at a huge garden-party at Limbe, she quietly but emphatically liberated herself from the little groups of senior officials who vied with one another to present chosen persons to her. Instead she made for people with whom, presumably on sight, she decided to chat. Thus it was that she approached the bulky figure of the Revd Job Mkandawire and they talked for a few moments. "Which is your church?" she asked him. Without hesitation and, overlooking the fact that the Church of Central Africa Presbyterian had been formally established 34 years earlier, he replied with a splendid roll of his r: "Church of Scotland, ma'am". Another who shook her hand was young Robert

Gwebe Nyirenda from Kaporo, north of Karonga, who had wept to me for his beloved land. "If only it was always like this", he told me later, "this would be a happy country. But tomorrow it will be Welensky's rule again".

Political window-dressing

The Nyasaland Governor, Robert Armitage, who had had an unhappy period in Cyprus, was now trying to appease the undeniable and growing black hostility to Federation by giving seats on his Executive Council to one or two hand-picked men of high standing whose presence there he obviously hoped, might persuade their voteless fellow countrymen that they had spokesmen in high places. The appointees would, of course, form a small minority in 'Ex-Co'. It was a window dressing job and fraught with failure. But it was interesting that the Governor addressed personal invitations to highly respected Christians. Thus it happened, one day when Stephen Kauta and I were staying in the manse at Karonga, that Andrew Kayira told us that he had had such in invitation and must reply very soon. He was troubled by it. As we chatted into the night, Kauta and I both told him that we believed that the Governor's device had come too late and that the way forward lay, not in such cosmetic acts, but in radical change that would open the way, without conflict, to universal franchise and so, inevitably, to Nyasaland's secession from the Federation. We knew that Kayira's own thinking accorded with ours. Our presence, however, helped to crystalise his decision and he sent his declinature to Zomba right away.

It was to Ernest Michael Mtawali, the pioneer of Mlowe Health Centre that the Governor then turned. Like Kayira, Mtawali was a man who wanted to see a peaceful resolution of the Central African crisis. I found in many such upright people a striking unanimity in their opposition to Chisazga as the Federation was called in the northern province. But they were too wise to believe that the answer lay in a physical conflict on racial lines. As the CCAP so often sang: "*Tiri ndipa zimoza, Mwati njumoza, Mtaski nayoso njumoza pera: toviranenge* - We are one blood with one Maker and one Redeemer: therefore let us help each other". But what was the right course of action at the moment? Sadly Ernest Mtawali had no close kindred spirits with whom to discuss the Governor's summons. With an immediate deadline for his reply, he wrote back and accepted the nomination. The sad consequence came later when he was harassed by Kamuzu Banda's Young Pioneers, after Independence, for his alleged collaboration with the enemy. I did not meet him again after we left Nyasaland in 1959. But I met his brother, Dr Charles in Dar-es-Salaam, and learned later of Ernest's premature death in exile.

Creatures great and small

At that period, early 1958, our family life was brightened by little Myra's joyous zest for each day's adventures, heightened by our acquisition of a playful kitten. But one morning while we were still in bed, Catherine and Jamie came in to see us, leaving Myra in her cot. "Oh, by the way", they said, "there's a snake under Myra's bed". So out I leapt and dashed to the children's room, to find that, sure enough, a long grey-green snake was lying along the cool, dark-stained floor boards under the cot, probably resting. The first weapon that came to hand was a tennis racket and that was good because of the spring in its frame. So I smacked the snake's head as it lay at peace. It died almost at once and I tossed its body far into the grass beyond our so-called garden. But there's no joy in such actions by which man, in Burns' words, breaks 'nature's social union' and pits his greater intelligence and cunning against his 'poor, earth-born companions and fellow mortals'. Alas, Isaiah's vision (chapter 11) is still far from fulfilment.

Chapter 18

DR BANDA
COMES HOME

In June, there came a report of a threat by some of Welensky's firebrands to stage a 'Boston Tea Party' if their demand for British recognition of a white-ruled Central African dominion was further delayed. On the sixth of July, Dr Hastings Banda arrived back in his native land after decades of self-exile. The territorial 'security forces' were in a state of alert lest things should get out of hand. But some senior government officers appeared to hope that Banda's arrival might reduce the tension and allow the Governor to deal with one man rather than a body such as the Congress.

Banda at once began an intensive tour of the country, uttering everywhere, in short sharp sentences the same message: "Federation must go. The people must now begin to take their part in government. If you want to teach a child to swim, you throw him in at the deep end. But I hate no man because of his colour. How could I hate white people when I have spent so many years in their countries?"

As he moved north, the Livingstonia Presbytery was meeting in Muhuju village at the foot of the Henga Valley. As the meeting began we heard that Kamuzu Banda was to address a rally at Rumphi the next day. I mentioned this to the Presbytery's executive committee and told them that the Doctor was an elder of the Church of Scotland. "Should we not invite him to visit the Presbytery?" I asked, and this was at once agreed. But the Moderator then asked me to go as their envoy. "We do not know him", he said. "You do. So you should carry our invitation."

When I arrived at Rumphi Boma, the rally had just ended. I had travelled in our rattly old Austin van which I parked well away from the crowd, thinking it better to approach on foot. As I drew near, I noticed that Banda, dressed as always like a British banker and wearing dark glasses, was sitting on a folding canvas chair,

looking small and apprehensive. He suddenly spotted me and it
was obvious that he was asking the men beside him who I was.
Then, hearing my name, he rose and came to meet me and embraced
me warmly, to the great surprise of many in the crowd. He was
clearly pleased to be invited to Muhuju, though some of the
Congress officials with him appeared less enthusiastic. However,
without much delay we set off, Kamuzu and I in the Austin and
some of the Congress men following in a landrover.

On arrival, I introduced him to the Moderator and Clerk of
Presbytery who welcomed him and asked him to address the 'fathers
and brethren'. He said he wanted to use English and the Moderator
told me to translate his message into Tumbuka. The Doctor became
at once much more relaxed than at the rallies he was addressing up
and down the Protectorate. Much of his address was about my late
father and about Banda's happy relationship with my family in
Edinburgh. Then in a word, he summarised his political message
and sat down to hearty applause. At the close of the meeting, he
accepted my invitation to spend the night at Livingstonia and so
off we went up the Henga valley. But Kanyama Chiume and another
senior Congress man were displeased that he accepted my invitation
without consulting them.

When Myra welcomed Doctor Banda at the Stone House, she
offered him a bath, which he accepted with barely concealed delight.
Nearly an hour later, he emerged from the bathroom and, with
considerable confusion, begged Myra to excuse him for being so
long. Then suddenly he turned to me. "Fergus", he said, "I hate, I
hate, the baths in the villages, standing on logs in a small grass
shelter, without a roof, with buckets of water for laving oneself -
and spiders. I hate them!" "I love them", I replied, "especially when
I've been cycling all day and at last reach a school where I am to
sleep at the teacher's house". And that was true. For when, as was
customary, a young girl of the house would enter the teacher's
living room, kneel on one knee and say quietly *"Turipo tumaji -
there is a little water"* (not "would you like a bath?" as if it were
debatable!) I knew that there would be gallons of hot and lukewarm
and colder water awaiting me in a little booth walled with thatching
grass, under the stars. Now my weary flesh would be rejuvenated
and I would find a generous meal awaiting me when I was clean.
But Kamuzu, I found, was still the same fastidious man I'd known
in Edinburgh 18 years earlier, hypersensitive on points of hygiene

and almost prudish in his attitude to such matters as bathing. His fiery expostulation against the kindly baths of his native land greatly surprised his Congress entourage.

The next day, I called all the students and staff of the Institution together to hear a short address from their new champion in the struggle against Federation.

The Unrest Grows

In those days it was impossible not to be aware of ripples of restiveness in the land. The deep-seated antipathy of women to the Federation may well have been the cause of the disquiet among young people. When politics kindle a fire in the mothers of the people, the 'powers that be' should take serious note. Thus unrest now and then erupted in some minor incident that showed how severely race relations were being strained by Welensky's perfidious brand of racism. Even in remote rural areas, such ripples would suddenly appear. The church, as an association based on superlative affirmations of 'fellowship in the Spirit' yet wounded every now and then by the infection of Central Africa's 'colour bar', was bound to be subjected to the glare of new criticisms from the younger generation. Movements of protest tend to be embarrassed and misjudged on account of what are sometimes called 'lunatic fringes'.

Thus it was that we were shocked one day by news of a short, sharp eruption of violence at Ifumbo in the Karonga hills area where Yoram Msopole was minister. On the previous Sunday, they told us, a small group of youths had rushed into the church building as children were gathering for Sunday School, driven the children out in fright and manhandled the simple forms that served as pews. There was a swift reaction of anger on the part of church members who had to clear up the mess of scattered and damaged forms and lead the children back to their Sunday School under escort. What heightened the people's anger was that their Chief appeared afraid and took no action against the rowdies. Mr Msopole and the elders decided then that the matter was serious enough to be placed before the Livingstonia Presbytery.

The Presbytery Executive Committee met at once and appointed Stephen Kauta, Andrew Kayira and myself a special commission to visit Ifumbo. For some reason, no mission vehicle was available and so our rattly green 'kalulu kachenjele' was quickly serviced, loaded with a 44-gallon petrol drum and despatched to the north. As we clattered over the rough track, that has since been signposted 'M1', my colleagues told me that a Congress member of very extreme political emotions was believed to have incited the attack by the youths. Our primary task, my companions believed, was to visit the Chief and express the grave concern of the whole church to him.

We were warmly welcomed by the Msopoles and fed sumptuously on a most tasty dish comprising duiker meat with chicken, marrows cooked in oil, served with heaps of fine local rice and topped by curds with a sprinkling of sugar. Then by the light of a pressure lamp we planned our strategy for the next day. A messenger was sent to the Chief seeking an audience in the morning, and his reply assured us that he would give time to 'the envoys of Christ'.

The royal audience was an unforgetable experience. We knelt briefly before him one by one and then sat on the stools provided. A pregnant silence followed and then our chosen spokesman, Stephen Kauta, began: "We who are pieces of rubbish (*vichwapi vya bantu*) in the presence of the Owner of the land (the Chief) praise your royal generosity in so receiving us". The chiefly head was bowed as those words were spoken and I stole a quick glance at Kauta. There he sat, my friend of the effervescent laughter and the keenest sense of the ridiculous, with not a twinkle of the eye to detract from the humble obeisance he was offering from the three of us.

Another silence followed, and then Kauta spoke again. Because chieftainship was so solemn a role, because the smile or frown of the chief could move his people to hope or to dread, the failure of a chief to quench a little fire before the forest was ablaze was a grave matter indeed. We had heard of the action of a group of ill-disciplined and disrespectful youths against the church. The local Christians had waited to hear the word of their father the Chief. But there was only silence. How could this be? It was whispered that the Owner was afraid of his grandchildren, and so he was doing nothing to restore the confidence of his people in his fatherly rule. Surely this was a heavy matter indeed. So our spokesman added, with carefully chosen words, to the weight of his rebuke; Andrew Kayira and myself nodding in solemn corroboration. And as he spoke, I noticed that bubbles of sweat were now beading the royal brow. The old Owner wiped them with a square of oriental silk, bought no doubt at the store at Tunduma on the Tanzanian border, owned by the Pakistani brothers Gilani. As Kayira added his endorsement of Kauta's statement and I then - to fulfil my commission - said a few words, the Chief had the semblance of contrition after just chastisement. Kauta then poured a little figurative oil on the weals his words had raised; the Chief assured us that he had heard and understood, and that he would now take counsel with his court. The audience closed with assurances of the loyalty of the church to the immemorial role of chiefs, after which we withdrew from the presence with solemn gestures of deference.

An unwelcome Visitor

1958 brought us another drama that was to bring into the open the depth of the black people's intellectual and emotional rejection of the Federation; and no less the necessity of a transcending fellowship to validate the whole Christian enterprise and its proclamation.

It happened this way. The Senatus met as usual one day to take counsel about the life and work of the Institution, and as usual, the secretary gave me a written list of our agenda. It was usual for the two of us to discuss the business briefly beforehand. But sometimes a late item would appear. That day as I ran my eyes down the agenda, an extraordinary inclusion of which I had heard nothing leapt up at me: 'Visit of the Governor General of the Federation'.

"What's this?" I whispered to the secretary but her reply was a shrug that clearly said, "Don't ask me. The one who mentioned it to me will speak himself, no doubt". So, after 'duly constituting' the meeting, we moved methodically into the business as listed. "We now come", I said, "to an item that I know nothing about. Is there someone to speak to it?" Sure enough, a senior missionary, on an awkward cough, began. The possible visit of His Excellency had arisen, he told us, from a chance meeting between himself and a senior government official at provincial headquarters. The official had indicated that planning an itinerary for the Queen's top representative was proving difficult because of 'African opposition to Federation'. The official wondered if Livingstonia would be willing to receive him. Under questioning, the senior colleague acknowledged that Government had been given an assurance that the big man would be received at our Institution. "This then is a matter for the Senatus to decide", I said, "though I am personally troubled by this news". For Northern Nyasaland was solidly anti-Federation and the Institution had added its protest to that of the Synod of Livingstonia against not only the imposition of Federation but also the sinister way it was developing.

A sensitive and somewhat nervous discussion followed until a senior Malawian summed up the mood of the Senatus thus: "It is our custom to receive strangers and not to refuse to receive them. So let us receive this person as we would receive any other visitor. But because he embodies the regime that we all distrust, we should be honest in telling him what is in the hearts of our people." And so it was decided, myself making it clear that I understood this consensus to mean that members of the community at Khondowe should be assured that, as Principal, I would endeavour to let them have an opportunity to express their views to the 'so-called Governor General', as some termed him. Written memoranda were favoured by the Senatus because the visit would inevitably be arranged on a limited time-table. Our office staff would type such memoranda willingly.

'Kwacha - the dawn is coming' was the slogan of the anti-Federation movement. "When he comes", the Teacher Training students asked the Scots lady in charge of their department, "shall we wear our Kwacha badges?" "Of course", she replied with wonted crispness, "but be sure they are neatly made". For each badge-wearer designed his own in that period of the Central African crisis.

When the day came, a car took the two secretaries, black and white, of the Joint Council (integrating Church and Mission) the Moderator of the Livingstonia Synod, the local minister and myself down to Vungu Vungu to meet the gubernatorial party. As Lord Dalhousie and his wife greeted us, he remarked on our splendid mountain scenery. One of our group, the senior man who had introduced the plan to the Senatus, moved with his wife into the Governor General's car and, as *quid pro quo*, the Acting Provincial Commissioner came into our vehicle. As we drove on to the plateau, the big limousine led and we followed. A few people watched as we moved through the '*madoda*' houses to what in a Scots village, would be called the cross. There, to my surprise, the local Brownie Pack awaited the 'motorcade' and as the Governor General passed, they raised a little cheer! "Jolly good for the Brownies", said the PC as we sat together in the old Chevrolet, "Jolly fine show."

The party moved up the plateau from the David Gordon Memorial Hospital by way of the industrial training department and on to the higher ground on which the 'college' buildings were shared by primary and secondary schools and the Teacher Training department, with the theological classrooms in newer accommodation nearby. Everywhere, the students and staff looked solemn and were undemonstrative, except at the Hospital where one medical orderly turned his back and bent down to pluck weeds as the Governor General passed. As agreed, the TTC students, to a man, wore Kwacha badges, some of which revealed notable artistic gifts. His Excellency paused for a moment to see what the badges represented. He was walking too far from the line of students to be able to observe them in detail. But he frowned slightly nonetheless.

I realised at once that this was not a visitor who sought or chose to risk person-to-person dealings with the local people. So, as we moved up the estate, I told him that we wanted to affirm what he would, I was sure, appreciate, namely the profound rejection by the people everywhere in the Protectorate of both the concept and the conduct of the Federation. His reply amounted to: "Ah yes. Pity. They don't seem to realise the economic benefits". My answer was to the effect that such benefits were hard to find. One or two memoranda had been given to me and those I now passed to him personally, but he did not read them then.

After 'walk-about', tea was served in the Council Chamber. HE thereafter said thanks on behalf of his entourage and commented enthusiastically on the splendour of the scenery. As hands were being shaken all round, the young colonial officer who was acting as Commissioner for the Rumphi district whispered to me his gratitude for the success of the occasion. "We know how the people feel about Federation and this tour has been a big headache. But best thanks to you all." The big limousine and its escorting vehicles then pulled away and we joined spontaneously in an enormous sigh of relief. But we shared also the impression of a useless visit, sustained by pretentious pomposity and vapid comments on trivia. Nothing whatsoever had happened to change the image of 'Chisazya' as the Federation was called in Tumbuka. No hint had been dropped of any intentions to heed the massive distrust and anger of black people in face of Roy Welensky's conduct as Federal Prime Minister. A highly paid nonentity had come and gone, having allowed himself only one dismissive comment on the political crisis by limply reiterating the trite 'official' claim that African anti-Federationism was due to innate ignorance, aggravated by self-seeking agitators.

Soon afterwards, our senior man, who had promoted the visit, went on leave with his wife to Scotland. As they passed through Zomba, the Protectorate capital not far from Blantyre, they were guests for dinner of the Governor, Sir Robert Armitage. A few days later I received a hurried note from that colleague telling me that the Governor had been informed that Lord Dalhousie had been 'jeered, booed and stoned' during his visit to Overtoun Institution. At the first opportunity, I showed the note to the Senatus and we all recorded a sense of shock at so malicious a lie. The first reaction of some was to ignore it completely. But "How would such a statement reach Government House in Zomba and gain such credence that the Governor would seemingly believe it unless it had been passed through governmental channels?" It was therefore agreed that I should call on the Acting Provincial Commissioner, who had sat with me in our vehicle as the limousine was driven on to our estate, and discuss the matter of the lying report with him.

I went to Mzuzu as soon as the 150-mile trip could be arranged. At the PC's office, I was asked to wait as he was busy. A good while later I was admitted and went straight to the point. His reaction was visibly psychosomatic. He wiped a rush of sweat from his brow and his smoking had a hint of desperation in the draw. He was slow to reply and so I filled in the silence by recalling how we had actually been together throughout the visit. "So we both know, don't we, that the report is totally false?" I said. His answer was something like this: "Well, everyone in government is aware of Livingstonia's well-known and publicised hostility to Federation." "Yes", I replied, "we have made known the opposition of the Presbyterian Church and of the Institution at Khondowe to the imposition and subsequent development of the Federation. We have done so from knowledge of the realities of 'white supremacy' in the south and central Africa. But to articulate such a protest as we have done consistently since before the Federation was established is wholly different from 'jeering, booing and stoning'." I then told him of the Senatus discussion when we first heard of the proposed visit by Dalhousie. The solemn agreement that it was right to receive him courteously and to tell him of the people's feelings had been fulfilled to the letter. "And you yourself know this is true", I added.

His next remark astounded me. "But didn't a little Brownie say 'Kwacha'? he exclaimed rhetorically. "Did she?" I retorted. "You and I were side by side in our car when HE passed the Brownies. They waved cheerily at his car, you'll remember, and you said to me, 'Jolly good for the Brownies'. I can think of no testimony more pertinent to our discussion today. And secondly, if perchance a little Brownie did say 'Kwacha', what happened in consequence? I saw or heard nothing of anything that could possibly have been called a disturbance. Since we were together throughout the afternoon, anything you had heard or seen, I'd have noticed too. And had such a disturbance included the 'jeering, booing and stoning' of the Governor General, the afternoon would have developed very differently from the way in which we experienced it together."

The PC tried again to return to our known opposition to Federation and the part played by missionaries in it. But I forced attention back to the specific points in the malicious report to Zomba. Our *contretemps* then began to run out of steam and so I made my final demand: "Since, as you say, you are responsible for the Queen's peace in this province and since peace involves the scotching of inflammatory lies, I have to ask you to inform the Governor at once of our shock and anger at this flagrant and malicious falsehood and to refute it pointblank as you can and we believe you must do since you were a participant in the visit from first to last." Clearly this riled him and he hedged. "If this is not done", I then said, "we shall find difficulty in suppressing the suspicion that the false report emanated from government circles in this province. I should think it highly unlikely that your young Commissioner in Rumphi sent the report personally and directly to Zomba, especially since he expressed his appreciation of our part in the success of the visit so warmly to myself. Please therefore advise the Governor that the story is totally false and do so urgently, with a copy to me." As I rose to go, he said that he expected to be in touch with the Governor shortly. But we received no confirmation that he had done anything at all about the matter.

A sudden and unique Emergency

One day in January 1959, during a spell of heavy rainfalls alternating with scintillating sunshine, I was busy at the desk in Dr Laws's spacious study that lay at the other end of the Council Chamber from our dining room at the Stone House. I looked up for a minute from my work and saw, about 50 yards away, a strange figure of a man waving a piece of paper, obviously to attract the attention of someone in the house. I rose and went out to greet him at once.

Our stranger was of short stature but with a body of striking slim strength, the muscles of his calves prominent like those of an Olympic runner. He wore a short cloak made from the skin of a deer and belted with a band of goat hide. His hair was brushed upwards to about two inches' length and the whiteness of his teeth was matched by ivory bracelets and anklets. As I approached him, he stiffened and raised his hand in salutation. Then, dropping on one knee, he presented the paper to me with both hands.

"To whoever receives this", said the folded letter, "please send help. Our aircraft has crashed up the mountain. There are seven persons here, two with injuries, though not very serious. We have had to abandon the aircraft. Thank you". I was due to chair a Senatus meeting that afternoon but I decided to organise a rescue party at once as we could not know how far they would have to climb before finding the pilot and his passengers.

I told the silent envoy from the mountains that we would send off rescuers, with a stretcher and First Aid box as well as food as soon as possible. "Will you please guide the team?", I asked and the hillman replied, "I will find them beyond Vungu Vungu and lead them".

Dr Chad Musk at once selected some of his hospital staff to join apprentices from the trades departments for the ascent; a team of around a dozen, accompanied by two of our missionaries. In a very short time, they were ready to start and I went to bid them farewell. "But we want you, our Principal, to come with us", said the young men of the rescue team and, realising they were serious, I had to send a note to the Vice-Principal asking her to chair the Senatus, and to Myra telling her to expect me when I got back!

I was ill-prepared for the climb. My shoes were not tough enough and I should have taken food before starting. But we all had a sense of urgency, and, black and white alike, we set off at an unwisely fast pace. As we became aware that our 'first wind' was spent and we'd not yet got our second wind, the hillman suddenly and noiselessly appeared from behind us, running uphill on light feet like a mountain gazelle. I noticed that he had taken time to do a spot of shopping at Mandala's Store on the estate but carried his purchases without strain. "Keep to the track", he said, "and you will not get lost".

When at last that longed-for 'second wind' revived us and soon afterwards we spotted our guide standing on a rock, waiting for us, I saw that the Phoka hillman had delivered his purchases to his home and was now ready to set the pace for us. It was a long haul but at last we found the stranded party with their aircraft sitting on the treetops, like a huge bird. The pilot was unscathed but his passengers, all white, were shaken and one man had a broken ankle. Two girls, flying from Kenya to boarding school in Natal had had their shoes off on the flight and abandoned them in the plane in the panic of the moment. The descent of Nyamkhowa, as the Phoka people call Mount Laws, was sore on their tender feet.

That night, beds were provided in various houses for the party and we arranged transport the next morning to take them south to Mzuzu. When at last we saw a report of the incident in the 'Rhodesia Herald', we felt some chagrin at the description of our famous Institution as 'a remote Anglican mission'. The tentacles of imperial English establishment were never far from us in colonial Africa!

Chapter 19
HOPE IN TIMES
OF CRISIS

For some time I had dreamt of a spectacular presentation of the passion of Christ by our students and staff. The plan was that we would read and re-read the record of the gospels on the events of the week before the crucifixion and become so familiar with it that, without the inhibiting influence of printed words, the participants would then enact it. The spontaneous ease of dramatisation which was so notable in central Africa was what originally inspired the idea. The first planning meeting took place on February 20 1959, soon after midday. About 150 atudents and a number of their teachers turned up and seemed to catch the excitement of the idea at once. Franklin Chunga was unanimously chosen to play the part of Christ and with equal alacrity, we found a Caiaphas and a Pilate, a Judas and a Mary Magdalene, a Peter, a Philip, a Barabbas and the rest. We then decided that a crowd scene would be a good way to involve everybody right away, and so we set ourselves to bring alive the 'trumphal entry' into Jerusalem. But we were suddenly interrupted.

"A European" - pronounced Yew-ro-payen - "wants to see you", a schoolboy came and told me. As I left the church, I found a tall young man outside, looking thoroughly scared. "They've stoned my store", he said and I realised that he was an employee of one of the trading companies that leased stores in one of our buildings. He was barely articulate but I knew that I'd better go and see what had happened. As I reached the store, a branch of Mandala (the African Lakes Corporation) I saw some of our industrial apprentices gathered at the workshops and Daniel McEwen Mkandawire, a young brother of our honoured accountant and a leading member of the local branch of the African Congress, standing near the store. I approached, pushing my bike and Mkandawire greeted me. The atmosphere was tense and a quick decision was needed. "Let's go up to the office", I said and the white store manager accompanied me along with Mkandawire and another Congress official.

The store manager had apparently dismissed Mandala's local *kapitao* on suspicion of theft. This was, in Mkandawire's view, unfair dismissal based on insufficient and unproved evidence. But the two Congress men agreed readily that the breaking of a window was unjustified. As we spoke, I heard a clatter and looked from the window to see that my bike had been thrown on the ground. Near at hand stood a well-known fellow from Vungu Vungu who was regarded as being 'tenpence in the shilling' mentally. It seemed best to ask the people who had gathered in a small crowd to disperse and Mkandawire agreed to support me in urging them to do so. After a moment's hesitation, the apprentices moved off and the rest of the bystanders drifted away too.

Meanwhile the Scots engineer had appeared and I told him what had happened. I then advised the store manager to suspend judgment on his employee and call it a day. He did not demur and climbed into his lorry. As Bill Hendry and I turned to leave, a rock was hurled at the lorry, fortunately causing no injury; and, as swiftly, a freak mist swept over the plateau reducing the visibility to a few yards.

A couple of uneasy hours followed, during which, as I heard later, a group of young people went to the Girls' School dormitory area and shouted into the mist. But when the Scots mistress in charge greeted them and asked their help in moving some bags of grain, they responded readily. Another such group, or possibly the same one, walked along our wooden verandah noisily and we heard some young voices chanting, "*Basungu chokani* - white people go away". But the account of this event in *The Rise of Nationalism in Central Africa* by Robert Rotberg, is not accurate in detail when it states that "Africans stoned missionaries at Livingstonia".

As the mist cleared so did the uneasiness. I had a quick consultation with senior black members of the community and we agreed to call all students and pupils together next morning and speak seriously about the day's events. That assembly passed off quietly and there were no interruptions as the senior teachers and church leaders called for mutual respect in the current political crisis. Everybody at the Institution knew that all the staff, black and white alike, were unanimous in our opposition to the Federation. A quiet week followed but the news from elsewhere in central Africa was disturbing.

The Crisis in wider context

At various places in the Nyasaland Protectorate minor incidents happened and in some police clashed briefly with angry crowds. The solidarity among the black peoples of the three Federated territories, was being doubly strengthened in those days. The inept and brash actions and utterances of Welensky and his white supporters were forcing black leaders to respond with increasing vigour. And the Accra meeting of the All Africa People's Conference in January 1959 had assured them of the moral support of the other peoples of the continent who had experienced what Kenneth Kaunda had once called "our uniform suffering under the jack boots of our capitalist and imperialist oppressors".

On 26 February, the Southern Rhodesia Government declared a 'State of Emergency' there and banned the African National Congress. On the evening of 2 March, the Nyasaland Governor was quoted on the radio as having stated that there would be no such Emergency Declaration in the Protectorate. But, just before midnight, when people were asleep, he announced a 'State of Emergency', banned the Congress and released the police and units of the Federal Army to arrest all ANC leaders and move them to already prepared 'concentration camps'. This action was called 'Operation Sunrise', a sour retort to the Congress rallying call 'Kwacha Ngwee - the dawn has come'.

It was true and noteworthy that, as Rotberg records, "most of the important leaders of the Congress offered no resistance". But there were some ugly events in the next day or two. At Loudon Mission of the Church of Central Africa Presbyterian, after failing to persuade the 'missionary-in-charge' to accept the evacuation of his family and his white colleagues, members of 'security forces' broke into the house of the local Congress chairman who refused arrest. In the struggle that followed, blood was spilled near his house. In the morning, after rain, the tracks of the Landrover tyres seemed to the local people to lead from that house to near the big house of the senior missionary. This sparked off an angry demonstration, made worse because that missionary had earlier publicly committed his personal support to the idea of Federation. What could have been a dangerous situation was resolved in the nick of time with the help of senior local people. The brutal arrest soon after of the young driver of the mission vehicle revived the tension there. The local leaders spoke later of a sense of hurt that they were excluded from 'confidential' discussions between the local District Commissioner and the missionaries about the imminence of the Emergency and the plan to evacuate white people. It was seen as confirming that 'white was white and black was black' and that race rather than fellowship in the church was the determinant in crisis.

The Emergency gave us at Livingstonia reason to believe that the Government was however aware that it should not expect missionaries at the Institution to be open to official 'confidences' as between white people only. Thus when 'Operation Sunrise' was being planned, no hint of it reached us as missionaries. The authority of the Senatus and not merely the Institution's Principal must have at least been noted by government officials. When therefore, the local ANC branch chairman, Mzumara, was arrested at night in a village near the Overtoun estate local leaders quickly scotched a rumour that one of the arresting officers who spoke Tumbuka was myself. The protest of the Senatus and the church leaders against the 'state of Emergency' confirmed that we were in sympathy with the voteless subjects of the Protectorate. But the Institution had more 'Europeans' on its staff than any other 'mission station' and we were soon to learn something of official anxiety as the crisis worsened.

Evacuation? - No thanks

Only a couple of days after the Governor's midnight declaration, a Rhodesian 'spotter plane' dropped about half a dozen empty teargas canisters on the open ground near to the Stone House where we lived. School children picked them up, opened them, and found in each a letter, marked 'Strictly Confidential' addressed to the Principal. As I collected them from the children who brought them to me at once, I found that the six letters were identical. Possibly the Provincial Commissioner at Mzuzu had decided to send a number of copies to ensure that at least one would reach me.

As I read his message, I remembered how, soon after reaching Livingstonia in December 1956, I had found a sealed letter to 'The Principal' in the strong room, dated some time well before the imposition of Federation in 1953. In it, the PC had asked one of my predecessors to give him, in confidence, a list of those white men on his staff who would be willing to 'bear arms' in the event of 'disturbances' among the local population. A copy of the Principal's reply was also in that envelope. To my dismay he had listed names of some colleagues and added a note to the effect that his own position would be affected by his having been a conscientious objector to military service during the Second World War. I could dimly appreciate that he had written under the pressure of fear and probably of loneliness. Certainly one colleague whom he listed as likely to agree to bear arms would, I knew, have been furious if he had heard of such a correspondence and of his own name included in it. What was so sad was that the colonial rulers of subjugated and exploited peoples had reason to assume that missionaries would, as it were, rally round the Union Jack, against the people they were sent to serve, because of a loyalty above their loyalty to Christ.

Now, on 5 March 1959, I had a strange letter in my hands. In view of the uncertain situation in the country, said the PC, he wished to offer missionaries and their families the opportunity of evacuation to greater safety at Nkhata Bay. A vessel would be off shore at Chitimba, at four am next morning. I should arrange for all who wished such 'safety' to go down the road to the lake under cover of darkness, as quietly as possible, to avoid disturbing the local villages. And, by the way, if any senior African members of our staff wished to be included in this exercise, they could be accommodated.

I immediately called a meeting of the Senatus. Because of the nature of the business, I forgot to say, "Please sit down everybody", and so we all stood. Without comment, I read the letter and then asked how my colleagues felt. Myra and I were sure of our own response but I first wanted to hear the free replies of those assembled. After a short silence, our Irish minister associated with the Karonga district said: "I'm sure I speak for Dorothy as well as for myself. We wouldn't dream of going away". In quick succession the rest of the missionaries echoed Bill's reaction. One of our older women colleagues was more emotional. "I don't know what is going to happen. Things could get worse. I'm very afraid. But I'm staying." After reporting our personal decision to stay, "Are there any other matters then?" I asked, for this was a time when the world was setting the agenda for us in a harsh way. "May I say something?" asked my beloved friend Stephen Kauta. "Surely", I replied. "Excuse me", he said, "but I want to speak in Tumbuka". His English was well tried and competent but I saw his heart was full and could best be released through his mother tongue.

In translation this is what he then said: "If you had decided to go, we would have understood. But, if you had gone, the body of Christ would have broken." Nowadays we hear tell of 'doing theology' in response to situations of crisis or persecution, as in South Africa and Guatemala, for example. "The Word was made flesh", says the Gospel, but how quickly and universally we seek to reverbalise it. It is in crisis, it seems, that Christ's people are forced to reverse this reverbalisation and to incarnate the liberating word in behaviour and conduct. Many years in which a measure of racism was apparently accepted by mission communities inevitably entrenched estrangements, that in turn closed up the springs of *agape*. Those quick months in 1959 surprised many of us with the joyful rediscovery that Paul's description of the church as 'the body of Christ' was not a random flight of fancy. "Please let my people be one", said Jesus to God just before his arrest, "so that the world may believe that it is you who have sent me".

A Nyasaland Sharpeville

Very soon after that Senatus meeting, we began to hear horrid rumours, soon to be confirmed, of what has to be called 'the massacre of Nkhata Bay'. One of the best of the colonial District Commissioners had been transferred from Rumphi to the Bay not very long before the Emergency. When 'Operation Sunrise' was carried out, before dawn on the third of March, the local people woke, as elsewhere, to discover that their Congress leaders had all been seized. As they gathered, in a large crowd and went down to the DC's office at the *Boma*, they could see a boat anchored out on the lake. "They must have our leaders in that boat", was the inevitable conclusion and so some spokesmen of the crowd asked the Commissioner to ring up the PC's office and find out what had happened. It may well have been that the PC himself did not know. It was clear that Roy Welensky wanted the Emergency to be operated by the Federal Army but that the Governor resisted this enough to ensure that, at least nominally, his PCs in the various provinces were in charge. We had reason to believe that some of the DCs were very unhappy not only about the declaration of a 'State of Emergency' but the Federation itself.

However much or little he knew, the DC at Nkhata Bay did try to contact his superior by telephone. But the cable had been cut by some ANC people who wished to hinder communications between police and soldiers. The DC was still in animated discussion with the people near the jetty but with no hint of violence when a posse of Rhodesian soldiers appeared. My friends at Nkhata Bay told me later that as the soldiers approached it was clear that the DC did not welcome them. A sharp disagreement, inaudible to my friends, took place between the soldiers and the Commissioner after which he stepped back and a soldier bellowed the words of the Riot Act at the crowd. For a few moments the people faced the soldiers and then the officer-in-charge issued the order to fire over their heads. Still the people stood and waited.

In the next few minutes the soldiers fired a number of times at the crowd, waiting for them to rise again from the ground before releasing another volley. At last, panic seized the people and they began to run in all directions. The local CCAP minister told me how a woman standing near him lay dead in a pool of blood with her baby, alive and crying, still tied to her back. When eventually Mr Justice Devlin came with members of the Commission of Enquiry appointed by the British Government, he told us, while staying in the Stone House at Livingstonia, that while the 'official figure' of the dead was around 45, there was reason to believe that many more had been killed by gun-fire. The local people who described the event to me believed that over 100 died.

A few weeks later, my black colleagues at the Institution suggested that I send a letter, on behalf of us all, to that DC at Nkhata Bay whom so many respected. My letter had to be carefully worded because the Emergency Regulations were still in force. I managed however to transmit to him the message of understanding which had been expressed by those who prompted me to write. In his also discreet reply, he said that he could never forget the horror of that day or 'the amazing forgiveness of the people'.

The Karonga district, north of our plateau, was to have its share of the drama, too. On the morning of 3rd March, a small crowd at Kaporo wakened the Revd Adam Mlagha with the news that Congress officials had been abducted in the night. "We are going to march to the *Boma*", they said, "but first, you must pray for us". "No, I won't pray", replied Mlagha, "until you put down your walking sticks. They will appear as weapons to the soldiers.

You will go without violence". The lake-shore people often carried walking sticks when trudging the beaches. But the minister's advice was taken and a heap of *ndodo* was piled up near his house. "Now let us pray", said Mlagha, "and then let me go with you to the *Boma*". His crisp prayer was for peace in the land, for wise reactions to dangerous events and for justice.

At each village they passed, the crowd grew larger. When they reached Mwanjasi school, they told the teachers there that it was useless to try to keep school going for that day. "The whole country is in bad trouble". Two young teachers and some pupils then joined the march. When they reached the *Boma*, soldiers were already at the DC's office, holding guns. Events moved fast. The Riot Act was read and the command to disperse was shouted. When the people did not obey, the soldiers fired and a child, around twelve, fell writhing to the ground. Seeing this, a senior man in the community stepped forward and gathered up the dying boy in his arms. Afterwards, some local people told me that the faces of some of the white soldiers had registered amazement at this quiet act. At a second volley, over their heads, the people turned and ran.

Piercing the Censor's Seal

Meanwhile at the Institution we became aware both that censorship of mail was to be part of the Emergency situation and that the crisis was such that we must send out messages somehow to friends and relatives outside the country. In addition to personal letters from missionary staff to their families abroad, it was important to get a description of the situation in the Protectorate to church leaders in Scotland. In a very short time we had a big bundle of mail collected, including a full report from myself to the Church of Scotland Mission office in Edinburgh and to Dr George MacLeod. Then we let it be known that we wanted someone to volunteer for the task of cycling northwest to the borders of Nyasaland with Tanganyika and Northern Rhodesia. Edward Musoni, a learner typist in our General Office, came forward at once, disappeared on his bicycle within minutes of tying a bundle on his carrier with our letters securely concealed inside, and returned in an amazingly short space of days. He brought with him a note from our colleague at Mwenzo confirming receipt and dispatch of our letters.

Somehow mysteriously word must have been passed to the 'forces of law and order' that Musoni had made that journey. Not long after he returned he compounded his felony by writing a personal letter to the DC asking him to understand the people's feelings about the Federation, and, as their 'father', to help them to be liberated from the power of Roy Welensky. Thus it happened that a young English colonial officer, turned special constable for the duration, called on me one day, very courteously, and asked if we had a student called Musoni. "Why do you ask?" I replied. "Well, it's a simple matter. He has written to the DC who would like to meet him and discuss his letter". There was more than one Musoni among our students so I asked what the first name was. My visitor had to take the letter from his pocket to check it. Suspicion had now come to my mind and so, politely, I took the letter from the 'special' and read it. "Does the DC really want to involve this student in a 90-mile trip to discuss this clear and honest letter?" I asked. "Well, yes! I'm not personally involved you'll understand, except to convey the DC's request."

I excused myself then and went over to the office, where Musoni was at his typewriter. When he heard about the DC's message, he said he was quite ready to go. My misgivings were increasing but I did not see how I could stop the process, especially since the young Englishman had a vehicle in which Musoni would travel. So off they went, but Musoni did not return. Instead he was sent to the stark concentration camp at Kanjedza for seven years detention, presumably on the grounds that his letter had mentioned the proscribed name of the Congress. Only the earlier end of the Emergency brought his release.

History reveals bullying as a major temptation to people 'in power'. Musoni's arrest and the bombing of cities have this as highest common factor: bullying to effect intimidation with not a trace of fair play. South Africa's story till 1990 was to bring the tragedy of racism to a grim climax; the Nyasaland emergency was a microcosm and a warning about the dogma of *herrenvolk*. As Welensky's 'pacification' of the Protectorate went on, villages were robbed of their domestic and field implements, their axes and hoes; women and children were frightened crudely; rape was unchecked and in some cases, houses were burned.

A farcical Facade

In June 1959, I visited the area where Scots Missionaries had made a temporary 'station' between Karonga and Mwenzo in 1882. We went to set in place a memorial of the pioneers who died there at Ibanda. As we walked in from the motor road we came to villages of which only fire-charred sticks remained. Live hens and a new sewing machine had been consumed by the flames that destroyed one house there; handiwork of the forces of 'law and order'. The destruction there differed from Dresden only in degree.

In the early days of the Emergency, it seemed not unlikely that the 'security forces' would visit Livingstonia where there was a bigger concentration of population than for many miles around. The arrival of soldiers would certainly have caused alarm and confusion among our pupils, students and estate families. I therefore wrote to the Provincial Commissioner, with the full approval of my colleagues to say that we would view visits by armed men with the greatest concern. The letter, though unacknowledged, seemed to have some effect: soldiers were never seen on the Institution's estate and, moreover, our one local university graduate, the deputy Headmaster of the secondary school was not detained. All the other graduates in the Protectorate were 'taken in' by the 'security forces' soon after Operation Sunrise.

Some time later there came an unexpected chance to chat briefly with the Governor about this virtually clean sweep of the country's university men who numbered less than 40 altogether. When it seemed that the army clampdown had silenced black opposition to the Federation, His Excellency undertook a tour of administrative stations (*bomas*) in the north. As Principal, I was formally invited, with Myra, to go to Rumphi for a reception. I consulted the Senatus and found my African colleagues unanimous that I should go '*kutiyowoyera tose*', to speak for us all.

Myra and I had a quick look through our wardrobe and found to our shock that my only semi-formal suit was heavily mildewed. Time was short. The nearest dry cleaner was 550 miles away. So we had to try petrol and managed to remedy the extensive stains. The suit was then hung out on the verandah for the smell of a filling station to be dissipated. I sniffed at it each time I came back to the house, but the powerful clinging ordour of our local motor fuel reached my nostrils before I reached the verandah. On the morning of the reception, I knew that I would just have to inflict the smell on my fellow guests. When it came our turn to talk with the great man and his lady I found some consolation in the fact that he matched my smell of petrol with that of a distillery: a conflict of spirits in every sense.

"Isn't it marvellous the trouble is all over?" piped the Governor's partner. "Robert has done a splendid job, don't you think?" she said as she shook our hands. There was nothing we could do but treat her banality as a rhetorical question. HE then made some reference to Livingstonia's long record of pioneering education and moved on to declare that by comparison with Ghana's graduates - "I know, I've served there" - the Protectorate's university men were outstanding. "Then why have you locked them all up?" I asked. "Well, they would dabble in politics" was his amazing rejoinder. He was giving them time to cool their heels, he said, and it was only 'for the duration', which should not be long now that 'law and order' had been restored. On that inane note he moved on to greet other guests. We stayed a little longer and pondered how the few black guests had been selected and what was the significance of their presence on such an occasion in relation to the popular determination to see an end to foreign rule and 'white supremacy'.

Good Relationships blighted

One cause of sadness was that the Emergency had spoiled a pleasant relationship that had started at Christmas 1958 between ourselves and the new District Commissioner at Rumphi. Soon after his arrival, we had learned that he was on his own for a while, his wife remaining in Scotland with their children. Myra and I therefore invited him to join us on Christmas day and he expressed real pleasure at being invited. When he came he brought gifts for our children and his manner told us that he was very much a family man. After the Emergency, he had occasion to call at Overtoun and reached the Stone House door in an ugly mood. As I greeted him, I noticed two *Boma* messengers in the back of the Landrover and was sure one of them was holding a gun. "I'm very angry at your people here", he said right away. "Not one of them greeted me as I drove on to the estate. What's wrong with them? Don't they realise I'm their DC? For sixpence I'd charge one of them with sullen insolence." He took a lot of persuading to accept that he was a relative newcomer, that because of the Emergency government Landrovers were naturally not welcome and that the sight of a messenger with a gun was sure to cause alarm and make people hide. "We hear here", I told him, "nasty news about what the security forces are doing in villages throughout the northern province and we know alas! that these are not just rumours".

Not long after I was down at Rumphi to see some of the church people. "Be sure you call on the DC", said Chiswakhata Mkandawire, giving further evidence of a fine sensibility to people as people despite the brutalities of white-led troops against village people. When I reached the *Boma* the DC's mien convinced me that the Emergency was hitting him hard and making him miserable. The presence of an army camp at the *Boma* could only make things worse for a man who, in his heart, wanted nothing of the blighting effect of the Federation. "Do you know what the army are saying about you?" he snapped. "They are saying you're running a communist cell up there on your plateau and that you should have been dealt with when you held a meeting for Banda to address your students without a police permit." The second statement was nonsense, I replied. The principal of Overtoun had every right to introduce an important visitor to the college and I would not dream of asking permission to do so. Moreover that visit of Dr Banda was before the Emergency with all its assaults on freedom. On the accusation about a communist cell, I had a question for himself. "Are we running such a cell?" "Of course not", he answered. "Then tell that to the army. You see them daily. I don't. And your refuting of this malicious charge should carry more weight with them than anything I might say." Alas, however, the tension in our relations persisted.

The Escalation of 'offical' Violence

Our Irish colleague made a visit to Karonga at that time to spend quite a few days with Andrew Kayira and the lake-shore congregation. He got a lift somehow or other and I promised to join him later and bring him back in the mission vehicle. When I got there I found my two friends very disappointed. Two days earlier the young teachers from Mwanjasi who had joined the community procession to the *Boma* with Revd Adam Mlagha on the morning march of March 3, had called on Kayira as their School manager to apologise for absence from duty for over a week. "You see, we were held like prisoners", they reported. "Where?" "In the

house of the white police officer." "And what happened?" With
the help of another white man, the officer had tied them up. "And
what else did they do?" They had been beaten, they said, by logs of
firewood, all over their backs. "Show us", said Kayira and they
stripped off their shirts, revealing widespread scars from their necks
to their legs. They walked in obvious pain, my friends told me.
The experience had shaken them badly. My two colleagues saw
them on their way, on foot, back to their little school and then sat
down to ponder what they'd heard.

The recently posted DC at Karonga, who had succeeded the
fine man in whose home Andrew Kayira and I had shared hospitality
in the previous two years, was a church attending Anglican. "We
must tell him", my friends agreed. "He ought to know about this
brutality". A message was passed in to the *Boma* telling the
Commissioner that the two ministers would like to meet him
confidentially. Within a short time he arrived by car and sat down
in Kayira's house to hear their report. He listened quietly as they
spoke, expressed gratitude to them for informing him and promised
to consider the matter. But a few hours later, he returned in a very
different mood. "Forget what I said before lunch", he told them.
"You had no right to give ear to such a statement against the security
forces. There's a State of Emergency, you know. So, Kayira, if you
repeat this offence, I can detain you up to seven years." "And you",
he said to my Irish colleague, "I order you to return to Livingstonia,
failing which I'll have to take action to make it plain how seriously
I must regard your action". Pleading that he was awaiting transport
from Overtoun, my friend obtained 'stay of execution' of this
peremptory order but was warned to lie low.

When I reached Karonga and heard this I decided to write to
the DC as one Christian to another and in confidence, expressing
shock and sadness at his *volte face* and his treatment of my colleagues.
But I received no answer. We had reason to believe that, in common
with other DCs he was under intolerable pressure from the braggart
military presence on his doorstep and the relish with which the
army was indiscriminately terrorising the countryside.

Meanwhile, another horrid situation awaited us at Livingstonia.
A delegation of church leaders, including myself, had been asked
to carry in person to the PC at Mzuzu, 80 miles to the south, a
solemn protest against the brutal attacks on village communities
and the seizing of their daily tools. We found the PC blandly

courteous but wanting to pooh-pooh the 'alarmist' reports. It didn't help, he said, to lend an ear to wild gossip. Indeed it could lead to a breach of the Emergency Regulations. Instead, he wanted us to try to appreciate the long-term benefits of the Federation. Turning to Sinoia Nkowane, recently designated to succeed me as Principal, he tried to find an ally. "As an educated man", he said, "surely you must realise that the Federation promises economic benefits to your people and merits our support?' Nkowane's answer came slowly and clearly: 'When you're lying on your back, it is not easy to appreciate what is being done above you'. It was as we returned in the afternoon from that mission of protest that I learned of what had been done the day before to the lake-shore village of Chitimba, 3200 feet below us.

Headman Mukhondowe was near the hospital when I saw him. Jumping from the Landrover I greeted him and confirmed that I would be at his village on the next day for Sunday worship. But though he answered quietly, his face showed pain. One eye seemed narrow and his voice came with difficulty. "What is wrong?" I asked and pushed aside his answer, "It's nothing". For it could not be concealed, and so he told me how a Landrover full of soldiers, had arrived on the previous afternoon and how when he left his little carpentry shop to go and meet them (as was his wont with all visitors), one of them struck him over the face. The blow had hurt his eye but had also split his inner cheek against his teeth. He then painfully showed me the inside of his mouth. "But to many others and to women", he said, "they did much worse".

There was nothing for it, I decided, but to collect a small team at once, including our doctor, and go down with the headman to see the situation for ourselves. What we found was sickening. One of the first victims to whom Mukhondowe took us was a very old woman who had been sitting on her reed mat looking out to the lake when suddenly she was attacked from behind and beaten with fists on her head and back. When we found her she was lying on her mat groaning softly: "*Ndirikufwa, ndirikufwa* - I'm dead, I'm dead". I took her hand and told her that the doctor would try to ease her pain and that she should not be afraid. But I was aware of a deep anger in my heart.

The next victim was a young woman who had given birth nine days before. Army boots had kicked her severely on her abdomen and breasts. Somehow her tiny baby had escaped this experience of what the Governor had referred to as 'the pacification' of the north. Then we met an upstanding young man who thanked us for coming and said he wished to make a statement for our record: "I am Sergeant Edwin Gondwe, Number such-and-such, Nyasaland Police. I am here at home on 3 weeks' leave. When the soldiers came yesterday I was bathing in the lake in a quiet little bay. Hearing some noise, I made for the shore here, wrapped in my towel and carrying my soap. As I was leaving the water, two soldiers rushed at me and threw me on the sand. I had difficulty in clutching to my towel. Then they began to drag me by my free arm up onto the grass and over the rough ground to their Landrover. A white officer was sitting there and at once he began to shout at me with swearing. I was kneeling now with the soldiers gripping my shoulders. Then I decided to speak and asked 'Is this legal?' This made the officer shout more loudly - 'What do you mean?' he roared. Then I gave him my name and number in the Police as I have told you. Somehow he didn't shout again. After being quiet for a moment he told the soldiers to let me go. So then as I rose, I said, 'I see you have been beating my people. I will report to my senior Bwana when I go back on duty'. It is good that I can now give evidence to you." "May I use your name?" I asked for I knew that these outrages must be reported. "Of course, yes, please", he replied and, as if on duty, saluted.

As darkness fell, we had a written record of over 40 assaults with the names of the victims. That evening at home I typed a detailed report with copies to the Governor, the PC, the DC and the Church of Scotland in Edinburgh. No replies were received from the colonial government officers. But not long afterwards, the DC went from Rumphi, past our road end, to Chitimba where he upbraided Headman Mukhondowe for not telling him but reporting instead to us. "Livingstonia is as a father to us", was the quiet answer. The DC was in an irascible mood. He must have been taken aback when the Headman asked him to go to the next village a few miles south along the shore. "If you are father too, you must tell our friends not to fear and to trust you", said Mukhondowe. His gentle words, as it were, cornered the DC who agreed to go, and so they went together. When they reached the next village, so the Headman told me later, he went ahead to call the people together. As the DC was entering the village clearing, Mukhondowe said something like this: "Everybody listen. I have come today with our Bwana DC. He wants to tell you that the evil thing that happened at Chitimba will not be done here."

A Snake in the Grass

In Uriah Heep Dickens portrayed a type found in every corner of the earth. We had one at Khondowe. On our arrival from Mwenzo in December 1956, this man - we'll call him Kangana - learned somehow that I was about to start on the typing of our Mwanga translation of selected Old Testament passages. He appeared at the back door and gave a tentative and self-effacing knock. When I asked him to come in, he said that it was not right to "trouble a big man"; he had brought a simple letter and would be honoured to be allowed to help in his own poor way to promote the Word of God. The letter spoke of his typing experience and named referees. Being very new to the area, I said I would want to consider his offer carefully and consult the people who knew of his work elsewhere.

"Employ him if it's just a typist you need. He types quite well. If there is any money involved, cash box or anything like that, let us help to find someone else for you." So answered the respected William Chiswakhata Mkandawire, accountant of the Institution; and so I said no to Kangana. When, not long afterwards, American missionaries rented an empty house on our estate for a few months, we heard that Kangana was selling them pawpaws locally priced at threepence for three shillings each - 12 times the price. To their ingenuous, "Are you sure this is enough, Mr Kangana?' he would answer generously that he was lowering the price to make them welcome! When the Emergency began in March 1959 we were to discover other talents in our Uriah. For it became known that he was employed in local espionage on behalf of the Federal Government.

At the period when the raiding of the northern province by the Federal soldiers was at its most savage, Myra and I were awakened at around 3am one night. Someone was knocking at the door and calling urgently for help. I was in so deep a sleep that the sudden leap from bed upset my circulation and, after a few moments, made me dizzy and near to faint. But in that gap of time, I opened the door to find Kangana trembling on the verandah. "You must come and help us please", he cried. "What's wrong?" I asked. "Soldiers have come to my village with guns and big torches. I can't go back. If you don't help me, I'll have to sleep on the hill. It is terrible." "But you don't need me or anyone else here", I replied. "Oh yes! Only you can help us." "What about your big friend?" I asked and he looked mystified. "Which friend, please? I have no friend to save me." "I'm talking of the big man in Salisbury (Harare)", I said, "the one who pays you to spy on your neighbours, the one who sent the soldiers. Go and tell them that he's your friend and see what they do then." With that, I closed the door and it was then that my head started 'swimming', my vision clouded and everything seemed far away. Myra managed just in time to keep me from falling to the floor.

Britain, the 'Protector', begins to face Facts

As the Emergency blanketed the country under censorship and seemed to have brought a hush that 'people at the top' misread as effective 'pacification', news from Britain was of growing opposition to the Tory Government's support for Welensky. In this, church leaders were prominent and the call was received for the dismantling or, as Dr George MacLeod called it, the 'unscrambling' of the Federation. That struck me as an odd term, for I knew no way of unscrambling an egg or anything else that people were accustomed to 'scramble' in daily life. But there was no misunderstanding the message that came from the May meeting of the General Assembly of the Church of Scotland. Rallied by a powerful speech by Macleod, that concourse of well over a thousand elders and ministers of the Kirk passed, by an overwhelming majority, a call to Her Majesty's Government to end the Emergency, release from detention all persons against whom there were no criminal charges, initiate consitutional talks with the recognised leaders of the African people of Nyasaland and concede the right of any of the three territories to secede from the Federation.

Not long afterwards, we heard that HMG had appointed a Commission, headed by Mr Justice Devlin, to enquire into the causes of the 'disturbances' in the Protectorate. The Commission, which included a former Lord Provost of Perth, wasted no time in preparing for the flight to Blantyre. But at once it became clear that the colonial government did not welcome this development, and of course officers of the occupying Federal army were furious. Thus, when I wrote to the Provincial Commissioner to ask him to ensure that Livingstonia was included in the Commission's itinerary, the cold official reply intimated that the PC was in no way involved in the movements of Lord Devlin's team - an astonishing statement! I therefore sent off telegrams to ensure that our invitation to the Commission would reach them at least at one of four points on the road to the north at which they would be bound to take evidence.

The Impact of Justice Devlin's visit

The reply from the Commission's Secretary cordially accepted our invitation and we planned to accommodate its members in staff house on the plateau. Mr Justice Devlin would be our guest at the Stone House. When their time of arrival was confirmed, and after consulting Senatus colleagues, I sent a 'round robin' in Tumbuka to all the villages within 70 miles north and south calling on all who had evidence to offer to come to Khondowe and testify before the Commissioners in person. "We cannot offer to feed you, so please bring food. Sleeping accommodation will be found, but bring your own blankets. If you wish your testimony to be typed, we can do this for you. Whatever testimony you have to offer, come with it to Livingstonia and come without fear."

It was wonderful to see columns of men, women and youngsters trudging up the main road of the estate in scores. By the time all the pilgrims had arrived, they must have numbered over 300. Chiefs and village headmen were among them, and their first evening was spent settling into their make-shift dormitories. Early next morning every typewriter in our general office was hammering away at the texts of a bundle of written testimonies.

It was while our clerks were out of the office for a brief midday break that our slippery Dickensian character, Kangana, stole into the office and up the stair, thinking to have escaped notice. But our great little estates manager, Titus Mkandawire, had spotted him and followed him swiftly to the typing room, Kangana was extracting a memorandum from one of the machines when Mkandawire entered. The fact that Kangana was some inches taller added piquancy to what followed. Titus emerged from the office building pushing his prey in front of him while he gripped the back of his jacket collar in an iron fist. A small crowd had gathered and the typists were returning to their task as the little man hustled our Uriah to the edge of the plateau. "We don't want snakes here. This is no place for snakes", he growled through clenched teeth and cheers from the spectators greeted his verdict. No violence was done to Kangana but he must have heard the message: Welensky's stooge was *persona non grata* on the Overtoun Institution's estate.

Devlin's visit gave heart to the people of a subjugated territory which, only five years later, would become the independent nation of Malawi. All of us, black and white alike, admired the way in which the Commissioners went about their business. Impeccable courtesy and consideration marked all their interviews and though they were rightly discreet, they gave us to understand how shocked they had been at various places further south by the clear signs that people feared to come forward to testify because of the threatening behaviour of the 'security forces'. We learned how, at one *Boma*, a lone witness had told them that soldiers outside the hall were preventing people approaching it. Only when a representative of the Commission went out to investigate did the soldiers pull back under cover. At another *Boma* the house of a church elder who gave his testimony was entered by soldiers who fired a bullet through the Kirk session minute book. Bully tactics up and down the country had thus denied the Commission the testimony of many who had a tale to tell. I was alarmed also to learn that, though the official figure of the dead at Nkhata Bay on March 4 was around 45, the Commission had reason to believe it actually exceeded a hundred. It thus belonged to the same level of wanton brutality as Sharpville.

Reconciliation before Departure

Our time meanwhile was running out. We had already stayed longer than we had expected when I was suddenly invited to be Principal of Livingstonia in 1956. We were glad, however, that there were now signs that the Federation could not long resist the massive opposition to it. In the remaining weeks before saying farewell in July 1959, I made a quick visit to the far north to collect seedling conifers for our afforestation scheme on the plateau. 15,000 were brought in what was quite a small load, from the Nyika Plateau nursery. One line of them was accidentally destroyed by a grass fire. But the great majority of them thrived and are giving shade and beauty to the estate today.

After Devlin, there was a noticeable relaxation of 'security' intimidation and so I went less anxiously to Karonga for a farewell celebration of communion with the lake-shore people who still cherished the memory of Matthew Faulds. It was a great open-air event, with thousands singing as they gathered and waited for the worship to start. Andrew Kayira, their splendid pastor, had invited the District Commissioner, the man who had treated him and our Irish colleague so strangely when they reported the beating of the two young teachers from Mwanjasi. I was amazed when I saw the DC arriving. He was obviously ill at ease as he sat down on a bench brought from the church building. For a few minutes he was alone. Then quietly some church elders went to sit beside him. It was very touching to see him receive the bread and the cup from the people among whom he had let his name be associated with the military fist of the hated Federation. It was a moment of healing. We were sojourning with a church strong in forgiveness.

Leaving Livingstonia was sad. The experiences we had shared with our friends of political injustice and its climax in the events of the Emergency had given us all a new understanding of the church as the body of Christ. We had been rediscovering the essential mutuality that makes fellowship in the Spirit so beautiful. Yet we knew that, for family reasons, we had to return to Scotland and could not hope to be in Africa again in the foreseeable future. In fact we were to spend only four and a half years away from the tropics. But that lay in the unknown future. So, for the sixth time in our eleven years of marriage, Myra and I had to pack up and move. And, of course, with no removal firms around, we had to do the crating and packing ourselves. Our firstborn was now nine and our youngest just eighteen months, and this meant all the extra packing of precious toys and the bulky apparatus of babyhood.

A Prison Visit

We had not travelled half the way to Blantyre when Myra discovered that chicken pox had entered the family circle by stealth. But what engaged our thoughts was not the identity of its source but what to do with an infectious disease when about to embark on a liner. In Blantyre the shipping agents had no clear answer for us and so they radioed a message to the Union Castle office in Dar es Salaam where the ship was then calling. The reply was a blunt negative: "Cannot accept passengers Macpherson". Fortunately Central African Airways were less rigid and so, after sending telegrams to Scotland about the delay, we flew to Bulawayo to spend some days with Myra's sister and brother-in-law there.

Southern Rhodesia was still under a 'state of emergency' but
white people were free to move at will. So with idle days suddenly
vouchsafed to us, I decided to visit Dr Hastings Banda and as many
of the other Nyasaland detainees as were locked up in the south.
Banda, who had been rudely wakened to be arrested on that first
night of 'Operation Sunrise', was in Gwelo with only one other
congress leader, Dunduzu Chisiza. About a dozen men were in
Khami. I therefore made contact with the Federal Director of
Prisons and put my request to him. His response was surprisingly
polite and he agreed on the condition that I would not publish any
part of my conversations with the detainees and concentrate on
'personal matters' when talking to them.

I went first to Khami and found, to my surprise, that the
Nyasaland men were all together. The room we met in may have
been 'bugged'. But after a hearty welcome they began to talk
confidently about the coming end of the Federation. They were
victors-in-waiting as it were, and the warmth and ease of their
conversation made me feel very much at home. Before I left, we
sang and prayed together for their country and for racial harmony
in southern Africa to replace the bitterness that spread from Cape
Town up to Lake Tanganyika. They sent special greetings to the
Church of Scotland. For men behind bars they were very well
informed about world affairs.

At Gwelo, my entry was less smooth. The Prison Governor
moved on to the offensive as soon as I arrived and made no effort
to conceal his fury that I had been given permission to visit Banda
and Chisiza at all. "You'll have only a few minutes", he snapped,
"and an armed warder will be present throughout. Only personal
matters may be discussed". I refrained from acknowledging this
condition and left him as soon as the warder came for me. The
warder was a pudgy, soft-looking fellow but well-armed. He put
me into the interview room and went for the Doctor who looked
no less dapper than ever in his neat dark suit, stiff white collar and
spotted tie.

After enquiring after my family, Kamuzu asked who was
succeeding me as Principal at Overtoun Institution. I told him that
it was Sinoia Nkowane, a Bachelor of Divinity of St Andrews
University. "I hope he is academically qualified", said the Doctor.
"I don't care about his colour, only about his fitness for the job."
More than I guessed then, that remark was an index of the way in

which, after 1954, Banda would measure fitness by British criteria and in consequence showed little zeal for 'Africanization' in the first years of Independence. But that's another story.

The interview with Dunduzu Chisiza was different. I had met him only once in the Protectorate and had not known he was locked up with the Doctor until the Director of Prisons suggested that I might as well see them both when in Gwelo. Like the men in Khami, Chisiza talked about the State of Emergency and the certainty that the Federation's days were numbered. To my surprise the warder did not interfere. He looked as though his thoughts were far away. Suddenly, however, Dunduzu spoke to him and asked him to go and bring a book on economics from the bed in the cell. Off went the warder and Chisiza told me that there was a letter in the book which he wanted me to take to a Scots missionary friend who supported the movement for independence. The warder brought the book and gave it to his prisoner with the courtesy of a waiter to a diner. When he moved to the doorway and turned his back, Dunduzu gave me the letter. Only three years later, in mysterious circumstances, Dunduzu Chisiza was to die in a road accident on the Blantyre to Zomba road in what had then become the Republic of Malawi. He was only 32 years old then.

On that brief visit to Gwelo, having a few hours in hand before going to the jail, I called on the Scots minister of the local congregation of the Presbyterian Church of Southern Africa. When I introduced myself as a missionary from Nyasaland, I sensed his embarrassment. In the course of a conversation that moved with the pace of a cat on broken bottles, he gave me to understand that in his relations with his all-white congregation, he had to disclaim any association with the Church of Scotland. The Kirk was suspect as being 'pro-African' and Livingstonia's attitude to Federation had increased this suspicion and bitterness. 'Meikles' (the big department store), 'munts' (a derogatory settlers' term for black people) and missionaries were often proclaimed as the three bêtes noirs of white Rhodesian society. It was sad to find further confirmation of how this infectious, irrational racism moulded the speech and behaviour of a minister of a church which in origin, creed and polity was so akin to the Church of Scotland. I remembered how Paul of Tarsus, as a converted racist, had warned of the danger of being 'conformed to this world', an insidious danger that has dogged the long history of the church in almost every land where it has been planted.

A new Hand - a new Hope

At last news came that berths awaited us on a Union Castle liner sailing from Cape Town in August. The voyage as always was refreshing. We enjoyed again the first whiff of sea air after a spell of years in land-locked central Africa. By December 1959 I was appointed as minister of a huge parish in a new housing area in the ship-building town of Greenock, west of Glasgow. But just before moving to our new home, I went to London at the instance of the General Secretary of the church's Foreign Mission Committee to call on the recently appointed Colonial Secretary, Iain Macleod.

The Personal Assistant to the Secretary of State told me that I could have fifteen or twenty minutes with his chief, and I wondered therefore what was the use of coming so far for so short a meeting. Macleod himself however, was welcoming and unhurried and we talked for well over an hour. "Let me say right away", he began, "that I am taking serious note of the views of the church in this matter of Nyasaland. And I don't mean just the Church of Scotland, which, as we know, had made a very clear call to HMG to open the way for a new approach to African opposition to the Federation. I'm concerned also with the outlook of the church in the Protectorate." He then told me that when the Prime Minister, Harold McMillan, had asked him to move from the ministry of labour to the Colonies, he had had to consider the idea very seriously. "If I take it", he had told McMillan, "we shall move to the rapid end of the emergency situations in Kenya, Nyasaland and elsewhere, and to the release of many hundreds of detained persons. I shall want to open the way to independence in these territories." The PM's reply was to the effect that that was why he had asked Macleod to take the colonial portfolio.

As I explained why and how I had come to see him and elaborated on my personal experience of the gross injustice and brutality of the Emergency forces, he listened attentively. His comment here about how the Hola camp atrocities in Kenya, in the Mau Mau period, had shocked him gave me a sense of real rapport. I then spelt out why I, and indeed most of my missionary colleagues, supported wholeheartedly the call of the Kirk's General Assembly in May. It echoed, I said, the deep longing of the black people of the three territories for the dismantling of the Federation and the opening of the way to independence. I gave my personal testimony to the non-violent positive action to which the people were committed in face of a system whose ready resort to violence seemed to promise the extension of the hated South African system of racial repression.

Later on, I was to discover that Kenneth Kaunda of Zambia and other black leaders had quickly come to respect the integrity and wisdom of Iain Macleod. When I interviewed him again over twelve years later, in connection with my book on Kaunda, I found the same perception that what Macmillan called "the wind of change in Africa" required new and positive responses from the old colonial power. But that is part of another *canto* of my story.

For the present, in the latter half of 1959, we were away from Africa, back in Scotland and plunging into a very different pattern of life. I had to hold on to the Zambian proverb that says: 'Where the rain finds you, there is the middle of the world'. Don't look backwards. Don't pine. Take your hoe and turn the earth. Respond to the rain - and there were 65 inches of it annually in Greenock. For wherever you are is always the most important place to be for the present. And as your days (Deuteronomy 33.25) so shall your strength be. So, whether you come or whether you go, move always 'with happy'.

Other books on Africa published by Handsel Press include:

The Story of Chogoria, by John Wilkinson

Robert Laws, Servant of Africa, by Hamish McIntosh